MW01145849

The Collector's Wodehouse

P. G. WODEHOUSE

Money in the Bank

THE OVERLOOK PRESS
WOODSTOCK & NEW YORK

This edition first published in the United States in 2005 by
The Overlook Press, Peter Mayer Publishers, Inc.
Woodstock and New York

WOODSTOCK
One Overlook Drive
Woodstock, NY 12498
www.overlookpress.com
[for individual orders, bulk and special sales, contact our Woodstock office]

NEW YORK
141 Wooster Street
New York, NY 10012

First published in the USA by Doubleday, Doran, 1942
Copyright © 1942 by P. G. Wodehouse,
renewed 1970 by P. G. Wodehouse

Cataloging-in-Publication Data is available from the Library of Congress

Manufactured in Germany

ISBN 1-58567-657-8

1 3 5 7 9 8 6 4 2

Money in the Bank

Mr Shoesmith, the well-known solicitor, head of the firm of Shoesmith, Shoesmith, Shoesmith, and so on, of Lincoln's Inn Fields, leaned back in his chair and said that he hoped he had made everything clear.

He accompanied the remark with one of those short, quick, roopy coughs by means of which solicitors announce that a conference is concluded, and Jeff Miller came out of his meditations with a start. Mr Shoesmith always reminded him of a bird, and in the attempt to decide just what kind of a bird he had allowed his attention to wander.

However, what he had missed must presumably have had to do with some aspect of the forthcoming case of Pennefather v. Tarvin, in which he had been briefed to appear for the plaintiff. That was what he had come here to discuss, and that was what Mr Shoesmith had been talking about at the moment when he had ceased to hang upon his lips. So it seemed safe to nod intelligently.

'I think I have covered the various points?'

'Oh, rather.'

'You agree with me that the case for the defence appears to rest upon the evidence of this witness, Lionel Green?'

'Absolutely.'

'Your task, therefore, will be to endeavour to discredit his story. You must shake Green.'

'Leave it to me.'

'Unfortunately,' said Mr Shoesmith, 'I am obliged to.'

He sighed. You would have said that he was not in sympathy with Jeff, and you would have been right. Jeff had his little circle of admirers, but Mr Shoesmith was not a member of it. About the nastiest jolt of the well-known solicitor's experience had been the one he had received on the occasion, some weeks previously, when his only daughter had brought this young man home and laid him on the mat, announcing in her authoritative way that they were engaged to be married.

He had said 'Oh, my God!' or something civil of that sort, but it was only with difficulty that he had been able to speak at all. He could see in Jeff little or nothing of a nature calculated to cause a father, receiving such news, to wave his hat in the air and dance about on the tips of his toes. He disliked his hair, which looked like straw; his character, which he considered unbalanced; and his manner, which struck him as flippant and slangy. He could think of no detail in which his future son-in-law's deportment during the interview which was just terminating had not differed from that of the ideal young barrister, receiving instructions for his first appearance in the courts, and he felt a sort of detached pity for this Pennefather, whose fortunes were to rest in such hands.

But Myrtle had insisted that her betrothed be given his chance of winning forensic fame – or as much forensic fame as can be won by appearing for a taxi-driver who is suing an interior decorator for hitting him in the stomach – and he had long ago become aware of the futility of trying to oppose Myrtle's wishes.

So now he merely sighed, and rose to his feet, to indicate that he had had as much of Jeff as he could endure.

'Well,' he said, with a wintry contortion of his facial muscles which might have passed in a dim light for a smile, 'we must hope for the best.'

'That's the spirit,' agreed Jeff cordially. 'Quiet confidence, and no weakening. You remember what Hengist said to Horsa before the battle of whatever it was?'

Mr Shoesmith's face betrayed surprise at this erudition.

'Why, er, no, I do not. What did he say?'

' "Horsa, keep your tail up!" Good afternoon,' said Jeff. 'Good afternoon.'

He left the office and made his way westward, walking with a long, swinging stride. For, whatever might be his spiritual shortcomings, Jeff Miller was a finely-built, athletic young man, one who did not have to call weakly for cabs to take him from Lincoln's Inn Fields to Halsey Court, Mayfair, where he had his modest residence, but was able to move thither under his own steam. A representative both of his University and of his country on the football field, with an impressive record at Twickenham, Cardiff Arms Park and other centres, he could have managed an even longer walk without distress.

As he threaded his way through the streets, he found himself once more brooding on Mr Shoesmith – not this time on his appearance, for his research work at the office had left him pretty straight in his mind that what the other looked like was a cassowary, but on his character and disposition. A cold, aloof, non-bonhomous old blister, he decided, one whose soul his own must always fail to touch. He tried in vain to think of a single subject on which it would be possible for Pop Shoesmith, on the one hand, and himself, on the other, to see eye to eye.

And yet there was such a subject, and that of the first importance. Jeff's engagement to his daughter Myrtle was, as we have seen, one of which Mr Shoesmith heartily disapproved, and it was one of which Jeff disapproved pretty heartily himself. Indeed, it is not too much to say that the thought of putting on a morning coat and sponge-bag trousers and accompanying Myrtle Shoesmith up the aisle chilled him to the marrow and made him feel as if he had been swallowing butterflies.

He was still quite at a loss to understand how the ghastly thing had happened. The facts seemed to suggest that he must have let fall some passing remark which had given the girl the impression that he was proposing to her, but he had no recollection of having done anything so cloth-headed. All he knew was that at a certain point of time at an evening party he had been a happy, buoyant young fellow, making light conversation to Myrtle Shoesmith behind a potted palm, and at another point of time, only a moment later, or so it seemed to him, he was listening appalled to Myrtle Shoesmith discussing cake and bridesmaids. The whole thing was absolutely sudden and unexpected, like an earthquake or a waterspout or any other Act of God.

But, blurred though his mind might be with respect to many essentials of the affair, on one point it was crystal clear – to wit, that the emotion which her personality inspired in him was not love.

Love, he felt, and he was a man who had thought about these things, should not manifest itself in such a strongly-marked inclination, when in the presence of the adored object, to stand on one leg and twiddle the fingers. In the days of his boyhood, he remembered, at his preparatory school, the retired sergeant-major, who came twice a week to teach the elements of drill and physical culture, had afflicted him with just the same nervous diffidence which he experienced in the society of Myrtle Shoesmith, and it would be straining the facts absurdly to say that he had loved that sergeant-major.

With a growing sense of being a good man snared in the toils of Fate, like somebody out of Shakespeare, he crossed Berkeley Square and arrived at Halsey Court.

The day was a smiling and gracious day, early June at his best. In a hundred thousand homes, barometers, tapped by a hundred thousand knuckles before breakfast, had declined to budge from Set Fair, and the blue sky showed how sound their judgement had been. Yet over this stuffy little backwater there brooded a sort of bilious twilight, as if an eclipse were in progress. Halsey Court never bothered much about sunshine. What it specialized in was the smell of cooking cabbage. And for the first time, Jeff found himself disliking this aroma and yearning for something more on the lines of roses and lavender.

This change of heart he attributed to the fact that he had been musing on his approaching nuptials, for hitherto he had been well content with Halsey Court. It might be dingy, but it was quiet, and quiet was of importance to him. For though he had passed his Bar examinations to please a wealthy godfather, and was about to plunge into active practice because Myrtle Shoesmith insisted on it, he was also, and primarily, a man of letters. He wrote stories about mysterious Chinamen and girls with hair the colour of ripe wheat and the corpses of baronets in panelled libraries, and he found the cloistral peace of Halsey Court assisted the composition of these.

He passed through the court's narrow entrance, and turned to the right. This brought him to Halsey Chambers, on the third floor front of which he lived. He climbed the stairs, and let himself into his flat, to be greeted by Ma Balsam, his stout and motherly housekeeper.

'Oh, there you are, sir,' said Ma Balsam, with that air of welcoming a prodigal son which always endeared her to her employer. 'Miss Shoesmith was wanting to speak to you on the telephone just after you went out.'

Jeff started.

'She's not back in London?'

'No, sir. She was talking from the friends in the country where she's staying. I told her you had gone to see her papa, and she said she would ring up again later. I hope everything turned out satisfactory, sir?'

'Eh?'

'Your talk with the young lady's papa.'

'Oh, yes. Quite satisfactory. Let me see, how deeply did I take you into my confidence about all that?'

'You told me you thought the gentleman was going to give you a job as a mouthpiece.'

'Well, he has. Yes, it's all settled, Ma. I appear for Ernest Pennefather, a licensed taxi-cab driver, who has invoked the awful majesty of the Law to help him pound the stuffing out of Orlo Tarvin, an interior decorator, claiming that in the course of a dispute about his fare Tarvin gave him a blow or buffet – whereby the said Pennefather goes in fear of his life. Interesting, of course, as showing what highly-strung, nervous men taxi-drivers are, but a bit on the minor side, one would have thought, for a man of my gifts. Still, the disembowelling of Green may give me some scope.'

'Sir?'

'It appears that a second interior decorator, of the name of Lionel Green, was present during the proceedings and maintains that the alleged blow or buffet was not a blow or buffet at all, but in reality more in the nature of a playful prod or tap. And the attitude of the defence, I gather, is "Laugh that off, J. G. Miller." Well, we shall see. I have been instructed to shake Green, and I propose to do it till he feels like a cocktail. I shall be very courteous, of course, very polished and suave, but by the time I've finished with him Green will know he's been in a fight. But what rot all this is, Ma. Pennefather *v.* Tarvin, forsooth! What have I to do with the petty squabblings of these fretful midges? I ought to be at my desk, immersed in literary composition. Was that the telephone?'

'Yes, sir. Miss Shoesmith, I expect.'

'You take a morbid view, Ma, but you are probably right.'

It was Miss Shoesmith. The voice which spoke was immediately recognizable as hers both from its beautifully clear diction and the note of authority which it conveyed. One of the things which prevented any real communion of soul between this girl and Jeff was the fact that she always addressed him like a governess talking to a problem child.

'Geoffrey?'

'Hullo?'

'I rang up before, but you were out.'

'Yes. Ma Balsam told me.'

'I wish you would not call Mrs Balsam "Ma". It's vulgar, and it must make her familiar. Is everything all right?'

'Fine this end. How are conditions where you are?'

'You know perfectly well what I mean. About Father. Has he given you the brief?'

'Yes, I've got it.'

'Good. Well, you will have no excuse, if you don't win the case. Father says the defendant hasn't a leg to stand on.'

'Awkward, if he wants to roller-skate.'

'What?'

'Nothing.'

'You said something about roller-skating.'

'No, I didn't.'

'Who has been roller-skating?'

'Let it go, let it go. Don't give the matter another thought. Yes, I shall win, all right. I anticipate a sensational triumph.'

'Well, we must hope for the best.'

'Exactly what your father said.'

'I shall be very annoyed if you don't win. All you have to do is follow Father's instructions. Mind you are respectful to the judge. Don't mumble. Don't grin. Don't hesitate. Be sure what you are going to say, and say it clearly and crisply. And your hair. See that it is tidy. But I was forgetting. You will be wearing a wig. Well, that is all, I think. Good-bye.'

'Good-bye,' said Jeff.

He replaced the receiver, and went to the window and stood there, looking out, his hands in his pockets, a frown on his face. Nature had intended him to be a cheerful, even exuberant young man, of ready laugh and face-splitting grin, but there was in his demeanour now a deep dejection. In the gutter below, sparrows were chirping their madrigals, but he showed no disposition to take the bass.

He could see no ray of hope on the horizon. With the feeling, which was his constant companion nowadays, for the wedding was fixed for the fifth of July and it was already the tenth of June, that if anybody cared to describe him as some wild thing taken in a trap, which sees the trapper coming through the woods, it would be all right with him, he threw a moody banana skin at the loudest of the sparrows, and went back into the room.

CHAPTER 2

Immediately opposite Halsey Chambers, face to face with it across the narrow court, stands Halsey Buildings. It is a ramshackle edifice given over to stuffy little offices, whose proprietors consider that the privilege of printing the magic word 'Mayfair' on their notepaper compensates for the lack of ventilation. And at the time at which this story begins, the window of the third floor bore the legend in large black letters:

J. SHERINGHAM ADAIR
(Private Investigator)

On the morning of the day following the trying of the case of Pennefather *v.* Tarvin, there turned in at the entrance of Halsey Court and started to make her way towards Halsey Buildings a young woman of stylish appearance and a certain rather bold and challenging beauty. Her golden hair gleamed brassily, her lips were ruddier than the cherry and her eyes sparkling and vivacious.

But they were not the sort of eyes which go with a meek and contrite heart, and one doubts if someone like the late John Knox would have taken to her very much. For, though a pleasing spectacle, she bore about her to the discerning gaze that subtle aura which stamps a girl as one of those at whose approach the prudent host packs away his knick-knacks and locks up the spoons. Her name was Dolly Molloy, and she was the bride of one Soapy Molloy, a share-pusher of some distinction.

Halsey Court was still its dishevelled self, and Dolly, as fastidious a girl as ever swiped a bottle of scent when the shopkeeper was not looking, eyed it askance. It was with a frown of distaste on her attractive face that she mounted the echoing stone stairs of Halsey Buildings and with the handle of her parasol – a present, though that institution was not aware of it, from Jarrow's Stores (Novelty Dept) – rapped on the grimy glass of the door marked 'J. Sheringham Adair'.

It is, of course, practically impossible for anyone really to have a name like J. Sheringham Adair, and it may be stated at once that the man who had established himself opposite Jeff Miller's flat missed it by a wide margin. He was a dubious character called Twist, known to his intimates as Chimp. And at the moment when the staccato sound of ivory impinging on glass broke in upon his peace, he was seated at his desk, consuming a frugal lunch.

The abrupt intimation that an unexpected caller had arrived brought him to his feet in sudden agitation, choking on a sandwich. As one whose business methods had led him to incur a good deal of displeasure in a good many quarters in his time, he always quailed when his privacy was invaded without appointment. Too often, on such occasions, he had been compelled to jump out of windows or to hide in cupboards. Indeed, his first act now was to cast a quick glance at the spacious closet behind his desk, and he had already started to make a move in its direction, when the door opened and the discovery of the intruder's sex stilled his alarm. A moment later, he was himself again. He had recognized an old acquaintance.

'Well, well, well,' he cried. Mrs Molloy was not a woman of whom he was fond, but relief lent an almost effusively welcoming note to his voice. 'Well, well, well, look who's here. Come along in and sit down, Dolly. Take the clean chair.'

'What clean chair?' asked the visitor, establishing herself, after an inspection which might have pained a more sensitive man, on a corner of the desk. 'Are you trying to grow mustard and cress in here, or sump'n? Well, Chimp, it's a long time since we run across each other. You look about the same as ever.'

This, if true, was rather a pity, for Mr Twist's appearance could scarcely but have been improved by alteration. He was a small man with the face of an untrustworthy monkey, the sort of monkey other monkeys would have shrunk from allowing to come within arm's reach of their nut ration, and, not content with Nature's handiwork, had superimposed on his upper lip a waxed moustache of singular hideousness. Nevertheless, he appeared to regard the remark as a tribute.

'Sure, I keep pretty good,' he said, curling the growth with a toothpick. 'How's Soapy?'

A cloud seemed to pass over Dolly's face. A keen ear might have detected a tremor in her voice, as she replied that Soapy was all right.

'And what brings you around?'

'Well, I happened to be in these parts, and I thought I'd look in. I'd sort of like your advice about something. And then there's that five smackers Soapy loaned you getting on for over a year ago and not a yip out of you since. I'll collect that while I'm here.'

'Soapy never loaned me any five smackers.'

'I've got your note in my bag.'

'I paid it him. Sure, that's right. I remember now. It all comes back to me.'

'And now it's coming back to Soapy.'

Mr Twist seemed cast down for an instant, but only for an instant. He was a resilient man.

'Well, we'll get round to that later,' he said. 'What do you want advice about?'

The rather predatory gleam which had been lighting up his visitor's lustrous eyes died away, and she heaved a sigh, like one about to reveal a secret sorrow. She dabbed at her nose with a delicate cambric handkerchief, one of a set of twelve for which a prominent West End haberdasher had been looking everywhere since he had last enjoyed her patronage.

'I'm kind of worried, Chimp.'

'What about?'

'Soapy.'

'I thought you would be one of these days. You were a sap to marry him,' said Mr Twist. His association with the absent Mr Molloy had been a long rather than an affectionate one. He could never forget the numerous occasions on which he, Mr Molloy, had double-crossed him, Mr Twist, just when he, Mr Twist, was preparing to double-cross him, Mr Molloy. 'What's the trouble? Has he started playing the old Army game?'

'It sort of looks like it.'

'The big chunk of boloney.'

'I'd be glad,' said Dolly, with womanly dignity, 'if you wouldn't call my husband chunks of boloney.'

'What else is there to call him?' asked Chimp. 'Slice him where you like, that's what he still is.'

Mrs Molloy bit a brightly coloured lip, but she refrained

from the belligerent retort which had trembled on it. Chimp Twist, whatever his defects, and no one was more alive to these than she, was a man of recognized judgement and acumen, and she was a stranger in a strange land and had nobody else to whom to take a young wife's problems. In her native Chicago, there were a dozen knowledgeable Solons in whom she could have confided the anxieties which were gnawing her bosom, with a reasonable certainty of getting aid and comfort. She could even have consulted Dorothy Dix. But this was England, and her advisory committee far away, probably behind bars. Except Miss Dix, of course.

Chimp returned to the matter in hand. His was a nasty little mind, that took pleasure in other people's recitals of their troubles. He anticipated particular enjoyment from a parade of the Molloy family skeletons.

'What's he been doing?'

'Well, it's this dame. I don't like the way he's acting. I think there's oompus-boompus going on.'

'What dame?'

'This dame he keeps sauntering in the rose garden with at this Shipley Hall place down in Kent, where we're visiting. They go off into this rose garden together, and she pins fragrant blooms in his buttonhole.'

Mr Twist seemed incredulous.

'She pins fragrant blooms in Soapy's buttonhole?'

'That's right.'

'In *Soapy's* buttonhole?'

'That's what she does.'

'She must be nuts.'

Again, Mrs Molloy was forced to bite her lip, and again she reminded herself how sorely she needed this man's advice.

'Twice I've caught her at it. I didn't like the look on his face, neither. Sort of soppy. Her name's Cork,' said Dolly, in an aggrieved voice, as if this somehow made it worse. 'Mrs Wellesley Cork. Soapy met her somewhere, and she told him about this joint she was running at this place she's rented from some lord or other, and Soapy would have it that we go visit there. It's a sort of crazy joint. You eat vegetables and breathe deep and dance around in circles. It's supposed to be swell for the soul.'

The description of the Clarissa Cork colony for the promotion of plain living and high thinking was not a very lucid one, but Chimp nodded understandingly.

'I know the sort of thing you mean. Yogi stuff.'

'Please yourself. Your guess is as good as mine. The place seems to me like a booby-hatch. I wouldn't mind breathing deep, if I was allowed to stoke up first, but all these vegetables are getting me down. When I reach for the knife and fork, I like to feel there's something in the old nosebag I can dig my teeth into. A little more of it, and I'll be cutting out paper dolls and sticking straws in my hair. The butler's gone bugs already.'

'I've sometimes thought of starting a racket like that myself,' said Mr Twist reflectively. 'There's money in it. But tell me more. Does Soapy dance around in circles?'

'Sure.'

'The big stiff. I hope he strains a muscle. What's that you were saying about the butler? Gone bugs, has he?'

'He could step straight into Bloomingdale, and no questions asked. He wanders around the place, like a lost spirit, with a strange, fixed look on his pan, like he was seeing visions or sump'n. And guess what. I found him in my room yesterdays burrowing under the dressing-table. Yessir, sticking up from under the dressing-table like Pike's Peak, and had the nerve to say he was looking for a funny smell. Funny smell, my foot. There wasn't a sign of any funny smell.'

Mr Twist agreed that this sounded, at the most charitable estimate, borderline stuff. He said with some interest that he had never seen a loony butler – adding in this connection, that he would rather see than be one.

'Yay,' said Dolly. 'It's certainly the by-Goddest joint I was ever in. But I didn't come here to talk about that. What do you make of this thing of Soapy and this dame? Talk quick. I've got to get a train in a minute.'

Mr Twist gave his verdict without hesitation. He had little faith in his fellow men and none in Soapy Molloy.

'The sooner you form a flying wedge and break up the play, the better off you'll be,' he replied, with all the emphasis at his disposal. 'He is your man, and he's doing you wrong.'

Dolly nodded sombrely. He had but confirmed her own view.

'That's the way I feel. This Cork dame is rich. Got it in gobs. And what I've been asking myself is, what's to prevent Soapy ditching me and making a pass at her? She would be a pushover for him. He's full of sex appeal, the sweet old pieface,' said Dolly, with a sort of mournful wifely pride. 'And he's just at what you might call the dangerous age. Young enough to have preserved that schoolgirl complexion, and old enough to have gotten tired of work and be looking around for a rich wife to take him away from it all.'

'You watch him like a hawk, and if you get the goods on him, jump on his neck.'

'You don't think it's just that he's sort of being civil, what with her being his hostess and all like that, what I mean?'

'No, I don't.'

'Nor me,' said Dolly regretfully. 'Well, I must be getting along, or I'll miss that train. Been nice, seeing you.'

'Drop in any time you're passing. That'll be five smackers.'

'What'll be five smackers?'

'My professional advice. Slip me that note of mine, and we'll call it square.'

Dolly Molloy quivered like a wounded deer.

'Five smackers for a measly coupla words which I'd practically made up my mind already to do like what you said? You've got a nerve.'

'We Mayfair consultants come high,' said Mr Twist complacently. 'Matter of fact, you're sitting pretty. Sherlock Holmes used to get jewelled snuff-boxes.'

Only a womanly fear of missing a train could have kept his client from lingering to express her opinion of him in blistering Chicagoese. But time was flying. She opened her bag, and placed a piece of paper on the desk. Too late, she was reminding herself that Alexander Twist had never been the man easily to be got the better of in a business transaction. It was precisely this keen commercial sense of his which had rendered spacious cupboards, into which to withdraw from exasperated callers, so necessary to his well-being.

Her heart was heavy, as she sped in the express towards the picturesque Kentish village of Shipley. A now solidified suspicion of a loved husband, coupled with the thought that there would be only spinach and potatoes for dinner, had robbed her entirely of her usual effervescence. Moodily she alighted at her destination, and with drawn brows started on the short walk up the hill to Shipley Hall.

Shipley Hall, ancestral seat of George, sixth Viscount Uffenham, and rented furnished from him by Mrs Cork, stood on a wide plateau, backed by rolling woodland, a white Georgian house set about with gay flower-beds and spreading lawns, commanding a comprehensive view of the surrounding countryside. Its grounds were looking their best in the June sunshine, and Soapy Molloy, pacing the terrace, was looking his best in a suit the colour of autumn leaves, a Panama hat, a red and yellow tie and a pair of those buckskin shoes with tan toecaps which add so much diablerie to a man's appearance.

Neither of these lovely sights, however, had the effect of lightening Dolly's despondency. The beauty of the grounds left her cold, and any uplift which she might have derived from the spectacle of her prismatic mate was neutralized by the fact that he was in the company of Mrs Cork. And, as if this were not enough, he selected the exact moment when he swam into Dolly's ken for taking his fair companion's hand and giving it a courtly pat. The couple then passed from view into the rhododendron walk.

Dolly sank on to a handy tree stump, and there remained for some little time, a prey to bitter thoughts. Presently she rose and made her way with leaden feet to her room. She was feeling that what she was suffering represented the limit which any young wife could be called upon to endure.

Opening the door, however, she found that she had been mistaken. Her view had been too optimistic. There was some more coming to her, and she paused on the threshold, tottering beneath the application of the last straw.

From under the dressing-table, rising like some *mesa* in a Western desert, there protruded a vast trouser seat. It quivered gently, like the butt end of a terrier at a rat hole.

On top of all her other troubles, Cakebread, the butler, was in again.

CHAPTER 3

Despite the fascination of Mr Molloy's society, Mrs Cork had
not lingered long in the rhododendron walk. She had a task to
perform which required her presence indoors. Some ten minutes
after Dolly had seen her on the terrace, she was in her study,
speaking into the desk telephone.

'Miss Benedick.'

'Yes, Mrs Cork?' replied a charming voice, like spring winds
sighing through pine trees.

'I want to see Mr Trumper immediately.'

'Yes, Mrs Cork,' said the charming voice.

Mrs Cork gave her powerful shoulders a hitch, and took up
her stand with her back to the empty fireplace, looking exactly
like the frontispiece of her recently published volume of travel,
A Woman in the Wilds, where the camera had caught her, gun
in hand, with one foot on the neck of a dead giraffe.

Nobody who is interested in dead giraffes will require an
introduction to Mrs Wellesley Cork. But in the wide public for
which the chronicler hopes that he is writing it is possible that
there may be here and there a scattered few in whom these
indiarubber-necked animals do not touch a chord. For the
benefit of this handful, it must be mentioned that she was a
very eminent explorer and big-game huntress.

It was the decease of Mr Wellesley Cork some twelve years previously, leaving her at something of a loose end, that had caused her to turn her great natural energies, until then expended in keeping a husband in order, in the direction of roaming, rifle at the ready, the wilder portions of Africa. And she had done it with outstanding success. You could say what you liked about Clarissa Cork, and a thousand native bearers in their various dialects had said plenty, but you could not deny that she was far-flung and held dominion over palm and pine.

When this dynamic woman wanted to see people immediately, she saw them immediately. She had trained her little flock to come at her call as if they had been seasoned relay racers toeing the mark with batons in their hands. The hour produced the man. Only a few minutes had elapsed before a shrimplike little figure came darting into the room. Mr Trumper, and no other.

Mrs Cork pierced him, as he entered, with a keen eye, as if he had been a gnu appearing through a thicket, and came to the point without delay. She was a woman who never wasted time in lengthy preambles.

'Well, Eustace, you know why I have sent for you.'

A gulp escaped the unfortunate man. The look on her face was a look of doom, bidding him abandon hope. He had worshipped Mrs Cork in a silent, shrimplike way, as men of his kind are so apt to worship her type of woman, for many years, and he had felt until this moment that the thought of this devotion might lead her to temper justice with mercy.

'You know the rule. Instant expulsion, if found eating meat. We must have discipline.'

One is not ashamed to say that the heart bleeds for Eustace Trumper. His great love had caused him to enrol himself among the foundation members of the little colony at Shipley Hall, but the Trumpers, father and son back through the ages, had always been valiant trenchermen, and Eustace in particular was noted in his circle for his prowess with knife and fork. At school, he had been known as Thomas the Tapeworm, and, grown to riper years, his abilities were so familiar at his club that when he appeared in the doorway of the luncheon-room, the carver flexed his muscles and behaved like a war horse at the sound of the bugle. If such a man, after nobly confining himself to vegetables for weeks and weeks, slips one day and is found in the potting shed with a cold steak-and-kidney pie on his very lips, who shall blame him?

Well, unfortunately, Mrs Cork, for one.

'Discipline,' she repeated. 'You'll have to go, Eustace.'

There was a pause. Mr Trumper raised pleading eyes, like a netted shrimp.

'Give me another chance, Clarissa.'

Mrs Cork seemed moved, but she shook her head.

'Impossible, Eustace. Suppose it got about that I had over-looked this flagrant violation of the rules. What, for instance, would Mr Molloy think? He has come here expressly to study our colony, with a view to starting something similar in America, if he finds it is a success. It would kill his enthusiasm.'

One would scarcely have supposed that at such a moment as this Mr Trumper would have had the spirit to frown. Nevertheless, he did, and darkly.

'I don't trust that man. I believe he's a crook.'

'Nonsense.'

'I'm sure he is. Nobody but a crook could be so smooth.'

'Nonsense. Mr Molloy is a charming, cultured American of the best type. A millionaire, too.'

'How do you know he's a millionaire?'

'He told me so.'

Mr Trumper decided to abandon the topic. It had often given him cause for wonderment that this splendid woman, so shrewd and capable in her dealings with head-hunters and wounded pumas, should be so inadequate when confronted with the pitfalls of civilization.

'Well, anyhow,' he urged, 'he'll never find out. Do let me stay, Clarissa. You know what it means to me to be near you. You are always such an inspiration to me.'

Mrs Cork wavered. She was a woman capable of checking a charging rhinoceros with a raised eyebrow and a well-bred stare, but she had her softer side. Except for her nephew, Lionel Green, there was no one of whom she was fonder than Eustace Trumper, nor had she failed, silent though it was, to note his devotion. She looked questioningly at a stuffed antelope's head which decorated the wall, as if seeking its advice. Then the struggle between principle and sentiment ended.

'All right. But don't let it happen again.'

'I won't, I won't.'

'Then we will say no more about it,' said Mrs Cork gruffly.

There was a silence, strained as silence always is after these poignant scenes. Eustace Trumper stood shuffling his feet softly. Mrs Cork continued to stare at the antelope. Mr Trumper was the first to speak, prefacing his words with a little cough, for the subject on which he was about to touch was a delicate one.

'Any news of Lionel, Clarissa?'

'I telephoned him this morning, directly after Miss Benedick had read me the report of the case in the paper.'

'I hope he is coming here?'

'He will be down this evening.'

'Capital. It will do him all the good in the world, being with you after such an ordeal. You are delighted, of course?'

Mrs Cork relapsed into silence for a moment. When she spoke, her words came as a surprise to Mr Trumper.

'I'm not sure.'

'Not sure?'

'I am rather wondering if Shipley Hall is quite the place for Lionel.'

'I don't understand.'

The french window of the study was open. Mrs Cork strode to it, and raked the adjacent scenery with a quick glance. A couple of disciples were breathing deeply at the far end of the lawn, but they were out of earshot, and she returned, satisfied. She had that to say which she did not wish to be overheard.

'Eustace, have you ever suspected that there might be something between Lionel and Miss Benedick?'

'Why, no. What do you mean?'

'I believe she's setting her cap at him.'

'Clarissa!'

'I may be mistaken, of course, but that is what I think. If she is, I'll soon put a stop to it. She may be Lord Uffenham's niece, but it's obvious that she can't have a penny, or what is she doing as my secretary-companion? That is why I am wondering if it is a good thing that Lionel is coming here. He is a sweet-natured, impulsive boy, just the sort to be an easy prey for a designing woman.'

'But what makes you think so?'

'I thought I saw signs of some understanding between them, the last time he was down here. Little things, but I noticed them. And I didn't at all like the way she behaved this morning, when she was reading me the newspaper account of Lionel's examination by that man, J. G. Miller. Her voice shook so much that I looked up, and I saw that her eyes were blazing. And when I said that I wished I could strangle J. G. Miller with my bare hands, she gave a sort of wistful sigh. I thought it most extraordinary. What possible reason was there for her to be so concerned, unless what I suspect is true?'

'You don't think it was just natural good feeling?'

'No, I don't.'

'It might very well have been. I can assure you that everybody here is most resentful about the whole affair. I was speaking to Cakebread after breakfast, and he told me that the cook had expressed herself very strongly.'

Mrs Cork stiffened.

'Cakebread? Are you in the habit of discussing the intimate affairs of the family with my butler?'

Mr Trumper blushed.

'No, no,' he said hastily. 'But I happened to come upon him unexpectedly in my bedroom, and you know how difficult it is on these occasions to think of anything to say. Especially to Cakebread. I confess I find him a little overpowering. He has such an odd way of staring at one.'

'He was in your bedroom? He doesn't valet you. What was he doing in your bedroom?'

'He appeared to be searching under the bed.'

Mrs Cork started.

'That's odd. Only the other day, I found him in my room, rummaging in one of the cupboards. He said he was looking for a mouse.'

'He told me he was looking for beetles.'

'I don't like this, Eustace.'

'It is disturbing. I certainly saw no beetles.'

'I hope the man's honest.'

'I am bound to say that that is a question which occurred to me. He looks completely so. But then all butlers do. Were his references satisfactory?'

'I didn't see them. There was no necessity. According to Miss Benedick, who looked after all the arrangements for taking the house, her uncle made it one of the conditions of letting me have the place that his butler should stay on. She told me that this was quite customary, and I saw no objection to it. But now—'

She paused, not because she had finished her remarks, but because there split the welkin at this moment the sound of a female voice raised in wrath, followed by a noise not unlike the delivery of a ton of coals.

'What the devil's that?' she asked, wondering.

Mr Trumper had skipped to the door. He vanished for a brief space, to return with first-hand information.

'It is Cakebread. He appears to have fallen downstairs. Oh, excuse me.'

The concluding words were addressed to Mrs Molloy, who had brushed past him at a high rate of speed and was now standing inside the room, breathing emotionally and exhibiting other signs of being a good woman wronged.

'Say, listen, Mrs Cork!' she cried shrilly.

Her tone was not the tone in which people habitually addressed the chatelaine of Shipley Hall, but feminine curiosity induced the latter to overlook this.

'Is something the matter, Mrs Molloy?'

'You bet your silk underwear something's the matter. Either you keep that darned butler of yours on a chain, or there'll have to be drastic steps taken. Hell's bells, there's a limit.'

'I'm afraid I do not understand you. What has my butler been doing?'

'I've just caught him rousting around in my room. For the second time in two days, by golly. Can you blame anyone for beefing? When we came to visit here, I understood that that room was reserved for I and my husband. Nobody ever mentioned that we were supposed to muck in with the butler. Hasn't he got a room of his own, or what is it?'

Mr Trumper had been punctuating this powerful speech with amazed squeaks.

'How very remarkable!' he now ejaculated. 'After what we were speaking about, Clarissa.'

'Mr Trumper has just been telling me,' explained Mrs Cork, 'that he found Cakebread in his room this morning, in most suspicious circumstances. And I was saying that not long ago I found him in mine. We were agreeing, when you came in, that something would have to be done.'

'I'll say something'll have to be done, and quick. You don't need any three guesses to tell you what the old blimp is after. He's getting around to cleaning out the joint and skipping. It's a wonder to me he hasn't done it already. Fire him out on his fanny pronto, is my advice, or we shan't have a darned thing left that we can call our own.'

'I quite agree with you. He shall go to-day.' Mrs Cork strode masterfully to the desk and spoke into the telephone. 'Miss Benedick.'

The delightful voice was right on the job, as usual.

'Yes, Mrs Cork?'

'Come here, please.'

'Yes, Mrs Cork.'

And after a brief interval, during which Mrs Cork made

some strong observations about dishonest butlers and Mr Trumper squeaked a good deal and Dolly Molloy fermented in silence, the door opened and Anne Benedick appeared.

Nature, in assembling Anne Benedick, had done a nice bit of work. She was a slim girl of twenty-three, one of those alert, boyish-looking girls of whom one feels what jolly children they must have been. She had a demure mouth, with a whimsical twist to it, and eyes that looked as if they saw the humour of things. The first thought any male observer would have had about her – except Mr Trumper, who naturally regarded such a position as a privilege – was that she seemed made for something better than sitting at a telephone saying 'Yes, Mrs Cork.'

Her employer, direct as always, came to the point with the decision of a machine-gun.

'Miss Benedick. Cakebread. Pay him a month's wages, and see that he leaves to-day.'

Her words were so definite, her tone so resolute, that one might have supposed that the girl's only possible reply would have been another 'Yes, Mrs Cork.' To that autocrat's astonishment, however, and to Mr Trumper's shocked disapproval, Anne Benedick did not take her cue.

'What!' she cried. 'Why?'

Mrs Cork had once had a native bearer who, when given his orders for the day, had said 'Why?' You can recognize him easily, if you happen to be in his village, by the dazed, stunned look which still lingers on his face and the way he has of jumping, if anyone speaks to him suddenly. That had been nearly ten years ago, and nobody had tried it since. Amazement, accordingly, held her dumb for an instant, and before she could rally from the shock Dolly Molloy intervened.

'I'll tell you why,' she said vehemently. 'I don't know who hired this darned Cakebread to haunt this house; nor what his charges were, but he's turning in a swell job. You can't go anywheres in the place without finding him floating around like ectoplasm. He's been in Mrs Cork's room, he's been in Mr Trumper's room, and he's been in my room, twice in two days. And what we kinda feel is that he'd best be shot out before he gets through with checking up on our stuff and deciding which of it to pack in his old kit bag and which is too heavy to lift.'

'Exactly,' said Mrs Cork. 'Get rid of him at once.'

Anne Benedick's mouth twitched. One would have said that she was amused.

'I'm afraid you can't get rid of him.'

Again, Mrs Cork was conscious of a sense of shock.

'Can't get rid of him?'

'I'm afraid not. I don't think you can have read the lease of the house carefully, or you would have noticed the clause about Cakebread. My uncle insisted on having it put in.'

'Clause? What clause?'

'That in no circumstances is he to be dismissed from his position.'

'What!'

'I'm afraid so.'

There was a silence. Then Mrs Cork said she had never heard of such a thing, and Mr Trumper said it was quite incredible. Mrs Molloy did not speak. She seemed to be thinking.

'It's annoying, of course.'

'Annoying!'

'But Uncle George refused to let the place under any other conditions.'

Mrs Molloy came out of her reverie.

'Well, say, listen,' she cried. 'There's nothing in the book of the words to prevent Mrs Cork having the bozo pinched and stowed away in the cooler, if he's a thief and gets caught with the goods?'

'Yes, I suppose she could do that,' said Anne. 'But really, Mrs Cork, you're quite mistaken about Cakebread. It's just that he has an enquiring mind.'

'Well, look,' proceeded Mrs Molloy. 'Lemme tell you how you can swing it. Hire a detective, and have him watch the bimbo.'

She gazed at Mrs Cork hopefully. Here, her agile mind had perceived, was one of those cases where a single stone may be utilized for the undoing of two birds. The sanctity of private property could be protected against any oompus-boompus, and at the same time she would have on the premises a trained ally, observing her Soapy's movements both in and out of rose gardens.

Mrs Cork's eyes lightened.

'An admirable suggestion.'

'Admirable,' agreed Mr Trumper.

'And I've got the very man for you,' said Mrs Molloy. 'Sheringham Adair, of Halsey Court, Mayfair.'

'Mayfair,' said Mr Trumper, impressed.

'Mayfair,' said Mrs Cork, well satisfied. 'That sounds all right.'

'He's as smart as a whip. One of the best men in the business.'

'Then I will put the matter in his hands. You have the name and address, Miss Benedick? Sheringham Adair, Halsey Court, Mayfair.'

'But really—'

'Please don't stand there, saying "Really." Go at once. If you start immediately in the two-seater, you will be able to reach him before he leaves his office. If possible, bring him back with you. I shall not feel easy in my mind till the man is in the house.'

'Nor I,' said Mr Trumper.

'Me neither,' said Mrs Molloy.

Anne Benedick gave an imperceptible shrug of her trim shoulders, but she knew better than to argue. Those who had the privilege of serving Clarissa Cork soon learned to acquire the Light Brigade outlook. What though the secretary-companion knew someone had blundered, hers not to reason why. What she had to do was go to the garage, get out the two-seater and make the seventy-minute trip to London.

Nevertheless, though outwardly acquiescent, it was not to the garage that she proceeded on leaving the room, but to the butler's pantry. She found its occupant seated at the table, playing chess with himself. From the contented expression on his face, he appeared to be winning.

He looked up, as Anne entered.

'Hullo, my dear. Come for a little chat, hey?'

There was a motherly severity in Anne's manner.

'No, I haven't,' she said. 'If you wish to know, my angel, I'm off to London, to engage a detective. Did you hear that? A detective. He's coming to stay at the house, and his task will be to watch your every movement with his magnifying glass.'

'Lord-love-a-duck! Yer don't mean that?'

'Yes, I do,' said Anne. 'Your conduct has aroused the liveliest suspicion. You've certainly made a nice mess of things, Uncle George.'

CHAPTER 4

At about the time when Anne Benedick, at the wheel of Mrs Cork's two-seater, was passing through the outer fringe of the suburbs on her way to Halsey Buildings, Jeff Miller stood leaning out of his third-floor window in Halsey Chambers, his eyes fixed on the entrance of the court. His air was one of anxiety and apprehension. He looked like Mr Trumper just before his interview with Mrs Cork.

Nor would anyone who had been placed in possession of the facts have been surprised at his trepidation. Earlier in the day, he had received a telegram from Myrtle Shoesmith, announcing that she would be with him in the course of the afternoon. And if Myrtle had cut short her visit to her friends in the country and was rushing back to see him in this impetuous fashion, it could mean but one thing. She had been reading about the case of Pennefather *v.* Tarvin.

Full reports of this had appeared that morning in all the brighter London journals, in some cases on the front page. And if this should seem strange, seeing what a minor case it was, it may be mentioned that what had caused light-hearted reporters to describe the proceedings at considerable length had been the football celebrity of plaintiff's counsel and his entertaining methods of cross-examination.

Jeff would not have done it for pleasure, but he could, if called upon, have recited those newspaper reports verbatim. They were graven on his mind. An excerpt from one flashed before him now, in letters of flame.

COUNSEL: Is it not a fact, Green—

JUDGE: Mr Green, if you please, Mr Miller.

COUNSEL: Oh, sorry.

JUDGE: Not at all, Mr Miller. Pray continue.

COUNSEL: Right ho. Thanks. Is it not a fact, Mr Green ... Look at me, if you please, and not at the jury—

JUDGE: Witness is looking at you, Mr Miller.

COUNSEL: Oh, is he? Right ho. Is it not a fact, Mr Green, that at school you were known as Stinker, and that we were given a half-holiday the day the news came out that you had had a bath?

WITNESS: Your worship!

JUDGE: It is more customary to address me as 'My lord', Mr Green, or, alternatively, as 'Me lud'. However, I find your emotion intelligible. Have these references to witness's apparently misspent youth any bearing on the case now before us, Mr Miller?

COUNSEL: I'm shaking him, me lud – showing what a louse he is.

JUDGE: Do not use the word 'louse', Mr Miller.

COUNSEL: As your ludship pleases. Well, anyway, Stinker, putting aside for the moment the question of your niffiness, wasn't it notorious that you couldn't tell the truth without straining a ligament? What I'm driving at is that this story of yours about the blow or buffet being really a prod or tap is a tissue of lies from soup to nuts. Come on now, come clean, you unspeakable wart.

JUDGE: The expression 'wart', Mr Miller—

There had been quite a lot of this sort of thing, culminating in Counsel requesting the Learned Judge for heaven's sake not to keep interrupting all the time, and His Lordship, ceasing to be urbane, speaking of contempt of court and advising Counsel to lose no time in adopting some other walk in life, for he, His Lordship, could see no future for him at the Bar. And the thought of Myrtle Shoesmith's eyes perusing it, and Myrtle Shoesmith coming to have a long, cosy talk about it, was not an agreeable one.

He craned his neck out of the window, scanning the horizon, and nearly overbalanced as Ma Balsam's voice spoke unexpectedly behind him. For one awful moment, he had thought that Myrtle had arrived unseen and sneaked up in his rear.

'When would you be wanting tea, sir?'

Jeff eyed her wanly. It seemed to him she had got a wrong angle on this interview which confronted him.

'I very much doubt, Ma, if the question of tea will arise.'

'Young ladies like their cup of tea, sir.'

'True. But I think you are overstressing the social side of this reunion. I have an idea that Miss Shoesmith will be far too busy talking to have leisure for refreshment.'

'I've made some nice rock cakes.'

'Even for nice rock cakes. You might tempt her with my blood, but a sip or two of that, as I see it, will be all that she will be requiring. I may be wrong, but I have an uneasy feeling, Ma, that she has been reading about the Case. You did, I suppose?'

'Oh, yes, sir.'

'You know, Ma, the whole thing is just one more instance of how one can regret doing something which seemed a good idea at the time. When I beheld this Lionel Green cowering before me in the box, and suddenly realized that he was the Stinker Green who had embittered my early boyhood, it appeared such an obvious course to slip it across him and bathe him in confusion that I didn't hesitate. "You are on the right lines, J. G. Miller," I said to myself.'

'Then you knew the gentleman, sir?'

'Didn't you gather that from the trend of my examination? Yes, we were at school together. He was a couple of years older than me. It was he who secured for me the repulsive nickname of "Socks", which I succeeded in living down, thanks to some lissomness on the football field, only in my last two years. "Socks", I may mention, was short for "Bed Socks". This blot Green spread abroad the foul canard that I wore bed socks at home and always had to sleep with a nightlight because I was afraid of the dark. Well, you know – or possibly with your pure mind you do not know – what hellhounds the young of the English leisured classes are. They were on to it like wolves.'

'Not nice of the young gentleman, sir.'

'Not at all nice. I was too small at the time to biff him in the eye, but I swore a dark oath of vengeance. I can now write that off.'

'I thought the Judge was very nasty to you, sir.'

'Very. I had always supposed that Counsel on these occasions was allowed to say whatever he liked, while the Judge leaned back and chuckled heartily at his ready wit, and it was a rude shock to me when His Lordship kept kicking me in the stomach. Still, these Judges have a great deal of penetration,

Ma. Shrewd fellows. You noticed what this one said, about how I ought to give up the Bar? He was merely putting into words what I have so often felt myself. From now on, I shall concentrate exclusively upon the work where I am convinced that my real talents lie. I shall write thrillers, and I shall do nothing but write thrillers, and if they come to me and plead with me to appear in the latest *cause célèbre*, I shall reply that I am sorry, but I cannot fit it in. You merely court disaster in these days of specialization, if you dissipate your energies. Oh, yes, Ma, I am quite clear that all this has been the best thing that could possibly have happened. But if you ask me if I am looking forward to the prospect of explaining that to Miss Shoesmith, I answer frankly...Oh, my God!' said Jeff, a powerful shudder passing through his well-knit frame. 'Here she is!'

He squared his shoulders manfully, endeavouring to over-come a sinking sensation in the pit of the stomach. Watching Myrtle Shoesmith, as she crossed the court, it would have been impossible for the dullest and least observant eye not to have seen that her walk was the walk of an overwrought soul. Mrs Cork, had she been present, would have noted instantly the resemblance to a leopard on the prowl. She disappeared into the doorway of Halsey Chambers, and Jeff, after a momentary hesitation, went out on to the landing to meet her, bracing himself for what was plainly going to be a sticky *tête-à-tête*.

For it had been evident to him, gazing down into the court, and it was more evident to him now than ever, as he peered over the banisters, that his betrothed was in no sunny and companionable mood. He had never really entertained the notion that they were going to have a good laugh together over the case of Pennefather *v.* Tarvin, but, if he had, it would have vanished when she arrived at the eminence where he stood. Reaching the landing, she halted, and regarded him for a moment in silence, panting a little, as if she had been some Empress of Emotion on the silver screen.

When she spoke, it was in a low thrilling voice, almost inaudible but packed with a wealth of pent-up feeling. It reminded Jeff of the voice of a Welsh forward, on whose head he had sat one muddy afternoon at Cardiff Arms Park.

'Are you mad, Geoffrey?'

The question was one to which a direct answer was difficult. Jeff decided to strike the soothing note.

'I think I know what you mean,' he said. 'You're referring to the Case, aren't you? I thought you might want to hear all about that. Come along in, and we'll have a long talk about it over a cup of tea.'

'I don't want any tea.'

'There are rock cakes.'

'When I read that report in the *Daily Express*, I nearly fainted. I couldn't believe my eyes. You must have been insane.'

'Well, I admit that I was just the slightest bit carried away and to a certain extent lost my calm judgement. As I was telling Ma Balsam, this man Green turned out to be a fellow who had embittered my youth with foul calumnies. When I recognized. him, I saw red. Green, too, of course.'

'I don't know what you are talking about.'

'I'm trying to explain why I wasn't suave and dignified, as I had intended to be. When this excrescence slunk into the witness box, and I realized that he was Stinker Green—'

'After all the trouble I took to get Father to give you the brief.'

'I know, I know. Oh, don't think I don't see your point of

view. All I'm trying to make you understand is that this boll-weevil Green—'

'He's furious. He keeps saying "I told you so." He pleaded with me to break our engagement.'

Jeff quivered from stem to stern. He had not expected this. A thorough cursing, yes. A proper ticking-off, quite. But not a complete remission of sentence. There came into his eyes a sudden wild gleam of hope, such as might have come into the eyes of some wretched man on a scaffold, who, just as the executioner is spitting on his hands with a cheery 'Heave ho!' observes a messenger galloping up on a foaming horse, waving a parchment.

'You wouldn't do that?' he said, in a low voice.

There was no weakness in Myrtle Shoesmith. She could see that her words had shaken this man to his foundations, and in a way, despite her justifiable indignation, she was sorry for him. But she was a firm believer in punishment where punishment had been earned. She removed her glove.

'I had already made up my mind to do it in the train. I am certainly not going to marry a man capable of behaving as you have done. I thought that I might be able to make something of you, but I see that I was mistaken. Here is your ring.'

Jeff, twiddling it between thumb and forefinger, was struck by one of those quaint thoughts which so often came to him when he was in joyous mood. With the idea of easing the strain and making the party go, he decided to share it with his companion.

'You know,' he said, 'this makes me feel like a pawnbroker.'

'What on earth do you mean?'

'Your giving me this ring. As if you had brought it in to the old pop shop and were asking me what I could spring on it.'

'Good-bye,' said Myrtle Shoesmith, rightly revolted, and was off down the stairs before Jeff knew that she had started. She understood now what her father had meant when he had described this young man as unbalanced and flippant.

CHAPTER 5

Jeff tottered back into his flat, and sank into a chair. He was feeling weak and spent. Sudden joy often has this effect, temporarily numbing the faculties. He was dimly aware that Ma Balsam was addressing him, and nodded absently. And from the fact that she went out, with a kindly word about drinking it while it was hot, he gathered that she must have been asking him if he would like his tea. And, sure enough, a few moments later she reappeared, bearing a loaded tray.

He eyed it without enthusiasm. Much has been said by writers through the ages in praise of tea, but there are occasions in a man's life when this pleasant, but mild, beverage, will not serve. Scarcely had Ma Balsam withdrawn, with another kindly word about hoping that he would enjoy the rock cakes, when he perceived that this was one of them.

In this supreme moment, he wanted to celebrate, and it seemed to him that the sort of celebration he had in mind called for something stronger than tea, something more authoritative, something that did not merely cheer without inebriating but bit like a serpent and stung like an adder. And it so happened that in his cupboard he had a bottle of the hell-brew required.

Five minutes later, he was sitting with his feet on the

window-sill, a lively glow permeating his entire system, his mood one of bubbling ecstasy. And so, for a space, it remained.

But after a while he found his thoughts taking a graver turn. At a time like this, he saw, it was not enough merely to rejoice. Nor was it enough, he realized, that we should have these great emotional crises in our lives. The important thing was to profit by them, to learn their lesson and act upon it: and he perceived that this wonderful piece of good fortune had been sent to him for a purpose.

It was easy, of course, to see what that purpose was. If he had a fault, it was, he knew, that in his relations with the opposite sex he was inclined to be a little too cordial, just a shade more chummy than was actually necessary. He liked girls. Tall girls, small girls, slim girls, plump girls, blonde girls, dark girls, he liked them all. And too often, when confronted with one, he was apt to start buzzing.

Yes, that was the blemish in his character which this experience had been sent to correct. He was a buzzer. Nature had dowered him with a ready flow of that small-talk which is part badinage and part sentiment, and far too frequently, when assisting at parties, routs and revels, he found himself backing the prettiest girl present into a corner and starting to buzz at her.

He had done it, he recollected with a shudder, even with Myrtle Shoesmith: and this whole Myrtle Shoesmith episode, with its hideous peril averted only at the eleventh hour, had been designed to warn him to watch his step and be a bit more distant with the sex in future.

There and then, he registered a vow that this should be attended to without delay. Girls in the past had spoken of J. G. Miller as 'dear old Jeff' and 'a scream'. Girls from now on would be asking one another in awed whispers who that cold, stern man with the strange, inscrutable face was, who leaned against the wall with folded arms and seemed unaware of their existence.

It was at this point that he happened to look round. His glance fell on the plate of rock cakes, lying untouched on their tray, and the sight brought him back to the present with a jerk.

His immediate thought was that he had never beheld anything so uninviting. The things seemed to be leering at him malevolently. Too many cooks, in baking rock cakes, get misled by the word 'rock', and it was into this category that Ma Balsam fell. And even if this had not been so, his stomach, which, though a healthy one, could be pushed just so far, rebelled at the thought of bilious *pâtisserie* on top of the generous spirit in which he had been indulging.

And yet it was impossible to leave that heaped-up plateful for Ma Balsam to take away. She was so sensitive, and it so plainly untouched. Jeff was a nice-minded young man, who shrank from giving pain. The feelings of Ma Balsam were sacred to him.

He was faced, accordingly, he saw, by the problem which was always bothering characters, in the stories he wrote – viz. How to get rid of the body? And it was as he stood brooding on this that his eye chanced to fail on the room opposite, the one that bore on the upper half of its open window the legend 'J. Sheringham Adair', and it was as if a sudden bright light had shone upon him.

From where he was standing, he could see into this room, and it had all the appearance of being empty. The odd little wax-moustached blighter, whom he had sometimes seen sitting at the desk apparently engaged in putting top dressing on his upper lip, was not doing so now. Private Investigator Adair's private investigations had apparently taken him elsewhere for the moment, to a consultation at Scotland Yard perhaps or possibly to Joe the Lascar's opium den in Limehouse in connection with the affair of the Maharajah's Ruby.

Whether this was so or not, on one point Jeff was clear. When Sheringham Adair returned, he might not have the Maharajah's Ruby in his possession, but he was going to be extraordinarily well off for rock cakes. With an accuracy of aim which gave evidence of the clear eye and the steady hand, he proceeded to hurl the contents of the plate across the courtyard.

It was the fifth and last of the jagged delicacies that hit Chimp Twist. It caught him squarely between the eyes, creating the momentary illusion that the top of his head had parted from its moorings.

For in supposing that Mr Twist's office was empty, Jeff had erred. Its lessee was there, but a few moments earlier he had gone down on his hands and knees in quest of a dropped sixpence. A curious impression, that the air had suddenly become full of strange flying objects, caused him to rise abruptly at precisely the worst time he could have chosen.

An instant's stunned inaction, and he was at the window, rubbing his forehead. His gaze rested on a young man with straw-coloured hair and a contorted face, who seemed to glare at him with an evil, ferocious hostility. And there came to Chimp the feeling that had come to him so often in the course of his dubious career, that things were getting too hot.

Nothing is more regrettable than the frequency with which these misunderstandings occur in life. We, who know the motives which had caused Jeff to throw rock cakes, are aware that his glare was one of horror and remorse. Quite inadvertently, meaning only to spare Ma Balsam's *amour propre*, he had gone and beaned one of the neighbours, and he stood aghast at his handiwork, too overcome to speak. Nobody, one would have imagined, could have failed to recognize him for what he was, a living statue of contrition.

But Chimp Twist was peculiarly situated. London, like the Chicago which a growing unpopularity had forced him to evacuate some years previously, was full of people who asked nothing more than to take a good poke at him, and his sensitive conscience suggested that Jeff must be one of these.

True, the latter's appearance was not familiar to him, but then one is so apt to forget faces. And the cardinal fact remained that this glarer had just been throwing lethal objects at him, though of what nature he had not yet had leisure to ascertain. Reeling back, he paused for a while in thought.

Jeff, meanwhile, had left his post. He had hurried from the room, and was clattering on his way downstairs to apologize. He was extremely doubtful whether any apology could really meet the case, but it was obvious that one must be offered. No right-thinking young man can sock a complete stranger on the frontal bone with a rock cake and just let the thing go without a word. There is a code in these matters.

And so it came about that when Chimp Twist leaped forth on to the landing, his momentary inaction ended and his whole being intent on making a getaway while the going was good, the first thing he beheld over the banisters was his implacable assailant bounding up the stairs, plainly with the object of renewing hostilities at close quarters. His escape was cut off.

But there was still a way. It was for precisely this sort of emergency that he kept that tall and spacious cupboard on his premises. To dart back into the office and dive for this sanctuary like a homing rabbit was with Chimp Twist the work of a moment. A few seconds later, he was curled up in its interior, breathing very softly through the nostrils, and Jeff, arriving at journey's end, found only an empty room.

There was the desk. There, scattered about the floor, lay his generous donation of rock cakes. But from any sign of wax-moustached little men coldly awaiting explanations the place was entirely free. The theory was one which would have been scouted by anyone at all intimate with Chimp Twist, but it really looked as if he must have been snatched up to heaven in a fiery chariot.

Jeff found himself running what might legitimately be called the gamut of the emotions – first, amazement at what seemed to him either a miracle or a first-rate conjuring trick; then, for he had never enjoyed the prospect of having to frame that apology, relief; and finally interest.

This was the first time he had ever been in the office of a private investigator, and it occurred to him that here was an admirable opportunity of picking up a little atmosphere, which might come in useful when the moment arrived for starting his next novel. He sat down at the desk, noting as Fact One concerning these human bloodhounds, that they apparently liked to work in dusty surroundings, no doubt in order to retain the fingerprints of callers.

And it was as he leaned back thoughtfully in the chair, wishing that a scrupulous sense of honour did not prohibit him from searching through the drawers and reading his absent host's correspondence, that someone knocked at the door, and there entered a girl at the sight of whom his head jerked back as if struck by a rock cake.

'Mr Adair?' she asked, in a charming voice, soft and musical like sheep bells at sunset.

'Absolutely,' said Jeff, coming to one of those instant decisions which were so characteristic of his eager, enthusiastic nature. The idea of not being the man she was looking for seemed to him too silly to be entertained for an instant.

It was true, of course, that he had registered a vow to be cold and distant to all girls, but naturally that had never been intended to apply to special cases like this.

CHAPTER 6

There was a brief pause. Jeff was too fully occupied on taking in the newcomer's many perfections to be capable of speech. His mind was in a sort of emotional welter, to the surface of which, like an egg shell in a maelstrom, there kept bobbing one coherent thought – to wit, that if this was the sort of girl who frequented the offices of private investigators, he had been mad not to have become a private investigator before.

It was true that almost anybody who did not look like Myrtle Shoesmith would have appealed to him at the moment, and Anne Benedick was supremely unlike Myrtle Shoesmith, but the thing went deeper than that. There was something about this visitor that seemed to touch some hidden chord in his being, setting joy bells ringing and torchlight processions parading through the echoing corridors of his soul. Romeo, he fancied, must have experienced a somewhat similar, though weaker, emotion on first beholding Juliet.

As for Anne, her reactions, if less ecstatic, were distinctly favourable. Halsey Court, and particularly the staircase of Halsey Buildings, had prepared her for something pretty outstandingly bad in the way of investigators – something, indeed, very like the Chimp Twist who might so easily have been there to receive her: and this agreeable, clean-cut young man came as a refreshing surprise. She liked his looks. She had also a curious feeling that she had seen him before somewhere.

'Good afternoon,' she said, and Jeff pulled himself together with a strong effort. His fervour was still as pronounced as ever, but the first stunned sensation had begun to wane.

'Good afternoon,' he replied. 'Do sit down, won't you?' He seized a chair and started mopping it vigorously with his coat sleeve, as Sir Walter Raleigh would have done in his place. He regretted that the lax methods of his predecessor's charwoman should have rendered the action so necessary. 'Quite a bit of dust in here, I'm afraid.'

'There does seem to be a speck or two.'

'One gets called away on an important case, and during one's absence the cleaning staff take it easy.'

'I suppose they have heard so much about the importance of leaving everything absolutely untouched.'

'It may be so. Still, there are too many rock cakes about, far too many rock cakes. I see no reason for anything like this number of rock cakes.'

'You don't think they lend a homely touch?'

'Perhaps you are right. Yes, possibly they do brighten the old place up. There,' said Jeff, exhibiting his handiwork, 'I think that's better.'

'Much better. And now would you mind dusting another? My uncle should be arriving in a moment. I thought he was coming up the stairs behind me, but he must have stopped to sniff at something. He has rather an enquiring mind.'

As she spoke, there came from outside the door the slow booming of feet on the stone stairs, as if a circus elephant in *sabots* were picking its way towards the third floor: and as Jeff finished removing the alluvial deposits from a second of

Mr Twist's chairs, the missing member of the party arrived.

'Come in, angel,' said Anne. 'We were wondering where you had got to. This is Mr Adair. My uncle, Lord Uffenham.'

The newcomer, as the sound of his footsteps had suggested, was built on generous lines. In shape, he resembled a pear, reasonably narrow at the top but getting wider and wider all the way down and culminating in a pair of boors of the outsize or violin-case type. Above these great, spreading steppes of body there was poised a large and egglike head, the bald dome of which rose like some proud mountain peak from a foothill fringe of straggling hair. His upper lip was very long and straight, his chin pointed. Two huge, unblinking eyes of the palest blue looked out from beneath rugged brows with a strange fixity.

'How do yer do?' he said. 'Haryer? I've been having a dashed interesting talk with a policeman, my dear. I noticed that he was the living image of a feller who took me to Vine Street on Boat Race Night of the year 1909, and I stopped him and asked him if he could account for this in any way. And I'm blowed if he didn't turn out to be my policeman's son. That's what you'd call a link between the generations, what?' He paused, and turned his glassy stare on Jeff, giving the latter the momentary feeling of having been caught in the ray of a searchlight. 'You ever been taken to Vine Street?'

Jeff said that he had not had this experience.

'Decent little place, as police stations go,' said Lord Uffenham tolerantly.

With which encomium, he lowered himself into a chair, with such an air of complete withdrawal from his surroundings and looking so like something which Gutzon Borglum might have carved on the side of a mountain that Jeff had an odd illusion that he was no longer there. He turned to Anne, to learn from

her what was the nature of the business which had put her on
J. Sheringham Adair's visiting list, and found her regarding
him with a puzzled look.

'I can't help feeling I've seen you before, Mr Adair.'

'Really?' said Jeff. 'I wonder where. You—' He paused. He
had been about to ask if she had been in court during the
trying of the case of Pennefather *v.* Tarvin, but perceived in
time that this would be injudicious. 'You never came to Cambridge for May Week, did you?'

'No.'

'Were you ever in Rome? Naples? Cannes? Lovely Lucerne?'

'Never. You seem to have travelled more than I have.'

'Oh, well, you know, one's cases. They take one everywhere.'

'I suppose so. I've never been about much, except just country
house visits in England. But I ought to be telling you my
business.'

Lord Uffenham came suddenly out of his coma, and at once
gave evidence that, though the body had been inert, the brain
had not been idle.

'Hey,' he said, once more subjecting Jeff to that piercing stare.
'Yes?'

'Do you know how you can tell the temperature?'

'Look at a thermometer?'

'Simpler than that. Count the number of chirps a grasshopper
makes in fourteen seconds, and add forty.'

'Oh, yes?' said Jeff, and awaited further observations. But
the other had said his say. With the air of a man shutting up a
public building, he closed his mouth and sat staring before
him, and Jeff returned to Anne.

'You were saying—'

'I was about to disclose the nature of my business, only the

Sieur de Uffenham got on to the subject of grasshoppers. You mustn't pay any attention to my uncle, Mr Adair. He's liable to pop up like this at any moment. Just say to yourself that now you know how to tell the temperature, and dismiss the thing from your mind.'

'The system would be a good one, mark you, if you had a grasshopper.'

'And hadn't a thermometer.'

'As might easily happen during a country ramble. The nature of your business, you were saying?'

'Well, to begin with, I have been sent here by Mrs Wellesley Cork.'

'I know that name.'

'I thought you might.'

'The big-game huntress?'

'That's right.'

'Of course. I saw a photograph of her in some paper the other day, looking sideways at a dead lion.'

'"Mrs Cork and Friend".'

'Exactly.'

'I am her secretary. My name is Benedick. She has taken my uncle's place in Kent – Shipley Hall.'

'Oh, yes?'

'And she wants to have a detective on the premises.'

Once more, Lord Uffenham emerged from his waxwork-like trance.

'Silly old geezer,' he said, like Counsel giving an opinion in chambers, and passed into the silence again.

Jeff nodded encouragingly.

'A detective on the premises? You interest me strangely. Why?'

'To watch her butler.'

'Worth watching, is he? An arresting spectacle?'

'She thinks so. And you were recommended by a Mrs Molloy.'

'Why does Mrs Cork want her butler watched?'

'She has an idea he's dishonest. She keeps finding him rummaging in rooms.'

'I see. Why doesn't she just fire him?'

'She can't. My uncle made it a condition of allowing her to have the house that the butler was to stay on and couldn't be dismissed.'

'Didn't she object to a clause like that in the lease?'

'She didn't pay much attention to the lease. She left it all to me. She told me to get her a house within easy distance of London, and my uncle wanted to let his, so I fixed everything up. It seemed all right to me. You see, I know Cakebread.'

'I don't. Who is he?'

'The butler.'

'His name is really Cakebread?'

'Why not?'

'It sounds too obviously butlerine. As if he had adopted it as a ruse, to lure employers into a false confidence. You're sure he's all right?'

'Quite.'

'As pure as the driven snow?'

'Purer.'

'Then why does he rummage in rooms?'

'Well—'

'Yes?'

'I don't know.'

Jeff permitted himself a moment's severity. It was, he felt, what J. Sheringham Adair would have done, had he been conducting this inquisition.

'Miss Benedick, do you ever read detective stories?'

'Of course.'

'Then you will be familiar with something that happens with unfailing regularity in all of them. There is always a point, you will have noticed, where the detective turns a bit sniffy and says he cannot possibly undertake this case unless he has his client's full confidence. "You are keeping something back from me," he says. Miss Benedick, I put it to you that you are keeping something back from me. What is it?'

He stared keenly across the desk. Anne had fallen into thought. A little wrinkle had appeared in her forehead, and the tip of her nose wiggled like a rabbit's. Very attractive, Jeff thought it, and so it was.

'I have just been working it out in my mind,' said Lord Uffenham, rejoining them after having preserved for some five minutes the appearance of being one of those loved ones far away, of whom the hymnal speaks, 'and I find that I could put the whole dashed human race into a pit half a mile wide by half a mile deep.'

'I wouldn't,' said Jeff.

'No, don't,' said Anne. 'Think how squashy it would be for the ones at the bottom.'

'True,' admitted Lord Uffenham, after consideration. 'Yerss. Yerss, I see what you mean. Still, it's an interesting thought.'

He ceased, and Jeff, who had waited courteously for him to continue, realizing after a pause that nothing more was coming and that this was apparently just another of the *obiter dicta* which it was his lordship's custom to throw out from time to time in a take-it-or-leave-it spirit, like the lady in Dickens who used to speak of milestones on the Dover road, turned to Anne again.

'What are you keeping from me, Miss Benedick?'

'What makes you think I'm keeping something from you?'

'My trained instinct. I'm a detective.'

'A very odd one.'

'Odd?'

'You aren't at all my idea of a detective. I thought they were cold and sniffy, like solicitors.'

'I know what you mean,' said Jeff. Association with Mr Shoesmith had taught him a lot about the coldness and sniffiness of solicitors. 'But in my case you feel—?'

'—as if I could tell you things without you raising your eyebrows.'

'Good Lord! Of course, you can. I may put the tips of my fingers together, but I wouldn't dream of raising my eyebrows. Confide in me without a qualm. I knew there was something on your mind, something that would throw a light on this butler business. You have special knowledge, have you not, which will bring faithful old Cakebread out of the thing without a stain on his character? Let's have the inside story.'

'I wonder.'

'Don't weaken.'

'Tell him,' boomed Lord Uffenham, abruptly coming to life in that surprising way of his. 'You came here to tell him, didn't you? You brought me along, so that I could be present when you told him, didn't you? Well, then. Lord-love-a-duck, what's the use of coming thirty miles to tell a feller something and then not telling him?'

'But it makes you look such a chump, darling.'

'It does not make me look a chump, at all. I acted from the

first with the best and soundest motives, and this young feller is a broadminded young feller who will recognize the fact.'

'Well, all right. You could help us a lot, of course,' said Anne, turning to Jeff. 'I mean, I suppose, as a detective, you're always looking for things, aren't you?'

'Always. Clues, Maharajahs' rubies, stolen treaties, anything that comes along.'

'And you would have special ways of finding anything?'

'You'd be surprised.'

'A sort of—'

'Technique.'

'Yes, technique. At present, it all seems so hopeless. It's like hunting for a needle in a haystack.'

'What is?'

'It's so difficult to know how to start telling you. Well, first of all, Cakebread isn't Cakebread.'

'Aha! Now we're getting somewhere.'

'He's my uncle.'

Jeff blinked.

'You said—'

'Cakebread is my uncle.'

'This uncle?' asked Jeff, indicating Lord Uffenham, who had once more become remote and was looking like a recently unveiled statue.

'Yes. You see, we decided that the only thing to be done, if he was going to let the house – and he had to let the house, to get some ready money – was for him to stay on, in case he suddenly remembered. And the only way he could stay on was by being the butler. It's quite simple, really.'

'Oh, quite. Remembered, did you say?'

'Where he had hidden it.'

'I see. Yes, that explains it all. Er – hidden what?'

Anne Benedick gave a sudden laugh, so silvery, so musical, that it seemed to Jeff that his great passion, in the truest and deepest sense of the words, really dated from this moment. Ever since she had come in, shimmering across the threshold like the spirit of the June day, he had known, of course, in a sort of general way that the strange emotion she awoke in him was love, but this laugh – hitherto she had merely smiled – seemed to underline the facts and clarify his outlook. There was all Heaven in Anne Benedick's laugh. It conjured up visions of a cosy home on a winter's night, with one's slippers on one's feet, the dog on one's lap, an open fire in the grate and the good old pipe drawing nicely.

'I'm not telling this story very well, am I?' she said. 'The word "it" refers to a small packet of extremely valuable diamonds representing the combined Uffenham and Benedick fortunes. My uncle hid them somewhere on the premises of Shipley Hall, and now hasn't the slightest recollection where.'

Inside the spacious cupboard, Chimp Twist, for all that he realized the imperative need of keeping his presence undetected, found it impossible to repress a startled snort. The thought of diamonds lying around loose in a country house – a country house, moreover, in which were established those old allies of his, Mr and Mrs Soapy Molloy, was one that spoke to his very depths. If this was not money in the bank, he did not know such money when he saw it. So he snorted.

Fortunately for his aims and objects, Jeff had snorted simultaneously on his own account, and with such abandon that the Twist contribution passed unnoticed. The idea did, indeed, cross Lord Uffenham's mind that there was a curious echo in the room and set him musing dreamily on acoustics, but that was all.

'That surprises you?'

'It does.'

'It surprised me, too, when he told me. I had always known that he had an original mind, but I hadn't been prepared for that.'

Jeff had recovered somewhat. He was even able, though a little feebly, to place the tips of his fingers together again.

'Let me get this clear,' he said. 'He put the entire family funds into diamonds?'

'Yes.'

'And hid them?'

'Yes.'

'And then forgot where?'

'Yes.'

'Like a dog with a bone?'

'Exactly like a dog with a bone.'

'Yes,' said Jeff, expelling a deep breath. '"Original" is correct. No need to consult the Thesaurus. You've got the right word.'

'You see,' said Anne. 'I told you it would make you look a chump. Mr Adair is stunned.'

As far as such an action was within the scope of a man weighing two hundred and sixty pounds, Lord Uffenham bridled.

'I refuse to admit,' he said stiffly, 'that it makes me look any such dashed thing. My motives, as I told you before, were fundamentally sound. Lord-love-a-duck, what's wrong with diamonds? One of the few good investments left in a world where everything else seems to be going to hell. It was only after considerable thought, after I had been shocked by the fall in value of some dashed railway shares to about half the value of waste paper, that I faced the problem squarely and made my decision.'

'Oh, there was a certain amount of method in your madness, I suppose.'

'What d'yer mean, madness?'

'There always is, bless him,' proceeded Anne, addressing Jeff with the air of an indulgent parent discussing the eccentricities of a favourite child. 'When he explains any of these weird doings of his, you find yourself nodding appreciatively and feeling that he has taken the only possible course.'

'Diamonds are always diamonds,' said Jeff, for the defence.

'Not if you can't find them.'

'It's nice, of course, to be able to find them.'

'Full many a gem of purest ray serene the dark, unfathomed caves of ocean bear, and a lot of good they are to a hard-up old peer of the realm and his impoverished niece. This also applies to gems which may or may not be stuffed up the chimney in the second housemaid's bedroom.'

'I don't think they are there,' said Lord Uffenham, having considered the suggestion.

'They may be.'

'True.'

'You haven't the slightest notion where they are.'

'At the moment, no. I keep getting what seem to be encouraging gleams of light, but they haven't led anywhere.'

Jeff touched on a point which, he felt, would not have escaped the attention of Sheringham Adair.

'Why didn't you put these diamonds in a safe deposit vault?'

'I don't believe in safe deposit vaults.'

'Ask him why he didn't buy a safe of his own,' said Anne.

'Why didn't you buy a safe of your own?' enquired Jeff obediently.

'I don't—'

'—believe in safes.'

'Well, I don't,' said Lord Uffenham, stoutly. 'A safe simply affords an indication to a burglar where to start looking. It gives the foul feller a sort of official assurance that if he is prepared to take a little trouble, he will find something to his advantage.'

'You are a deep reasoner, Lord Uffenham.'

'Always have been.'

'Doesn't he remind you a little,' said Anne, with a niece's candour, 'of the White Knight in *Alice Through the Looking Glass*? When he passes into those trances of his, I always feel that he's thinking of a way ... I forget how it goes, but a way of doing something or other quite different from anything anybody else would have thought of. Safe deposit vaults? No. He doesn't believe in them. Safes? Not for the Last of the Uffenhams. Coal scuttles, yes.'

'Coal scuttles?'

'He tells me he once hid them in the drawing-room coal scuttle. He used to think of a different place every night.'

'It amused me,' said Lord Uffenham. 'I found it an entertaining test of my ingenuity.'

'Which, of course, has rather complicated things. His memory has got back to what you might call the fitful stage, and he keeps remembering clever places he once thought of. And then he goes and rummages there. So now you will understand how all this anti-Cakebread feeling started. Every time he rummages, somebody always comes in while he is halfway through. You can see what he's like – rather a large man – tall, broad, lots of firm flesh. If you come into a room where he is hunting for diamonds, you can't miss him.'

Jeff nodded. He quite saw how the other would catch the eye.

'Very embarrassing.'

'Most.'

'And how did you – er – get this way, Lord Uffenham?'

'Mr Adair means,' interpreted Anne, 'how did you lose your memory? You tell him. I want to see if it sounds as funny as it did when you told me.'

Lord Uffenham exhibited a certain testiness.

'You will exaggerate so, my dear. There's no question of my having *lost* my memory. All that's happened is that it's a bit uncertain for the time being, owing to that motor accident of mine.'

'You aren't telling it nearly as well this time, darling. My Lord Uffenham,' explained Anne, 'is a man who will never just accept conventions. He likes to brood over them and examine them, and if they seem to him unreasonable, he takes a resolute stand against them. He was driving on the right of the road, taking a resolute stand against the English convention of driving on the left, and an orthodox thinker in a lorry came round the corner. When they let Uncle George out of the hospital, the places where the stitches had been were healing up nicely, but his memory was a blank. The doctors said it was a most interesting case. They loved it.'

'It was a happy thought of yours, considering Lord Uffenham's views, to instal him in the house as a butler, and not a chauffeur.'

'Yes. Though I'm afraid he's not very pleased.'

'I am not,' said Lord Uffenham decidedly. The subject was evidently one to which he had devoted much brooding thought. 'I hate cleaning silver. I dislike waiting at table. It irks me to be thrust continually into the society of a cook who insists on telling me about the state of her inside, going into a wealth of detail which is quite uncalled for. And I particularly resent having to answer to the name of Cakebread.'

'Tell me,' said Jeff, 'did it take you long, thinking up that name?'

'Oh, no,' said Anne. 'It came in a flash.'

'You are a very exceptional girl.'

'Thank you. With quite a fairly exceptional uncle, don't you think? Well, will you help us?'

'Of course.'

'It will make all the difference in the world. I mean, nobody can object to a detective nosing about. It's what he's there for. Uncle George can give you his selections for the day, and you can try them out. Sooner or later, we're bound to strike oil.'

'The mere process of elimination.'

'Exactly. There's just one thing. I'm afraid you won't enjoy being at Shipley. The place is run on the strictest vegetarian lines.'

'This is grave news.'

'Mrs Cork is a fanatic on the subject. In the course of a recent expedition into Africa, she was greatly struck by the glowing health and simple, unspoiled outlook of a tribe called the Ugubus, who, except for an occasional missionary at Christmas, live entirely on fruit and vegetables. She took Shipley with the idea of making it a sort of nucleus or cell for propagating the Ugubu doctrines throughout England. The programme calls for high thinking, tribal dances and, above all, vegetarianism. I just want you to know what you are letting yourself in for.'

'No exception is made in the case of visiting detectives?'

'Of course not. Naturally, you will have to pretend to be an ordinary member of the colony, so as to deceive Cakebread.'

MONEY IN THE BANK

'I see. Still, you will be there.'

'Yes, I shall be there.'

'Then say no more.'

'Well, that's fine. And, anyway, if you find it getting too much for you, you can always drop in on Uncle George in his pantry, and he will give you a glass of port.'

Jeff cast a grateful eye at this lifesaver.

'Will he?'

'Certainly,' said Lord Uffenham. 'The cellar's full, and it all belongs to me. Swill till your eyes bubble.'

'What a disgusting idea,' said Anne. 'I'm sure Mr Adair is most abstemious.'

'Mr Adair,' Jeff pointed out, 'has never been tried as high as he seems likely to be at Shipley Hall.'

Anne rose.

'Then the only thing we haven't settled is when you are to come.'

'When would you like me to come?'

'Mrs Cork spoke of my bringing you back in the car.'

'Excellent.'

'But there won't be room. She didn't know I was going to have Uncle George aboard. How long will it take you to pack?'

'Twenty minutes.'

'Then there's a good train you can catch quite easily. Are you going to your club, Uncle George?'

'Yerss. I thought I might look in.'

'Well, I can give you half an hour. I want to go and see Lionel. I'll call for you.'

It was not for Jeff to comment on this desire of hers to visit male acquaintances, but he had a distinct feeling that for the first time a jarring note had been struck. Then, for he was a fair-minded young man, he decided that he need not make too much of the matter. A girl like this would obviously not be lacking in male acquaintances. His task must be to make it clear to her – taking his time over it, of course, and not alarming her by too instant a display of the Miller fire and impetuosity – that these Lionels and what not were a very poor lot compared with some of the men she had met more recently.

'Good-bye,' he said, pressing her hand with respectful tenderness.

'Good-bye, Mr Adair. And thank you for helping us.'

'Thank you for giving me the opportunity of helping you,' said Jeff.

She hurried out, and Jeff, turning to bid farewell to Lord Uffenham, found that mountainous individual regarding him with an unwinking stare.

'Ha!' said Lord Uffenham. 'Ha! Hey, what?'

Jeff inclined his head in courteous interrogation. Lord Uffenham jerked a thumb at the door through which Anne had passed.

'In love with her, ain't yer, hey?'

The question was so sudden and unexpected that Jeff found himself answering with the automatic candour of a hypnotized subject on a platform.

'Yes,' he said.

'Thought as much,' said Lord Uffenham. 'Stuck out a mile. She's like me, that girl.'

'Er – in what way?' asked Jeff, who had not been struck by any resemblance.

'No woman has ever been able to resist me,' said Lord Uffenham modestly, 'and no young feller I've ever seen has been able to resist her.'

He navigated laboriously through the door, to reappear like the Cheshire Cat and fix Jeff with that tense, unblinking stare.

'Well, wish yer luck,' he said, and disappeared again, this time permanently. And Jeff, after a few moments of profound meditation, made his way slowly down the stairs and went back to Halsey Chambers.

Some minutes later, when it had become absolutely clear to him that he had the office to himself, Chimp Twist emerged from the cupboard, gave his moustache a thoughtful twirl and sat down at the desk to smoke a cigarette.

His brain was working briskly.

CHAPTER 7

Anne Benedick had been waiting in the hall of Lord Uffenham's club some ten minutes before his lordship finally appeared, descending the broad staircase with one hand glued to the arm of a worried-looking Bishop, with whom he was discussing Supralapsarianism. At the sight of Anne, he relaxed his grip, and the Bishop shot gratefully off in the direction of the Silence Room. Lord Uffenham eyed his niece with a guilty sheepishness which he endeavoured to conceal beneath a bluff exterior.

'Hullo, my dear. Just arrived, hey? Capital. Late, ain't yer?'

'No, I am not late,' said Anne, with the severity which she was so often called upon to employ in her dealings with the head of the family. 'And I have not just arrived. They took my name up to you a quarter of an hour ago.'

'So they did, so they did. I remember now. I was showing some of the boys a trick with matches, and lost track of the time. I'll fetch my hat.'

'You've got it on.'

'Have I? Then let's go.'

'We'd better. I shall have to drive with terrific speed, if I'm to get you back before you're missed.'

'Didn't I tell you it was my afternoon out?'

'No, you didn't. Do you mean you've let me fret myself to a shadow, when all the time I needn't have worried?'

'It's this memory of mine. Very uncertain it has become in many respects.'

They made their way to where the two-seater stood, and Anne moved back to allow her companion to enter. There had been a time when, sharing a car with him, she would have taken her seat first, but a few experiences of having the vehicle play cup-and-ball with her under the impact of that enormous mass had taught her prudence. It was Lord Uffenham's practice, when he intended to sit, to hover poised for a moment and then, relaxing limply, to come down with a bump, like an avalanche.

Silence fell between them at the outset of the journey. Anne preferred not to talk in London traffic, and Lord Uffenham was thinking of all the good things he could have said to the Bishop, if he had not been so pressed for time. That rigid look came over his face and limbs, and until they had passed through the suburbs he was simply not to be numbered among those present, the impression he conveyed being that he could now be reached only by transatlantic telephone.

'Well?' said Anne, as they came into the smoother waters of the arterial road. She detached a hand from the wheel, in order to prod her relative in the ribs and show him that he was expected to wake up and converse. 'How do you feel about it all, my poppet?'

'Hey?'

'This business of having a tame detective to help us. I think it has improved our prospects, don't you?'

'Oh, yerss. Decidedly.'

Anne looked wistfully out through the windscreen.

'Something must happen now, don't you think? If it doesn't, it will break my heart. You don't know how sick I am of being a secretary-companion.'

'You don't know how sick I am of being a butler.'

'Let's hope that Mr Adair will restore the family fortunes. What did you think of him?'

'Smart young feller.'

'That's how he struck me.'

'Just like what I was at his age.'

'Were you slim and muscular?'

Lord Uffenham considered.

'Muscular, yes. Never very slim. What I mean is that I was the devil of a young chap; and this young chap is the devil of a young chap. Got some go in him. Not like that pestilential poop of a pop-eyed plasterer you've gone and got engaged to.'

'I've told you before, darling, that you mustn't call Lionel a poop. His eyes never popped in their lives. And he isn't a plasterer, he's an interior decorator.'

'Worse, much worse. I was shocked, when you told me you were going to marry him. Shocked to the core.'

'I know you were.'

' "What, that chap?" I remember saying. "That slimy, slithery, moustache-twiddling young slab of damnation? Lord-love-a-duck!" '

'You did, didn't you? But never mind about Lionel. He's a subject we've agreed to differ upon. I'm glad you thought Mr Adair clever. I must say I was impressed by the quick way he seemed to grasp everything. I suppose detectives are like that.'

Lord Uffenham uttered a hoarse, gurgling sound, like some strong swimmer in his agony. It was his way of chuckling.

'He isn't a detective.'

'What?'

'Didn't fool me for a second.'

The clearness of the road ahead justified Anne in detaching her gaze from it and turning to stare at her companion. The sight of a sort of film beginning to fall over his eyes indicating to her that he was about to go into another trance, she prodded him in the ribs again.

'What do you mean?'

'What I say. D'yer think I don't know a private detective when I see one? I was brought up on them. When I was a young feller starting out in life, they used to follow me about in droves. Private detectives are shocking bounders. You can tell 'em a mile off. This young chap was just some young chap that happened to be in the office. What did you say, when you went in?'

'I said "Mr Adair?" Like that. With an enquiring lilt in my voice.'

'To which he replied—'

'Something like "Definitely," I think. Or "Absolutely."'

'Well, there you are. A real private rozzer would have said "At your service, madam," or some greasy remark of that kind, rubbing his grubby hands together and smirking like a waiter. Did this chap smirk?'

'No. He just stared.'

'Exactly. And why? Because you had bowled him over. You always do bowl these young fellers over. It's a gift you inherit from my side of the family. I've always bowled women over. It was my great trouble in the old days. I'd start out meaning to be merely ordinarily civil, and before I knew where I was, another home wrecked. That's why I used to be followed about by private detectives.'

'I wish your memory was as good about diamonds as it is about your horrible juvenile excesses, my angel.'

'So do I. No pleasure to me to remember juvenile excesses,' said Lord Uffenham, virtuously.

Anne's gaze had returned to the road. Her eyes were thoughtful, and she pressed a tooth against her lower lip. She was reviewing the facts in the light of this new evidence. And as Lord Uffenham had allowed his mind to float off and engage itself with the problem of why birds sit in rows on telegraph wires, when these must be uncomfortable for the feet and there are plenty of trees handy, the silence lasted till they were approaching their destination.

'But it seems so mad,' said Anne, at length.

'Hey?'

'Mr Adair.'

'What about him?'

'I say he must be mad.'

'Why?'

'To masquerade like this.'

'Nothing mad about it, at all. Dashed sensible thing to do, considering the way he feels. Isn't it natural for him to want to be at your side, when he's fallen head over ears in love with you?'

'In love with me?'

'Certainly. I told you you had bowled him over, didn't I? He fell in love with you at first sight.'

'Don't drivel, darling.'

'I'm not drivelling.'

'He couldn't have fallen in love at first sight.'

'Why not?'

'People don't.'

'Don't they, by Jove? I'd like to put all the women I've fallen in love with at first sight end to end—'

'Well, you mustn't. I'm sure you're mistaken.'

'Had it from his own lips.'

'What?'

'Certainly. After you had left, I looked him in the eye and said "Are you in love with her, hey?"'

Anne gasped.

'You didn't!'

'I did.'

'But why?'

'I wanted to have my suspicions confirmed by a reliable source. Nothing like going to the fountain head, when you need information.'

'And what did he say?'

'He said "Yerss."'

'A man of few words.'

'You don't need a lot of words to answer a simple question like that. "Love her, don't yer, hey?" I said. And he said "Yerss." So there you are. I'd grab him, if I were you. Splendid young feller. I took to him from the first.'

'And what about Lionel, my betrothed?'

'Lionel? Bah! You wouldn't give that poop Lionel Green a second thought, if he hadn't the sort of tailor's-dummy good looks that women seem to be incapable of seeing through, poor misguided creatures. Give me two lumps of coal and a bit of putty, and I'll make you a better man than Lionel Green, any time. Lord-love-a-duck, I'd have liked to have been in court yesterday, and heard that feller putting him through it.'

Anne stopped the car. They were only at the entrance of the drive of Shipley Hall, and though it would have been impolitic for the secretary-companion and the butler of the establishment to bowl up to the front door together, there was no need for her to drop him for at least another two hundred yards.

But, unlike Myrtle Shoesmith though she was in every other respect, she shared that disciplinarian's view that males who have behaved badly should be punished.

'Out you get, angel.'

'What, already?'

'This minute. And I hope you get bitten by wild snails. You know perfectly well how naughty it is to talk of Lionel like that.'

'You wouldn't mind it, if you didn't know in your dashed heart that it was true.'

'Out,' said Anne. 'Really wild snails. Ferocious ones, with long horns.'

Lord Uffenham descended like some monarch of the forest felled by a woodman's axe, and Anne drove on. Her eyes were once more pensive, and that tooth was again pressing against her lip. She was thinking how intensely she disliked that fiend in human shape, J. G. Miller. She wondered if it would ever be her good fortune to meet him and tell him just what she thought of him.

She hoped so.

CHAPTER 8

The shadows of the great trees that flanked the lawns of Shipley Hall had begun to creep across the smooth turf when the station cab, bearing Jeff, pulled up at the front door. The ringing of the bell produced Lord Uffenham, looking extraordinarily official.

'Hullo,' said Jeff, greeting him with the warmth of an old crony. 'So you got back all right? Listen. Give me ten minutes to fraternize with the Black Man's Burden, and we'll go into the matter of that glass of port you spoke of.'

'Sir?'

The frigid monosyllable, and the blank and unrecognizing stare which accompanied it, told Jeff that he was in the presence of an artist. Lord Uffenham, when buttling, evidently permitted no echoes from a sociable past to interfere with his conception of his role. When in the public eye, he was Cakebread, the whole Cakebread and nothing but Cakebread. Jeff modified the exuberance of his demeanour, infusing into it something of the other's formality.

'Is Mrs Cork at home?'

'Yes, sir. What name shall I say?'

'Mr Adair.'

'If you will step this way, sir.'

With the same reserved aloofness, in a silence broken only by the sound of his boots, which squeaked, Lord Uffenham conducted the young visitor along a passage, coming to a halt outside a door through which, as he opened it, there proceeded a strong and resonant voice saying something derogatory about rogue elephants. A moment later, Jeff found himself in the presence.

His first emotions on beholding Mrs Wellesley Cork were rather similar to those experienced by the numerous elks and wapiti which had encountered her in their time. Like them, he felt startled and a little nervous. Mrs Cork, even when not armed to the teeth, was always a somewhat awe-inspiring spectacle, when seen for the first time in the flesh. She was a large, powerful woman in the middle forties – handsome, if you admired the robuster type of beauty, less attractive if your taste lay in the direction of the more essentially feminine. A series of African summers had tanned her features to the consistency of leather, causing her to look like an older Myrtle Shoesmith who had been sitting out in the sun.

At the desk, Anne Benedick was seated with a notebook on her knee. She appeared to have been taking dictation.

'Yes, Cakebread?'

'Mr Adair, madam.'

'Oh? Come in, Mr Adair. How do you do? That will be all for to-day, Miss Benedick.'

Anne, during these exchanges, had been eyeing Jeff with covert interest. It always interests a girl to re-examine a man, who, so she has been assured since her last meeting with him, has fallen in love with her at first sight. She found herself feeling kindly and well-disposed towards him. She liked people to like her – or, if they preferred it, to love her.

Furthermore, courage in the male was a quality she particularly admired, and there was no question but that this pseudo-Adair, in insinuating himself into the Cork home under false pretences, was displaying heroism of a high order. Most of the young men of her acquaintance, given the choice between indulging in practical pleasantries at Mrs Wellesley Cork's expense and stirring up a nest of hornets with a short stick, would have chosen the hornets without hesitation.

Less rigid than her uncle in her views on unbending to old acquaintances, she smiled dazzlingly at him, as she passed from the room, causing him to feel greatly strengthened. After a smile like that, he was able to regard Mrs Cork as a mere bagatelle, to be taken in his stride.

That dynamic woman was subjecting him to a keen scrutiny.

'Sit down, Mr Adair. You are very young,' she said, finding a flaw in his make-up in the first minute. 'I had not expected that you would be so young.'

Jeff apologized for being young, considered saying that his father had been the same at his age, thought better of it. Something about his hostess told him that she might not appreciate buzzing.

'Still, you have had plenty of experience?'

'Oh, lots.'

'Good. I suppose Miss Benedick explained my reasons for wanting you here?'

'Fully.'

'That was Cakebread who showed you in.'

'So I deduced.'

'Keep an eye on him.'

'I will.'

'The man's either a lunatic or a thief, and I want to know

which, when I make the strong protest to Lord Uffenham which I intend to make. The idea of putting a clause like that in the lease.'

'Unusual.'

'I cannot understand why Miss Benedick did not draw my attention to it. By the way, what was your impression of Miss Benedick?'

The theme was one on which Jeff could have become lyrical. Rightly divining, however, that his companion would not desire any poetic rhapsodies, he confined himself to the reply that Anne, in his opinion, had seemed very charming.

'The way she wiggles the tip of her nose,' he said, allowing himself a moment's licence. 'Most attractive.'

Mrs Cork looked a little blank.

'I have never seen her wiggle the tip of her nose.'

'I suppose a detective observes these things.'

Mrs Cork remained for some moments in thought. She seemed to be musing on the mobility of Anne's nose. Then, catching the eye of the antelope on the wall and appearing to read into its glassy stare a suggestion of rebuke, she returned to business.

'I am not easy in my mind about Miss Benedick.'

'You mean about Cakebread,' said Jeff, genially correcting the slight slip.

'I do not mean about Cakebread,' replied Mrs Cork, with petulance. 'I said Miss Benedick, and I meant Miss Benedick. When Mrs Molloy suggested bringing a detective to Shipley Hall, I welcomed the idea principally because it would enable me to find out a good deal about Miss Benedick which I would very much like to know. Your principal duty, while you are here, will be to watch her. I don't trust her. I think she's sly.'

Jeff could not let this pass. The revolting adjective had caused his soul to turn a handspring. He had no objection to Mrs Cork smirching Lord Uffenham with her foul innuendoes, but when it came to Anne, it was time to pull her up sharply.

'Sly? What do you mean, sly? She's nothing of the sort,' he said warmly. 'She has a beautiful nature, as frank and open as a – well, you know the sort of thing.'

Mrs Cork began to dislike this young man. She preferred those about her to be Yes-men in the fine old Hollywood tradition. There came into her eyes a hard, steely look, which any of her native bearers and a variety of half-caste traders through the dark continent would have recognized. It was the look which had caused her to be known in native bearer and half-caste trader circles as 'Mgobo-'Mgumbi, which may be loosely translated as She On Whom It Is Unsafe To Try Any Oompus-Boompus.

'You appear to have made up your mind about her on very slight acquaintance,' she said, frostily.

'The primary asset of the detective is the ability to read character at a glance.'

'Very possibly. But I happen to have had the opportunity of observing her in my nephew's society. And I believe she is trying to entangle him.'

The monstrous word affected Jeff like a bradawl through the seat of his trousers. He sat up sharply. 'Sly' had been bad enough, verging closely on the frozen limit. 'Entangle' reached this limit, if it did not actually pass it.

'My ability to read character at a glance tells me that you are entirely wrong.'

'Will you stop talking about your ability to read character at a glance. I am not employing you to contradict me.'

Jeff's immediate impulse was to thunder that she was not employing him at all and to rise and turn on his heel and stalk from the room. Only the reflection that this would interfere a good deal with his project of seeing plenty of Anne in the near future restrained him.

'What has given you the idea that there is anything between Miss Benedick and your nephew?' he asked, more pacifically.

'The way she looks at him. And I was telling Mr Trumper only this afternoon that her behaviour when she was reading me the newspaper report of my nephew's examination in court was most suspicious. Her voice trembled, and when I said I would like to strangle this man Miller with my bare hands, she gave a sort of wistful sigh. I looked up at her sharply, and saw that her eyes were blazing.'

'Miller?' said Jeff, interested by the coincidence.

'A man of the name of J. G. Miller. A barrister.'

Once more, the bradawl had come shooting through the seat of Jeff's chair, causing him to leap like a salmon in the spawning season. It is always disconcerting for a young man to learn that he is enjoying the hospitality of a woman who is anxious to strangle him with her bare hands. He looked at Mrs Cork closely. He had the advantage in reach, but she conveyed the impression that she might be a nasty customer in the clinches.

'My nephew, Lionel Green, was a witness yesterday in the law courts, and this J. G. Miller, who acted as counsel for the other side, abused and vilified him in the most outrageous manner. And, as I say, it appeared to affect Miss Benedick, as she read about it, with an indignation which struck me as quite uncalled for. Mr Trumper says it was just natural good feeling. Stuff! The girl's in love with Lionel. At least, I strongly suspect so. What you are to do, while he is down here – he arrives this evening – is watch them and make sure. I don't want to lose her, if I can help it – she is an excellent secretary, I grant her that – but if I find out that my suspicions are correct, she goes immediately.'

It was fortunate for Jeff that the speech which has just been recorded was on the long side, for it gave him time to reassemble his faculties, which had been disordered as if by the touching off beneath him of a bomb. The discovery that he had strayed into the home of Stinker Green's aunt was in itself a disturbing one. Even more disturbing was the news that Stinker Green in person was expected to arrive here this very evening.

That really did call for careful, constructive thought. Unless restrained – and how he was to be restrained was not immediately obvious – this Green, who had presumably been burning briskly with resentment since their last meeting, would undoubtedly denounce him in the first five minutes, or more probably in the first five seconds. After which, even if he escaped strangulation at the hands of Mrs Cork, which years of healthy exercise on shikarri had rendered peculiarly capable of strangling anything, from a hippopotamus downwards, it would be good-bye to Shipley Hall for Sheringham Adair.

'And while on the subject of Lionel,' proceeded Mrs Cork, 'there is another thing. I don't know if Miss Benedick told you, but here at Shipley Hall we are a little colony who have pledged ourselves to discipline the body.'

She paused. The tenseness of his thoughts had caused Jeff to sink into a trance of almost Uffenhamian calibre. She gave the desk a sharp rap.

'Discipline the body,' she repeated, wondering why Mrs Molloy had recommended an investigator who, in addition to being as fresh as an April breeze, was also apparently deaf.

Jeff came to himself with a start.

'Oh, ah, yes. You mean all that vegetarian—' He, too, paused. He had been about to use the word 'bilge', and something told him that it might be better to search for a synonym. 'That Ugubu stuff?' he substituted.

'Exactly. Have you ever been in Africa, Mr Adair?'

'Never. Lovely Lucerne, yes. Africa, no.'

'Then you have never seen the Ugubus. They are the most splendid physical specimens in existence, with the hearts of little children. This is entirely due to their vegetable diet and the rhythmic dances they dance. I am hoping eventually to spread this Ugubu cult through England, and everything, of course, depends on the earnestness and enthusiasm of our little band. I am sorry to say that not all the members of it are as wholehearted as I could wish. Only this morning I found one of them eating steak-and-kidney pie in the potting shed.'

Jeff seemed stunned.

'Steak-and-kidney pie?'

'Yes.'

'Hot or cold?'

'Cold.'

'In the potting shed?'

'Yes.'

'My God!'

'And I strongly suspect Lionel of going off to the local inn and obtaining surreptitious supplies of meat while he is at the Hall. And I won't have it. I have warned the innkeeper that he is under observation, and reminded him that his application for the renewal of his licence will be coming up shortly before the local Bench, of which I am a member, and I fancy I have frightened him sufficiently. But I want you to watch Lionel and see that he finds no other source of supply. You will report to me the slightest lapse on his part, and I shall take steps. I may tell you that my nephew is entirely dependent on me, so I am in a position to apply pressure. I can rely on you?'

Jeff inclined his head.

'Implicitly. You were enquiring of me just now, Mrs Cork, if I had ever seen an Ugubu. I now ask you, in my turn, if you have ever seen a one-armed paperhanger with the hives?'

'I don't understand you.'

'I merely wish to assure you that that is what I shall be as busy as. "Watch Cakebread," you say. "Watch Miss Benedick," you add. "Watch my nephew," you conclude. I will do so. I will watch them all. And if it gives me a crick in the neck, that is just one of the perils of the profession – an occupational risk, as you might say – which a detective must face with a stiff upper lip. And now,' said Jeff, 'I think my best plan will be to lose no time in making your nephew's acquaintance. I always try to become acquainted at the earliest possible moment with people I am employed to watch. I ingratiate myself with them, thus winning their confidence and causing them to become clay in my hands. I shall, for instance, try to see a good deal of Miss Benedick while I am here. Similarly with Mr – Green, did you say was the name? You mentioned, I think, that he was arriving this evening?'

'His train is due in half an hour.'

'I will meet it. And I shall hope, by the time we get to the house, to have laid the foundations of a firm friendship. What does he look like?'

'What does that matter?'

'I always think it is a help, when you are meeting a person who is arriving by train, to be able to recognize him.'

'Oh, I see. He is tall, slender and very good-looking. He has a small, silky moustache, and his eyes are a soft hazel.'

'Then I will be starting now, so as to be on the platform in good time,' said Jeff.

There was no actual need for him to have torn himself away from his employer's society for another ten minutes or so, for the walk to the station was a mere step, but it irked him to remain in the company of anyone who could consider Stinker Green's moustache silky.

CHAPTER 9

When a sensitive young man with a high opinion of himself alights from a train and finds confronting him on the platform the barrister who has recently made a public spectacle of him in the witness box, some slight constraint is inevitable. Almost never in such circumstances does the stream of conversation flow from the start with an easy effortlessness.

Lionel Green's eyes, as they rested on Jeff, remained hazel, but the fondest and least discerning aunt could not have described them as soft. He recoiled like one who sees a snake in his path, and, drawing himself to his full height, would have passed on without a word, had not Jeff attached himself to his arm.

'Hullo, there,' said Jeff, genially. 'We meet again, what?'

Lionel Green endeavoured, without success, to disengage himself.

'Don't wriggle,' said Jeff. 'You seem disinclined to chat, Stinker, and I believe I know why. You have not forgotten that little dust-up of ours at the bar of Justice yesterday. Or am I wrong?'

Lionel Green assured him that he was not wrong.

'I had a feeling that that might be it. My dear old man, you mustn't take a trifle like that to heart. I was purely the professional. No animus whatsoever. If I had been briefed for the defence, I would have made Ernest Pennefather look just as big a piece of cheese. Don't you feel that outside the court we can be the best of friends?'

Lionel Green said he did not.

'I feared as much. Well, this makes things rather awkward. You see, our interests are bound up together, and only by the exercise of mutual toleration and the old give-and-take spirit can we both obtain our full helping of life, liberty and the pursuit of happiness. You will have to curb your resentment.'

'Will you kindly let go of my arm. I want to find the station cab.'

'I will lead you to it. Our paths lie in the same direction. You are headed for Shipley Hall. I am already in residence.'

'What!'

'Yes.'

'Do you know my aunt?'

'I do, indeed. A charming woman. And this will make you laugh. She thinks I'm a detective – you know how one is always getting mistaken for detectives – and is employing me to watch her butler, whose conduct has been arousing suspicion. So when we fetch up at the Hall, will you remember that my name is Sheringham Adair.'

Lionel Green's sombre eyes lit up with a stern joy.

'You mean you have wormed your way into the house under a false name?'

'I dislike the word "wormed", but you cover the facts.'

'I'll have you kicked out the moment we get there.'

Jeff nodded.

'I had anticipated that some such project would have occurred to you, for I see that you are in difficult mood. But there is no terror, Stinker, in your threats, for I am armed so strong in honesty that they pass by me as the idle winds, which I respect not. Weren't you listening when I said that our interests were bound up together? I see that I shall have to explain. I'm afraid what I am going to tell you will come as something of a shock. In engaging me to watch her butler, Mrs Cork made it clear that that would be only part of my duties. I am to keep an eye on you, also.'

'On me? What do you mean?'

'She suspects you of having fallen into the toils of her secretary, a young person of the name, I believe, of Benedick. And she intends to stop it in no uncertain manner.'

The belligerence faded from Lionel Green's demeanour, leaving him deflated. As Jeff had predicted, this item of news had affected him powerfully.

He gazed at his companion wide-eyed, his shapely jaw drooping like a lily on its stem. The fear that had been haunting him for weeks had been proved to possess a solid foundation. Something had revealed the position of affairs to his lynx-eyed aunt, and she had begun, at the worst possible moment, to sit up and take notice. Another day or two, he was thinking bitterly, and he would have been safe.

In stating that her nephew was entirely dependent upon her, Mrs Cork had spoken the exact truth. It was from her that he received the handsome allowance which enabled him to eat well, dress well, smoke well, belong to the Junior Arts Club and go about in taxi-cabs like that of the neurotic Ernest Pennefather. She also financed the microscopic interior decorator's shop in the Brompton Road, where he sold an occasional olde-worlde chair or Spanish altar cloth to personal friends of his Oxford days.

At any time, her displeasure would have worn a portentous aspect, but circumstances had so arranged themselves at the present moment as to render it particularly lethal. He had recently been given the opportunity of buying a partnership in a larger and really prosperous shrine of interior decorating, that conducted by his friend Mr Tarvin, situated in a more fashionable neighbourhood and catering rather to the great public than to a handful of ex-college chums imbued with the spirit of Auld Lang Syne.

It was to plead with Mrs Cork, whom he had already approached with regard to providing the sum he required, that he had forced himself now to visit Shipley Hall. His spirits had sunk at the thought of going there, for he was a young man who preferred, like Mrs Molloy, to know, when he sat down to dinner, that something would be coming along that would be worthy of his steel. But he was prepared to undergo privations, convinced that a little earnest persuasion would enable him to consummate the deal.

Everything depended on it. With the partnership signed and sealed, he would be in a position to announce his engagement to Anne; to defy Mrs Cork – preferably, of course, over the telephone; in short, to take a strong and independent line. But if his aunt's woman's intuition had led her to suspect, failure and disaster stared him in the eye.

'I don't suppose, of course, that there is anything in it,' continued Jeff, 'but that is what she thinks, and it would be best if you were to avoid this Miss Benedick's society as much as possible, while you are at Shipley Hall. It is always wisest on these occasions to leave no loophole for criticism. Well, you see now what I meant when I spoke of our interests being bound up together. Pursue that impulsive plan of yours of getting me kicked out, and what happens? There arrives in my place another detective, a tougher specimen altogether – not an old school friend who has always liked you, though you may have been deceived at times by his surface manner, but a cold, businesslike professional who will turn in an adverse report to your aunt before you can say "What ho." I merely mention this for your information and guidance.'

He massaged Lionel Green's arm affectionately, ignoring its unresponsive stiffness. It was almost a pity, he was feeling, that he had decided to abandon his career as a pleader at the Bar, for there was no question but that he had a way of putting a case extraordinarily well. Still, what the Bar lost, literature gained. You had to look at these things from every angle.

'And another point, Stinker,' he proceeded, as they stepped into the station cab. 'Mrs Cork, in instructing me to watch you, had in mind not only your relations with Miss Benedick, but your practice, as she suspects, of sneaking off on the sly and supplementing her wholesome Ugubu fare with carnal snacks at the village inn. I may tell you that she has warned mine host that her eye is on him, and that if he attempts to slip you so much as a chump chop and chips he will get it right in the neck at the next quarter sessions, when the question of renewing his licence comes up. You spoke?'

Lionel Green had not spoken. He had merely uttered a hollow groan. He had been relying on the village inn.

'So you will need my kindly services more than ever. Not being, like you, a marked man, I shall be able to act as an intermediary or go-between, establishing a liaison between you and this provider of the necessaries of life. Place your orders with me, and I will see that they are filled.'

Lionel Green brightened. Nothing would ever make him

actually fond of this old schoolmate of his, but he was willing to concede that the fellow had more good in him than he had supposed.

'That's very kind of you, Miller.'

'Not at all. It will be a pleasure. And now tell me something of this Miss Benedick – her tastes, I mean. Just give me a list of her favourite topics of conversation, the books she likes, the subjects to avoid when chatting with her and all that sort of thing. You see, in order to convince Mrs Cork that I am not loafing on my job, it will be necessary for me to see something of the girl from time to time. In which case, it is always a good thing to know what to talk about.'

Five minutes later, having stopped the station cab at the gates and alighted with renewed assurances to his companion of his good wishes, Jeff started to saunter through the grounds of Shipley Hall, lost in agreeable meditation.

He was well pleased with the success of his diplomacy. He had eliminated Lionel Green as a menace, and he had acquired a sound working knowledge of Anne Benedick's tastes and preferences, which could scarcely fail to come in handy. He knew nothing of the real Sheringham Adair, apart from the fact that he had a waxed moustache and an uncanny knack of dissolving into thin air, but he doubted if even that trained expert could have handled a situation better.

It was now the gloaming of the June day, and the air was full of soothing sounds and scents. Birds chirped drowsily in the bushes, insects droned as they passed on their way to supper and bed, the grass was fragrant under the falling dew. He strolled along at random, enjoying these phenomena until presently he found himself on the margin of a small pond not far from the house. Here he paused, to study the activities of certain water beetles which were skimming about its surface in the fussy, energetic way so characteristic of water beetles all the world over.

From the scrutiny of these he was roused by the sound of voices, and, looking round, saw that his solitude had been invaded by a young woman of boldly attractive aspect and a man in the middle forties whose appearance suggested vaguely an American Senator.

They were, though he had as yet, of course, no means of identifying them, that interesting and enterprising couple, Mr and Mrs Soapy Molloy.

CHAPTER 10

The news, conveyed to him some quarter of an hour earlier by his wife, that his old acquaintance, Chimp Twist, was on his way to Shipley Hall, had startled and disconcerted Mr Molloy. And when it had become clear to him that it was through her instrumentality that this unwanted addition was being made to the strength of Mrs Cork's little group of serious thinkers, he was more amazed than ever.

'For goodness' sakes, honey,' he exclaimed, 'what ever did you want to go and do a thing like that for?'

Mrs Molloy was looking cold and proud.

'Oh, I thought I would.'

'But Chimp, sweetie!' Mr Molloy had as poor an opinion of the sleuth hound of Halsey Court as the latter had of him. 'You know what he's like. As slippery as an eel dipped in butter. A bird you can't trust an inch.'

'Chimp's all right.'

'He's not all right. His work is raw. You know that as well as I do. The first thing that'll happen when he fetches up here is that he'll see something that takes his fancy and isn't nailed down, and he'll swipe it and be gone like the wind. And then what? We're in bad for recommending him. I give us a coupla days. After that, we'll be handed our hats and told to get the hell out.'

'You wouldn't like that.'

'You betcher I wouldn't like it.'

'No. It would break your heart, wouldn't it, to have to part from your Mrs Cork.'

'What do you mean, pettie? You're acting strange.'

All the banked-up fires in Dolly Molloy burst out.

'So you don't know what I mean? That's a laugh. You think I haven't been hep to your goings-on, do you? Well, I have. Who roamed with her in rose gardens, having blooms stuck in his buttonhole?'

Mr Molloy gaped.

'But, sweetie—'

'Who patted her hand on the terrace this very afternoon, trying to look like great lovers through the ages? You don't know I seen you, did you? Well, I did, and it was like as if someone had batted me over the bean with an iron casing. I'd never of thought it of you, Soapy. After all that stuff the minister put across about forsaking all others and sticking around me in sickness and in health, and you nodding as much as to say that it was okay by you.'

'But, sweetie, you've got me wrong.'

'You patted her lunch-hook.'

'Sure I patted her lunch-hook. And why? Because I was trying to sell her oil stock.'

'What!'

Mr Molloy looked like a Senator clearing himself of the trumped-up charges of a foul and corrupt opposition.

'Sure. When you're married to a business man, you've got to let him have his sales methods. She was telling me about her nephew Lionel and what a hell of a time he'd been having in the law courts and how she feared it might have bruised his eager, sensitive spirit permanent, and I threw in a pat just to help things along. It worked, too. It wasn't more'n a coupla minutes later that I was interesting her in a block of Silver River. We had to break off the conference just then, on account there was a guy she wanted to see indoors, but it's all fixed. She's giving me her cheque to-morrow.'

The stony expression had faded from Dolly Molloy's piquant face, as if erased by a sponge. As she realized how she had wronged this good man, tears of remorse dimmed her bright eyes.

'Oh, Soapy! What a sap I've been.'

' 's all right, sweetness.'

'But why didn't you tell me?'

'I was keeping it as a surprise for your birthday.'

'How much do we cop?'

'Close on a thousand.'

'Dollars?'

'Pounds.'

'A thousand pounds? Oh, Soapy!'

She flung herself on her husband's ample bosom, sniffing emotionally. Nothing marred the ecstasy of this supreme moment, except those pangs of remorse which still continued to rend her. 'Sap', she was feeling, was the exact word. She must have been a super-sap not to have understood from the start that her Soapy would never have dreamed of bestowing caresses upon another woman, unless actuated by the soundest commercial motives.

Presently, the long, tender embrace ended. Mr Molloy said 'Gee!' and lit a cigar. Mrs Molloy said 'Gosh!' and powdered her nose. They walked along together in silent contentment. 'Oh, blessings on the falling out that all the more endears,' they were possibly saying to themselves. Or possibly not.

'You know, sweetie-pie,' said Mrs Molloy dreamily, touching on an interesting point, 'I've sometimes wondered if somewhere or other there really is a Silver River oil well.'

'Me, too.'

'There might be.'

'There might.'

'Funny, if there was.'

'Very funny,' agreed Mr Molloy. 'What you would call a coincidence.' He smiled, then struck a graver note. 'But about Chimp, honey. I'm free to admit that I don't like the notion of that little grifter being let around loose in this joint.'

'I wouldn't worry.'

'But I do.'

'I mean, you don't have to. Chimp likes his home comforts. He won't stick it out here a day. Not when his stomach gets on to it that all that's coming to it is vegetables.'

'Something in that,' said Mr Molloy, brightening, and the conversation turned to other topics. They were debating the chances, if Mr Molloy played his cards right, of Mrs Cork putting in a repeat order for Silver River, when they rounded the corner of the shrubbery and perceived before them, standing on the brink of the pond, a personable young man whose air was that of one who watches water beetles.

'Hello,' said Mrs Molloy.

'Who's here?' said Mr Molloy. 'Looks like a new internee.'

They approached, and Mr Molloy, in pursuance of his policy of being a ray of sunshine to all men, for you never knew who might not be wanting a sound investment in oil, gave Jeff a cheery good evening.

'Good evening,' said Jeff. He found the other impressive. The sweeping removal of Mr Molloy's hat had revealed a fine, high forehead, rather like Shakespeare's.

'New member of our little community, sir?'

'Just arrived. Nice place.'

Dolly uttered a mirthless laugh.

'There's nothing wrong with the place. But, oh baby, wait till that dinner gong goes!'

'The wife,' said Mr Molloy explanatorily. 'My name is Molloy.'

'Mine is Adair,' said Jeff, and was surprised to observe that the affable couple seemed startled.

'Ad-what?'

'Adair. Sheringham Adair.'

Mr Molloy looked at Mrs Molloy. Mrs Molloy looked at Mr Molloy. Then they transferred their gaze to Jeff, subjecting him to a penetrating stare. The lady's eyes were particularly questioning in their bright intentness.

'Something wrong here,' said Mr Molloy.

'Oompus-boompus if you ask me,' assented Dolly, whom a strenuous life had rendered peculiarly swift in the identification of oompus-boompus. 'What's the game?' she demanded coldly.

Jeff's heart had given a little jump. When Mr Molloy, with that air of his of bestowing a public honour on a deserving recipient, had told him his name, that name had had a vaguely familiar ring. But only now did he realize that this woman, whose eyes were boring into his with such unpleasant fixity, must be the Mrs Molloy who had recommended Sheringham Adair to Mrs Cork. He had not anticipated that on arrival at Shipley Hall he would meet someone presumably well acquainted with his neighbour of Halsey Court.

But then, he reminded himself, he had not anticipated that he would meet Lionel Green. And look how he had handled him. He braced himself to handle with equal smoothness this new menace.

Mr Molloy, though shaken, had not abandoned his suavity of manner. He agreed with his wife that something was toward that had all the appearance of oompus-boompus, but he was prepared to listen to explanations.

'What Mrs Molloy means,' he said, 'is that we were expecting a friend of ours named Sheringham Adair around these parts to-night.'

'The private investigator,' said Dolly.

'And you're not him.'

'You're dead right he's not him.'

Jeff smiled. He had suddenly perceived that this was going to be absurdly easy.

'How very amusing!'

'I haven't started laughing yet,' said Dolly austerely.

'I don't wonder you're surprised. How long is it since you saw your friend?'

'I was talking to him this morning.'

'And he didn't tell you he had sold the business?'

'Sold the business?'

'Lock, stock and barrel, with all the goodwill and everything. I took over this afternoon. Of course, one naturally assumes the trade name.'

Mrs Molloy looked at Mr Molloy.

'Chimp Twist never said a word to me about selling out.'

'He didn't?'

'No, sir. Not a syllable.'

'You have found Mr Twist a secretive man?' said Jeff, interested. 'I noticed the same thing. A valuable quality, no doubt.'

Dolly was still unconvinced.

'You don't look like a detective.'

'Surely,' said Jeff, throwing in a 'dear lady' for good measure, 'that is just how a detective ought to look, in order to lull suspicion in suspects. Hullo,' he went on, looking at his watch, 'it's later than I thought. I suppose one ought to be going in and dressing. Good-bye, Mrs Molloy. Good-bye, Mr Molloy. For the present, of course. In the not distant future I hope that we shall see much of one another.'

He disappeared with long strides, trusting that he had not been abrupt but convinced that he had chosen a very suitable moment for breaking off the conversation, and Mrs Molloy turned to her husband.

'How about it, Soapy?'

'Maybe it's on the up and up.'

'But wouldn't Chimp have mentioned he was selling out?'

'He doesn't mention much.'

'And why would he sell out, sudden like this?'

'Maybe he had to skip, quick. He often does have to skip quick, the dishfaced little weasel.'

'That's true.'

They fell into a thoughtful silence, which remained unbroken till they had passed through the front door.

CHAPTER 11

A helpful housemaid directed Jeff to the room which had been allotted to him, and he had finished dressing and was relaxing over a cigarette, when the door was pushed open as by some irresistible force and a vast body of familiar aspect appeared on the threshold. From the kindly smile on the slablike face that topped it, Jeff saw at once that he was now in the presence of George, Viscount Uffenham, not of Cakebread. There was about the visitor none of that cold aloofness which had prevented a fusion of soul at their last meeting.

'Haryer?' said the mountainous peer affably. 'Just came to see if they'd made yer comfortable. Everything all right?'

Jeff replied that everything was splendid.

'Capital,' said Lord Uffenham. 'Capital.'

He spoke absently, for while he had not actually fallen into a trance, he had ceased to allow his attention to be riveted on what his young friend was saying. He was pottering about the room like a ruminative elephant, examining its contents with an abstracted eye. He picked up Jeff's pyjamas, and inspected them solemnly. There was a book on the table by the bed. He picked that up, and turned its pages for a moment. He also picked up and dropped into the fender a small china ornament which had been standing on the mantelpiece.

The sharp, splintering sound caused by the descent of this *objet d'art* seemed to rouse him from his reverie. Returning to the centre of things and lowering himself into a chair, he reached out a massive finger and gave Jeff a nasty blow on the knee with it. His face was benign and fatherly. In the way in which he regarded the younger man, there was genuine affection, as well as something suggestive of a stuffed owl in a taxidermist's window.

'I've been wanting a chat with you, young feller,' he said.

Jeff replied courteously that he, too, had been counting the moments.

'Remember what we were talking about in that office?'

It seemed to Jeff that the other, if he was expecting him to have forgotten this already, must be crediting him with a memory as uncertain as his own. He said, with a touch of surprise:

'The diamonds, do you mean?'

'Lord-love-a-duck, no, not the diamonds. About you being potty about my dashed niece.'

Jeff would have preferred him not to allude to the divinest of her sex as his dashed niece, but he abstained from rebuke. Policy dictated a friendly and respectful attitude towards this old codger.

'Oh, yes.'

'Still love her, hey?'

Jeff assured him that the passage of two and a half hours had made no difference in his fervour, except perhaps to deepen it, and Lord Uffenham seemed relieved.

'That's good. Because I told her you did, and if you had changed your mind it might have made me look a silly ass.'

Although a young man not ill-equipped with *sang froid*, Jeff found it impossible to restrain a start.

'You told her I loved her?'

'Yerss.'

'I see. Er – how did she appear to take it?'

'Looked a bit thoughtful, it seemed to me.'

'I see.'

'Gave me the impression she was turning the thing over in her mind.'

'I see.'

'What's the matter? You sound stuffy.'

'Oh, no. It only occurred to me that she might have thought it a little sudden.'

'You've got to be sudden with a girl like Anne. Listen,' said Lord Uffenham, once more driving a piston-like finger at Jeff's knee, 'I'll tell yer something. When I saw yer this evening, I took an instant liking to yer.'

'That was very nice of you. I can assure you that I, for my part—'

'Don't interrupt, blast yer. An instant liking, I say. I'm a great reader of character – got an eye like an X-ray – and I saw at a glance that you were a fine young feller. I have neither chick nor child – at least, I don't think so,' said Lord Uffenham, after a moment's hesitation, 'and I regard you as a son. As a son, dash it. You're just the sort of feller I'd like to see married to Anne. You're like I was at your age, a hell of a young chap. They don't seem to breed 'em nowadays. Most modern young men are squirts and perishers. D'yer know Mrs Cork's nephew, Lionel Green?'

'We have met.'

'There's a perisher for you. There's a squirt, if you want one. A Hivite and a Jebusite, no less. And Anne goes and gets engaged to him.'

'What!'

'That's right. With the pick of the land at her disposal, she goes and gets secretly engaged to Lionel Green.'

Jeff was shaken to his foundations. The hideous news had found him utterly unprepared. Not for an instant had he suspected the possibility of this dreadful state of things.

True, Mrs Cork had hinted at such a possibility, but he had naturally paid little attention to her wild theories. If Mrs Cork, he had felt, had observed anything in the relations of Anne Benedick and Lionel Green, it had no doubt been the wart Green persecuting the girl with his loathsome addresses. And as for all that stuff about her eyes blazing when she read of his, Jeff's, pitiless *exposé* of the man, he had simply not believed it. What had happened, he presumed, was that her eyes had shone with a pretty delight, as what girl's would not, who read of a pill who had persecuted her with his addresses being put on the griddle by a brilliantly incisive young cross-examiner.

He stared, aghast.

'You don't mean that?'

This seemed to puzzle Lord Uffenham.

'What d'yer think I mean?' he asked.

'It's too frightful.'

'Ghastly.'

'We must save her.'

'Exactly. You must cut him out.'

'I will.'

'How do you propose to set about it?'

'Well—'

Lord Uffenham raised a hand, like a policeman directing traffic.

'That's enough. That tells me the whole story. You aren't

thinking along the right lines. If you were, you wouldn't have said "Well—"; you'd have said "Set about it? I'll tell yer how I'm going to set about it. By setting about *her*, dash it, and sweeping her off her dashed feet!" That's what you would have said, and that's the only way you'll do it. Grab her! Seize her! Fold her in a close embrace. A really close embrace. One that'll make her ribs creak. Kiss her, too, of course. Kiss her repeatedly. At the same time saying "You are my mate, dash it," or something to that effect. That'll do the trick. That'll divert her mind from that oily French polisher of hers.'

He ceased. The glow faded from his eyes, which took on the glazed and corpselike look with which Jeff had now become familiar. His thoughts had drifted away to the year 1911 and a girl in a hat like a herbaceous border, whose name, if memory served him aright, had been Maudie.

Jeff was glad of the silence. He took advantage of it to try to fight down the rising feeling of nausea with which these revolting words had filled him. He had become very fond of Lord Uffenham, but it was plain to him that the old gentleman's soul, if you could call it that, and his own were, like his own and Mr Shoesmith's, poles apart. Their whole outlook on love and the way in which it should find expression was diametrically opposed. A costermonger, sporting with his donah on Hampstead Heath on a Bank Holiday, would probably have felt that Lord Uffenham had the right idea. To Jeff, who since meeting Anne Benedick had become practically pure spirit, his whole technique was appalling. The thought of soiling Anne, that ethereal being, with this knock-'em-down-and-drag-'em-out type of wooing got in amongst his finer feelings as if they had been hit by a black-jack, and, but for the fact that the latter was in a trance and in any case had got to be conciliated and kept friendly, he would have given the loose-thinking peer a severe look.

Lord Uffenham came to life in that sudden way of his, like a male Galatea.

'Got any money?' he asked.

The abrupt question startled Jeff, but he prepared to do his bit. It occurred to him that in the peculiar circumstances he would presumably have to tip Lord Uffenham at the conclusion of his visit. He could only suppose that the other preferred to collect in advance.

'How much do you want?'

'To marry on, I mean.'

'Oh?' said Jeff, enlightened. 'Well, I'm not rich. Just a few hundred a year, left me by a godfather. And I make a bit by writing.'

'What d'yer write?'

'What are usually called thrillers. I shall be starting a new book any day now. Do you read thrillers?'

'Oh, yerss.'

'Then you will enjoy this one. It has an absolutely original central idea.'

'It that so?'

'A good many authors of goose-fleshers, you may have noticed, in order to chill the spinal cord, have given their Master Criminal a twisted ear. I am breaking fresh ground and striking an entirely new note by allotting mine two. You see the extraordinary cleverness of this? We shudder at a fiend in human shape, even one of whose aural appendages looks as if it had been chewed by a wild cat. Let him have a couple, covering both port and starboard sides, and our blood turns to ice.'

Lord Uffenham seemed only mildly impressed.

'Sounds pretty dashed silly,' he said. 'Don't suppose there's much money in writing, anyway. Mrs Cork wrote a book about her adventures in Africa, called *A Woman in the Wilds*, and I expect it sold about a dozen copies. She can't even give the thing away without exerting the full strength of her personality. I've seen her force copies on visitors, regardless of their age or sex, like a nurse making a child swallow liquorice powder. No, you'll have to find those diamonds.'

'I mean to.'

'It's an odd thing,' said Lord Uffenham. 'Just now, turning out some old papers, I came on a diary I'd lost, and there was an entry against April the fourth – the word "Bank". I couldn't understand it. That was the way I sometimes used to jot down a reminder of where I'd put those dashed diamonds, when I happened to think of a particularly out-of-the way place. There was another entry, for instance, which said "Rover". That was when I hid 'em at the bottom of the dog's bag of biscuits. But what the devil "Bank" can have signified, I can't tell you. I would never have dreamed of putting the things in any bank. I don't believe in banks, except for keeping a little small change in. Yet there it was, dated April the fourth, and it was on April the fifth that I had my motor accident.'

'Curious.'

'Very curious. I can only suppose the note must have referred to something else. Probably my bank manager had asked me to call. No, if you find the things, it'll be in some dashed ingenious place, where no one would ever have thought of looking. But don't you worry. I never forget anything, not permanently. I can remember the exact tone of voice in which a certain gal used to say "Don't!" as far back as the year '09.'

'I suppose girls often used to say "Don't!" to you in '09?'

'Pretty often. Yerss, fairly frequently. And that brings me back to Anne. She'll say "Don't!" But pay no attention. Grab her. What yer looking like that for?'

Jeff hastily erased from his features the look of revolted austerity which he had injudiciously allowed to appear there, and substituted for it the smile of good-fellowship.

'I was only thinking,' he said, putting the suggestion forward with a diffidence which robbed it of offence, 'that while the method which you advocate might be admirable – how shall I put it? – well, might be admirable with a certain type of – subject, isn't there the danger in this particular case that it might have unfortunate results?'

'Don't see your point.'

'Miss Benedick is so spiritual.'

'Nothing of the kind. Healthy, normal girl, with a normal liking for romance.'

'That's exactly what I mean. Is there anything really romantic in the course of action which you suggest? I should have said not. I can see such methods as invaluable in helping to win a bar-room scrap, but... Well, what I really mean is that I should have thought Miss Benedick would have preferred the troubadour to the stevedore type of wooer.'

'Troubadour? What d'yer mean?'

'The Troubadours were minstrels of the Middle Ages, who used to get their results – and it was universally admitted that they did get results – by means of the honeyed word rather than the quick smash-and-grab. I confess that I was thinking of relying on the honeyed word.'

'You'll be a fool, if you do.'

'You don't think that if the word were really honeyed—'

'No, I don't. I know Anne. Known her ever since she was so high.'

'Tell me about her when she was so high.'

'Haven't time. Just remembered I've got to give that feller Molloy a telegram. Came half an hour ago. I was on my way to his room, when I stopped in here. Well, you be thinking over what I've said. I'm an older man than you, an older, wiser man, and I know a thing or two. Troubadours, indeed! Of all the dashed nonsense.'

And with these withering words, Lord Uffenham heaved himself to his feet and plodded ponderously from the room.

He left behind him a young man unconvinced and still more than a little revolted. Despite his proficiency as a buzzer, Jeff was at heart modest and diffident. He was inclined to idealize the other sex. Anne, in particular, filled him with a deep and worshipping humility. This would not prevent him, should he find himself alone with her, talking easily and well – the love behind the humility would, indeed, stimulate him to new heights of eloquence – but it acted as a definite bar to any idea of behaving towards her with the physical abandon of a greyhound pouncing on an electric hare.

He lit another cigarette, and fell to musing on the apparently wilful eccentricity which had led a girl like her to plight her troth to so outstanding a human gumboil as Lionel Green.

Lord Uffenham, meanwhile, had presented himself at the door of the Molloy apartment, had delivered the belated telegram and departed. Soapy opened it, and uttered an exclamation.

'From Chimp,' he said, his eyes widening. 'Wants to see me to-morrow. Reply paid, and the address he gives is "Halsey Buildings, Halsey Court, Mayfair".'

He passed the communication to his wife, and she, too, read it with widening eyes.

'Then he's still there!'

'Still there.'

'He hasn't sold out.'

'No.'

'I knew all along,' said Mrs Molloy, her teeth coming together with a little click, 'that it was oompus-boompus.'

CHAPTER 12

The fine weather was still holding up on the following morning, but no ray of sunshine penetrated into the murky interior of Halsey Court when Mr and Mrs Molloy entered it. It looked dingier than ever, and the number of people cooking cabbage in the immediate neighbourhood seemed to have increased.

In Chimp Twist's manner, as he received his visitors, there was an impressiveness befitting the sensational nature of the tale he was about to tell.

'Sit down, Dolly. Park the carcass, Soapy. So you both came along. I was only expecting Soapy.'

Mr Molloy's fine face expressed surprise, and Dolly interpreted.

'I was telling Chimp yesterday about you and the Cork dame, sweetie, and he prob'ly got the idea that we were *p'fft*. We got Soapy all wrong, Chimp. He's explained everything. It seems he was just trying to sell her oil stock.'

'Oh?' said Mr Twist. 'Is that so?'

He eyed Mr Molloy with such open admiration for his ready resource that Dolly felt obliged to comment on it.

'You think he was stringing the beads, do you? Well, he wasn't. You tell him, Soapy.'

'I sold the Corko a block of Silver River yesterday afternoon,' said Mr Molloy proudly. 'She's giving me her cheque to-day.'

'For a thousand pounds.'

'For a thousand pounds,' said Mr Molloy, rolling the words round his tongue.

Chimp Twist winced. The thought of somebody else, especially somebody he disliked as much as he did Soapy Molloy, securing such a sum affected him like an aching tooth. Only the reflection that he had something on the fire which would make a thousand pounds look like chicken feed enabled him to regain his composure.

'Well,' he said, dismissing the other's petty triumphs with a wave of the hand and coming to the thing that really mattered, 'I guess you two got kind of a surprise yesterday.'

'You mean the guy with the hay-coloured hair? Surprise,' said Mrs Molloy feelingly, 'is right. When we found him doing a song and dance around the garden, claiming that he was J. Sheringham Adair, you could have knocked the both of us cold with a coupla feathers. Who is the bimbo?'

'Search me. All I know about him,' said Chimp, giving a little shiver as that fearful scene of the previous afternoon rose before his mind's eye, 'is that he's someone who doesn't like me.'

'Can't you get closer than that?' asked Dolly. She seemed to be feeling that this rendered the field of identification too wide.

Chimp shook his head.

'I've been trying to place him, but I'm darned if I can remember where we ran across each other. Still and all, if a bird throws things at you, and then comes charging up the stairs to finish you off, you can pretty well label him as somebody that isn't too fond of you.'

Mr Molloy raised his eyebrow.

'Throws things ... What things?'

'Well, I've been having a look at them, and they seem to me like flints of some kind. I tell you, when I saw him coming up those stairs, I was into the closet quicker than forked lightning. And it was on account I was in the closet that I come to hear the story this girl Benedick told him.'

'What story?'

'About these diamonds.'

'What diamonds?'

'Ah!' said Chimp. 'That's just what I'm going to put you wise about. Start listening.'

His visitors did so, with the alacrity which is always the result of mentioning diamonds to a certain type of auditor. When he had finished his narrative, Dolly's eyes were shining like stars, and Mr Molloy's breathing had become so stertorous that he resembled a Senator suffering from a troublesome attack of asthma. The news that they were residing in a sort of Tom Tiddler's Ground or Cave of Ali Baba, where parcels of valuable diamonds might leap to the eye at any moment, had affected both of them profoundly.

'Fancy old Cakebread being a Lord!' said Dolly, breaking an ecstatic silence. 'I'll tell you sump'n, Soapy. From now on, I'm going to give that lobster a rush, in a big way. When that memory of his starts hitting mid-season form again, I want to be the little playmate from whom he can conceal nothing.'

'Ah,' said Mr Molloy, still having trouble with his bronchial cords.

'And meantime you be hunting around.'

'I will.'

'The stuff must be somewheres.'

'Sure, it must be somewheres.'

'And maybe you'll find it.'

'You betcher it won't be for want of trying. Diamonds are my *dish*.'

'I've nothing against 'em myself.'

'And now,' said Mr Molloy, his old, easy-breathing self once more, 'about terms.'

Mrs Molloy seemed perplexed.

'Terms?'

'The divvying up,' explained Mr Molloy. 'Don't forget, honey, that it's only fair to give Chimp his cut.'

'Oh, yay,' said Dolly, enlightened. She had overlooked this side-issue. 'You mean, he ought to get a little sump'n for putting us on to this?'

'I think so,' said Mr Molloy. 'Yes, I certainly think so. Chimp has been of considerable assistance. Of considerable assistance,' he repeated: and if in his manner, as he beamed benevolently at his old friend, there was something a little patronizing, it is always hard for a man who is doing a kindly act to avoid a certain complacency. 'I feel that Chimp should have his share.'

'Maybe you're right,' agreed Dolly. She seemed to be thinking her husband's attitude a shade quixotic, but was prepared to yield a point. 'What ought we to give him? Twenty-five per cent?'

'I would suggest thirty. You've got to take the big, broad view, sugar. Come right down to it, if it hadn't of been for good old Chimpie, we might never have gotten on to this.'

'Just as you say, sweetness. Then we pencil Chimp in for thirty per.'

'That's how I see it.'

'It's a lot of money.'

'Quite a good deal.'

'Still, he's an old friend.'

'A very old friend.'

'I've always liked him.'

'Me, too. I don't know a man,' said Mr Molloy, again with that slight suspicion of the patronizing in his manner, 'whom I esteem more highly than I do good old Chimpie.'

A sharp, unpleasant, rasping sound broke the pause which followed these eulogies. It was good old Chimpie clearing his throat.

'Jussa minute!' he said. 'Juss a minute, juss a minute!'

The atmosphere up to this point had been one of such jolly friendliness and good will that his words struck a discordant note. His two admirers could not conceal it from themselves that his tone had been acid. Furthermore, he was looking like a monkey which observes a couple of other monkeys trying to chisel it out of a banana.

'Something wrong, Chimpie?' enquired Mr Molloy solicitously.

Mr Twist's waxed moustache seemed to have been infected by its proprietor's emotion. It had the air of bristling at the ends.

'Yep,' he replied briefly. 'Your figures.'

For one who had openly confessed her affection for this man, Dolly Molloy was not looking very loving. Her delicate brows had come together in a frown.

'Oh, Gawd!' she exclaimed, and it would be idle to pretend that she did not speak peevishly. 'Here he is, acting up again! Every time we have one of these business discussions, he always opens his mouth so wide, it's a wonder he don't swallow himself. What's your beef about taking thirty per?'

'Yes, Chimpie,' said Mr Molloy, dignified and reproachful. 'What's eating you? Thirty per is nice money.'

'Not so nice as ninety per.'

'Ninety?' cried Mr Molloy, with a start of pain, as if he had been bitten in the leg by a brother.

'Ni-yun-ty?' echoed Mrs Molloy. She, too, seemed to have felt a loved one's teeth closing on a lower limb.

Chimp Twist fondled his moustache, as if soothing it and assuring it that all would come right in the future.

'That's what I said. I'm the promoter of this scheme. If it hadn't of been for me, there wouldn't be any scheme. Naturally, I expect you to do the simple, rough work for the customary agent's fee of ten per cent.'

There was a silence.

'This would happen just the day when I've gone and gotten a cracked lip,' said Mrs Molloy, at length. 'All the same, I guess I'll risk a slight guffaw.'

She did so, and Chimp eyed her bleakly.

'So you think it's funny?'

Dolly replied that that was the impression which she had intended to convey, and her husband's quizzical smile showed that he, too, was not blind to the humorous aspect of the proposition.

'You can't say it's not enough to hand us a laugh, Chimpie,' he protested. 'The point you're missing, if you'll excuse me mentioning it, is that the madam and I are inside the joint and that you're outside, looking in.'

'Yes, that's the point you're missing, you poor dumb brick,' assented Mrs Molloy. 'It's only purely and simply our kind hearts that makes us slip you a cut at all.'

'And here's the point you're missing,' said Mr Twist. 'A phone call from me to the Cork dame, putting her wise about the sort of oil stock you've been selling her, and you'd be out of the place in half an hour. Less, maybe. Depends on whether she lets you stay and pack. Chew on that.'

Mr Molloy was shocked.

'You wouldn't do that?'

'I would.'

'But it's low. It's not gentlemanly. I wouldn't have thought you'd have been able to stoop to such an act, Chimpie.'

'I've been doing bending and stretching exercises lately,' explained Mr Twist. 'I can stoop to anything now.'

Mrs Molloy, finding speech, of which this revelation of what was possible in the way of human baseness had momentarily deprived her, gave utterance to a remark so packed with thought and meaning that, although running to only about ten words or so, it provided a complete critique of Mr Twist's appearance, manners, morals, moustache and parentage. A sensitive man would have been wounded by it, but Chimp Twist had heard too much of this sort of thing in his time to pay attention to it nowadays.

'That stuff won't get you nowhere,' he said reprovingly.

'No,' Mr Molloy was forced to agree, 'there's no percentage in cracks, honey.'

'But you aren't going to let him get away with this customary agent's fee boloney, are you?' demanded Dolly, quivering.

Mr Molloy, never a very sturdy fighter, looked unhappy.

'I don't see what else we can do, sweetness.'

'Well, that's where you're different from me.'

'But, pettie, he's right. If he spills the dirt to the Corko, it's outside for you and me. I've found her a nice, smooth-working sucker, always ready to listen to a spiel, but she's got a certain amount of sense, about enough to make a duck fly crooked, and she'll start asking questions. And I can't afford to have her asking questions. Don't forget I haven't gotten her cheque yet.'

'That's the way to talk,' said Chimp. 'I like to listen.'

'Then listen to this,' shrilled Dolly. 'This ice you're talking about – how do you reckon you're going to get it, except through I and Soapy?'

Chimp Twist gave his moustache a final twirl.

'Easy. Simple as pie. You told me yourself about this Yogi joint this dame is running, and when I was in the closet the girl was giving that guy the lowdown on it. So I understand the workings. All I got to do is simply drive up to the front door and say I'm a rich millionaire from the other side, who's heard about the place and wants to sit in, and they'll lay down the red carpet for me, same as they seem to have done for Soapy. How's that?'

'Not so good.'

'No?'

'No. You'd never get to first base.'

'What's to stop me?'

Mr Molloy had been asking himself the same question. To him, it seemed that the day was lost and that it would be futile to struggle further. He was experiencing all the complex emotions of a man who finds himself in a cleft stick, and he was at a loss to account for his loved one's apparent confidence. However, he had so often found her equal to situations by which he himself was baffled that he eyed her now with a certain faint hope.

'I'll tell you what's to stop you,' said Dolly, once more showing herself worthy of a husband's trust. 'That straw-headed gazook that's got it in for you. He'll be the first thing you bump up against when you breeze into the joint, and then what? He'll immediately start chewing your ugly little head off at the roots, same as he was planning to do before.'

Chimp's jaw fell. His moustache drooped limply. He had completely overlooked this obstacle.

'Personally and speaking for myself,' proceeded Dolly, 'I hope you will come down to the place, doing a buck and wing about being rich millionaires, because then everything'll be nice and simple for I and Soapy. All we'll have to do is buy a wreath and attend the funeral, and there we'll be, all set to start hunting for this ice without nobody interfering with us. Come along and join the party. There's good trains all through the day.'

There was a silence. Chimp Twist was once more fingering his moustache, but nervously now, like a foiled baronet in an old-time melodrama. Mr Molloy's eyes had lost their haggard look, and were alight with love and admiration. Dolly was touching up her lips with a lipstick.

'Remember yesterday in the garden, Soapy?' she said, 'when we come on this bird by the pool? Remember how he stood there, sort of silhouetted against the evening sky, with all his muscles rippling like snakes?'

'Ah!'

'You thought he must be a prizefighter or sump'n.'

'A wrestler.'

'That's right, a wrestler. One of those all-in boys that get a holt on people and tear great chunks off of them with a flick of the wrist.'

Chimp Twist had heard enough.

'Well, what's your proposition?' he asked sullenly, a beaten man.

'Fifty-fifty,' said Dolly promptly. 'Okay by you?'

Mr Twist, though not with enthusiasm, replied that it was

okay by him, and presently Mr and Mrs Molloy took their leave, the latter all smiles and amiability, the former a little thoughtful.

'You were too easy with him, pettie,' he said, as they made their way through the cabbage-scented court. 'The way you'd gotten him by the short hairs, why ever didn't you gouge him for seventy?'

'Well, I'll be darned!'

'Oh, I'm not sore,' Mr Molloy hastened to add. 'I think you were swell. It's just that the thought of splitting Even Stephen with that little buzzard sort of goes against my better nature.'

'Well, for the love of Pete!' cried Mrs Molloy, astounded. 'You don't suppose he's going to get anything, do you? Where's your sense, honey? Once we get our hooks on the stuff, natch'ally we sim'ly pick it up and fade away. I just said fifty-fifty to keep him happy.'

The cloud cleared from Mr Molloy's Shakespearian brow. It seemed to him incredible that he could ever, even for an instant, have questioned the sagacity of this wonder-woman.

Board meetings take time, even if they run with far more smoothness than had been the case with the one at No. 3, Halsey Buildings, and the day was well advanced by the time Soapy and Dolly alighted at Shipley station. After the excitements of the morning, both were feeling pleasantly ready for the mid-day meal.

A quick dash in the station cab would just have enabled them to beat the Hall luncheon gong by a matter of minutes, but Soapy was not in favour of this. His, like Eustace Trumper's, had been from boyhood a healthy appetite, and his personal view of the Ugubus and their chosen bills of fare was that the latter were loathsome and the former weak in the head. He had little difficulty in persuading his wife that here was an admirable opportunity for avoiding Mrs Cork's hospitality for once, and the hour of two found them seated in the coffee-room of the Stag and Antlers in Shipley High Street, squaring their elbows at a smoking dish of ham and eggs, with a second on order in the kitchen.

It was not for some little time that either felt in the vein for conversation. But when the first keen edge of hunger had been blunted, they began to talk, and their talk, as was natural in the circumstances, turned to the local cuckoo in the nest.

'We'd best attend to that straw-haired guy first thing, before we do anything else,' said Dolly, replying to her husband's wistfully expressed hope that Jeff would choke on a forkful of spinach. 'We can't do no constructive work till we've gotten him out of the place. Having him in our hair all the time would cramp our style.'

'Ah,' agreed Mr Molloy, lowering ham into his interior with the air of a Senator laying a foundation stone. 'But how do we get him out?'

'Easy. Tell the Cork dame he's a ringer.'

'But won't she wonder why we didn't do that yesterday?'

'Why would we? He had us fooled yesterday with his story about having bought the business. We was completely took in. But after a while we thought it over and seen where it seemed kind of funny, so we went to London this morning and saw the real Sheringham Adair, who was shocked, horrified and surprised to learn that he was being impersonated. No holes in that?'

'Not a one.'

'I'll get together with her as soon as we're back. I'd say, at a guess, that we'll be kissing this bird good-bye around three o'clock, standard time. Is that good? Or is it good?'

'Honey,' began Mr Molloy, and broke off abruptly. He had been about to pay the light of his life a marked tribute, but the second dish of ham and eggs had just appeared in the doorway. And when the maid had withdrawn, after setting it before him, the door opened again, to admit the very straw-haired guy of whom they had been speaking.

Jeff, always considerate, had lost no time in coming to the Stag and Antlers to procure sustenance for Lionel Green. Watching that elegant young man during the meal which had recently terminated in the dining-room of Shipley Hall, he had been greatly touched by the wanness of his aspect as he picked at his peas and carrots. The sight had left him feeling that now, and not after an interval of delay, was the time for all good men to come to the aid of the party. He had never been fond of Lionel Green, and saw little prospect of being fond of him in the future, but there are moments when common humanity makes us sink our prejudices.

In his mind, it must be confessed, there was also the thought that, while at the Stag and Antlers, he might also procure a little sustenance for himself. His first luncheon as Mrs Cork's guest had left him, like Mr Molloy, marvelling at the tastes of the Ugubu tribe. These simple aborigines might, as his hostess had claimed for them, be the most perfect physical specimens in existence, but it was possible, he felt, to pay too high a price for mere muscle.

Having placed an order for a large consignment of beef sandwiches, he had strolled off to kill time while they were being prepared, and the rich smell of ham which percolated through its doorway led his wandering feet to the coffee-room.

His arrival was the signal for the coming into Mrs Molloy's eyes of the battle light. It flared up like a beacon. Mr Molloy, who was gazing at the ham like one who sees the Taj Mahal for the first time, did not immediately observe it. Only when his wife said 'Hey!' did he perceive that she and he were no longer alone.

The ejaculation 'Hey!' can never be made to sound anything but abrupt, and Mrs Molloy had taken no pains to soften its brusqueness on the present occasion. The word had left her lips like a bullet, and it commanded Jeff's immediate attention.

It needed but a glance, as he approached the table, to tell him that Mrs Molloy was in no friendly mood. There had been certain moments during their conversation of the previous evening when he had had this same feeling that they were not in sympathy, but he had supposed that he had overcome all mistrust on her part with his ready explanation of his presence. This, apparently, was not the case, for her eyes were gleaming with suspicion and hostility. And even if he had been unable to read the language of the eyes, her opening words would have enlightened him.

'So here's Mister Smartie!' she said. 'Mister Smartie himself in person!' And there was no possibility of mistaking the observation for a tribute. Nor, taken in conjunction with the set features and the glittering eyes, was it to be classified as genial banter. Dolly Molloy was an attractive woman, but there were times when she could look more like a cobra about to strike than most cobras do.

But if Jeff was startled, it was only for an instant. He was an intelligent young man, and it was borne in upon him immediately that something had gone wrong with the works. He braced himself to cope with this new development.

'Good afternoon,' he said, with a genial smile. 'So here you are. We missed you at lunch.'

'Is that so?'

'It is, indeed. We were all wondering what had become of you.'

'Oh? Well, I'll tell you, shall I?'

'Do.'

'We were at J. Sheringham Adair's office, chewing the fat with J. Sheringham Adair. And when we told J. Sheringham Adair that there was a guy down here that claimed to have bought the business off of him, J. Sheringham Adair said "What the hell?"'

'Strong words.'

'"I never sold no business to nobody," he said. So try that one on your pianola.'

Jeff nodded. The circumstances being as she had outlined, he quite saw how she might wish him to try it on his pianola.

'I see,' he said, thoughtfully. 'I had been asking myself if something of the kind might not occur.'

'Well, now you know the answer. It has. You'd best go and start packing.'

'Packing?'

'So's to be good and ready to leave quick, when I've dished the dirt to Mrs Cork.'

'You wouldn't do that?'

'Wouldn't I? Why not?'

'Well, for one thing, you would be depriving yourself of a lively and entertaining companion, in a house where there seems to me, from what I have observed during my brief stay, to be rather a shortage of entertaining company. Think of being left with nobody to talk to except that bunch of stiffs up at the Corkeries.'

Mr Molloy seemed to find his words lacking in tact.

'She's got me,' he pointed out.

Jeff considered the point.

''Myes. Yes, she's got you, I suppose. Still—'

'Anyway,' said Dolly, dismissing the subject, 'I'll risk being bored. Don't you go worrying yourself about me, baby. I shall get along swell. I've only two things to say to you, my lad. One is "Get the hell outa here," and the other is "Do it quick."'

'But why this extraordinary eagerness to get rid of me? What harm am I doing you by being here?'

'That's a laugh, Soapy?'

'A big laugh, honey.'

'I'll tell you why,' proceeded Mrs Molloy. 'We know all about that ice.'

'Ice?'

'The diamonds,' interpreted Dolly impatiently. 'We're after them, same as you.'

'What!'

'That's what.'

'But they don't belong to you.'

'They soon will.'

'Egad! This sounds like dirty work.'

'Call it what you like.'

'Well, well, well!' said Jeff. 'Well, well, well, well!'

He stood staring at them, his manner that of one from whose eyes the scales have fallen. Neither Dolly, who was returning his gaze unblinkingly, nor Mr Molloy, who was getting along with the ham and eggs, had a twisted ear, let alone two; nevertheless, it was plain to him that he was standing in the presence of a brace of Napoleons of the Underworld, and he was a little piqued that he had not seen through their crust of respectability earlier. Inspector Purvis, the hero of his novels, would, he felt, have done it at their first meeting.

Dolly returned to what Mr Shoesmith would have called the *res*.

'So out you get, Sonny Boy.'

'You really intend to expose me to Mrs Cork?'

'What's to hinder me?'

'Your kind heart, I would have said. Your sweet, gentle nature. But those don't seem to be functioning at the moment.'

'No.'

'So I suppose I shall have to fall back on the fact that, if you do, I on my side shall instantly tell her that I have seen you wolfing ham and eggs in this wayside inn. You know her rigid views. We shall be able to travel up to London together.'

It was a telling shot. For an instant, Dolly had nothing to say. Mr Molloy had, but as he was in the act of swallowing ham at the moment, only the concluding words were distinguishable.

'... deny it,' said Mr Molloy.

Dolly recovered herself. She shot a swift glance of approval at her helpmeet for the timely suggestion.

'That's right. We shall sim'ly and totally deny it. And it's not likely Mrs Cork will believe the word of a barefaced impostor.'

'Ah, but it won't be merely the word of a barefaced impostor. There will also be that of a whiskered innkeeper. The proprietor of this caravanserai will support my story. He has already been warned by Mrs Cork to serve no proteins to the members of her private loony-bin, and it is going to be a shocking blow to him to learn that a couple whom he mistook for bona fide travellers are in reality guests at the Hall. He is far too scared of our hostess to try any funny stuff on her. He will babble out the hideous facts.'

Dolly looked at her husband, hoping for another bright suggestion, but he had shot his bolt. From the expression on his fine face, it was evident that he had accepted defeat. And Dolly, though it cut her to the quick to do so, was obliged to accept it, too.

'You win,' she said, briefly.

'Personally,' said Jeff, 'I would be inclined to call it a draw. We seem to be in the position of a bunch of the boys who, whooping it up at the Malemute Saloon, have all gone and got the drop on one another simultaneously. I can't expose you. You can't expose me. The only thing I can suggest is that we observe a mutual toleration and good will. And now I fear I must leave you. I have duties which call me elsewhere.'

He had just remembered that the sandwiches must be about ready, and he had no desire to have them delivered to him in his present company.

He left behind him a thoughtful silence, which Mr Molloy was the first to break.

'There's no getting away from it,' said Mr Molloy ruefully, but with a certain unwilling respect in his voice, 'that that boy knows all the answers.'

Mrs Molloy writhed in anguish. Jeff had paused at the door to bestow upon them another of those genial smiles, and it had gashed her like a knife.

'I'm going to put it across that slicker,' she said, speaking thickly in her emotion, 'if it's the last thing I do.'

'But how, pettie?' asked Mr Molloy. He was one of those men who are always asking 'How?'

'Don't you worry. I'll fix him.'

Mr Molloy started. He was a nervous man, and he knew his wife's impulsive nature. Once she embarked on an enterprise of the kind at which she was hinting, he feared lest the sky might be the limit.

'How do you mean, fix?'

'Just fix.'

'You wouldn't croak him?'

Mrs Molloy laughed merrily at the whimsical thought. She had quite recovered her spirits.

'Don't be silly, sweetness.'

'Well, mind you don't,' urged Mr Molloy, still apprehensive, and started to pick rather feverishly at an egg which he had overlooked.

CHAPTER 13

Anne Benedick came out on to the terrace, and started to make her way slowly across the sunken garden beyond it. Her destination was the little pond where Jeff, a week earlier, had studied water beetles.

From childhood days, this had always been a favourite retreat of hers in moods of depression, and one of these had her in its grip now. It would be exaggerating to say that her heart was bowed down with weight of woe, but she had the feeling that the state of her relations with the man to whom she was engaged to be married was not one hundred per cent satisfactory, and that always tends to lower the spirits.

When she had learned that Lionel Green was arriving for a visit, Anne had been uplifted. She had looked forward to much delightful rambling at his side through the shady walks and murmurous groves with which the ancient home of the Uffenhams was so well provided: and it had come as a shock to her to discover that he proposed during his stay to avoid her society altogether.

And though, when he had explained the motives which had led him to take this decision, she could see that they were based on good sense and prudence, she still felt that there was something a little ignoble in so rigorous a policy of Safety First.

It blurred the picture she had formed of him as a king among men.

In addition to this, there was the matter of the stuffed antelope.

She was musing on these things, struggling to overcome a feeling of forlornness and disillusionment, when Jeff came curvetting through the garden on his way back from the station. He had spent the morning and the earlier part of the afternoon in London.

Several reasons had taken him to London to-day. In the first place, it had suddenly occurred to him, talking it over with his conscience, that a written apology to J. Sheringham Adair, sent round to his office by district messenger boy, would amply compensate for his omission to tender verbal regrets. It would also be considerably easier to compose than one thrown together on the spur of the moment under the man's personal, and probably incandescent, eye. The great objection to apologizing face to face with a fellow human being whom you have knocked cock-eyed with a rock cake is that unavoidable sense of *gêne* and embarrassment in the early stages.

He also wanted to buy a copy of that book of Mrs Cork's, *A Woman in the Wilds*, to which Lord Uffenham had alluded, for it seemed to him a useful thing to have by one in case of emergencies. A large box of chocolates for Anne was another purchase he had in mind. And, finally, there was the matter of accident insurance.

It was a few days after his chat with Mr and Mrs Molloy at the Stag and Antlers that Jeff's thoughts had first turned in the direction of accident insurance. What had supplied the impulse was the falling within a foot of his head of a handsome ormolu clock, as he stood smoking a cigarette in the hall, waiting for Anne to come and join him in a saunter round the grounds. It brought home to him the fact that, now that there existed open warfare between himself and so spirited and resourceful an antagonist as Mrs Molloy, his position had become one of considerable delicacy.

With the passing of the days, a solid respect for this great woman had begun to burgeon within Jeff. Her dignified husband he regarded as a mere stuffed shirt, hardly worth a passing thought, but Dolly herself inspired him with something akin to awe. How, for instance, she could possibly have come to learn of Shipley Hall's hidden treasure was still an unsolved enigma to him. It suggested the possession of something almost in the nature of second sight. And in addition to her psychic gifts, it now appeared, she had also this remarkable capacity for direct and rapid action.

True, after swallowing most of his cigarette and looking up with a jerk that nearly dislocated his neck, he had not actually observed her leaning over the banisters, but an ormolu clock, last seen on an antique chest of drawers on a first floor landing, does not descend into the hall of its own volition, and he had no hesitation in assuming that Dolly's was the hand which had started it on its downward course. He might be wronging her, but he did not think so.

Far too many things, he reminded himself – vases and bricks and watering-cans and things like that – had been falling in his vicinity since the breaking off of diplomatic relations. And there was no question but that the loose stair rod, which he had detected just in time to avoid coming the purler of a lifetime, when about to hurry downstairs to dinner, had been made loose by someone interested in his movements who knew that he would be coming along at that moment.

It seemed to him that, circumstances, having brought him up against a woman endowed with the temperamental outlook and able executive abilities of Lady Macbeth, he was faced, unless he cared to go about in a crash helmet, by two alternatives – the first, which he declined to consider, to accept her suggestion of leaving the Hall; the second, to run up to London as soon as possible and take out accident insurance with some good company.

A word to Mrs Cork to the effect that he had succeeded in securing an excellent set of her butler's fingerprints and proposed to go with them to the Records Office at Scotland Yard, the boys there being always ready to assist a personal friend, and he was on his way to the metropolis with the comfortable feeling that, while this would not actually spike his adversary's guns, it would at least place him in a position to save something out of the wreck, in the event of her target practice improving.

He was now back in the grounds of Shipley Hall, and there, right ahead of him and alone, stood Anne. His spirits, already high, rose higher. That he should have found her like this, first crack out of the box, seemed to him proof that Providence recognized a good man when it saw one, and took care that his merits should not go unrewarded.

During the past week, Jeff had had many pleasant conversations with Anne, and they had confirmed him in his view that the slow, steady attack by means of the honeyed word was the method to pursue. He broke into a run and began speaking honeyed words now, as soon as he was within earshot.

'So there you are!' he said. 'I had expected to have to conduct a long and laborious search for you, ending probably in the discovery that you were in Mrs Cork's study, taking down in your notebook tedious reflections on elephants.'

He drew up beside her, and found that she was looking at him in that curious, intent way which he remembered from their first meeting.

'It's a funny thing,' she said. 'When you started to run just then, I felt that I was on the verge of a revelation. I thought I was going to remember where I had seen you before.'

'You still think you have seen me before?'

'I'm sure I have.'

'And my running seemed to provide a clue?'

'Just for a second. But the vision faded.'

'I'll run a little more.'

'No, don't bother. It's not important.'

'But it is. You are being cheated out of what should be one of your most beautiful memories. Seeing me for the first time marks an epoch in most people's lives. They live over the moment again, to cheer themselves up in moods of depression. Are you sure, now that you have had time to think it over, that you were never in Lovely Lucerne?'

'Quite sure. Is it very lovely?'

'Beautiful. Nice and blue, and crowded with fascinating tourists with Baedekers.'

'If it's as good as all that, I could hardly have forgotten being there. Especially if I had seen you.'

'That's true. Then one can only assume that we must have met in some previous existence.'

'Perhaps.'

'In which I was perpetually running.'

'Yes. It will be a great day for me, when I remember.'

'A gala day,' said Jeff.

He agreed with his conscience that all this sounded very like buzzing, and did not attempt to deny that when saved from the firing squad in the matter of Myrtle Shoesmith he had vowed never to buzz again, but, as he went on to point out, it was not really buzzing. The depth of feeling behind the words was the thing to go by. When you really loved a girl with every fibre of your being, it did not matter if superficially you might seem to buzz. Quite simple, when you thought it out, he told his conscience, and his conscience said Quite.

Anne found that her spirits had risen. They always did, she had noticed, when she was with Jeff. She could not recall having met a man with whom she had felt so immediately in sympathy. It was almost, it sometimes seemed to her, as if someone had told him which were her favourite topics, her pet books and everything of that sort. Quite a part of her recent depression, she was honest enough to recognize, had been caused by his sudden disappearance after breakfast.

'What became of you all day?' she asked. 'I was afraid you might have decided that the Ugubu diet was too much for you.'

'No, no,' said Jeff. 'As a matter of fact, I am so intensely spiritual that I scarcely know what I'm eating. I had to go to London. I've brought you some chocolates.'

'How absolutely noble of you. Strictly forbidden, of course.'

'I guessed as much. You must nibble them in the privacy of your bedroom. It will bring back memories of dormitory feeds at Roedean.'

'I didn't go to Roedean. I was "privately educated", as they say in *Who's Who*. What took you to London so suddenly?'

This was an easy one. Jeff replied that he had had to attend to a few little matters at the office which required the personal touch. More difficult was the problem, which had been vexing him a good deal since Mrs Molloy had so frankly revealed the predatory leanings of herself and husband, of whether to confide this new angle of the situation to Anne or preserve a prudent silence.

The question was one which was beginning to assume major proportions. Twice, visiting Lord Uffenham in his pantry in quest of port, he had found him closeted there with Mrs Molloy: and there seemed to him no doubt, from the way they were getting along together, that if the old buster ever did remember where he had put those diamonds, the first person whom he would take into his confidence would be this golden-haired specialist in oompus-boompus.

Clearly, Lord Uffenham should be warned. But to warn him involved confessing to Anne that he had deceived her, and one never knew how girls were going to take these things. On the whole, he decided that silence was best.

'How did you pass the day?' he asked.

'Not too well.'

'Don't tell me that Simone Legree made you work on an afternoon like this?'

'No. We finished before lunch.'

'Then what went wrong?'

'Uncle George was a little strong on the wing, and it led to a certain amount of unpleasantness. In fact, I have been through the furnace.'

'He had one of his sudden inspirations?'

'He did. He thought he might have put the diamonds inside the stuffed antelope's head in Mrs Cork's study.'

'Surely not?'

'Why? It's just the sort of ingenious place he would have thought of.'

'But that sawn-off sample of African wild life wouldn't have been there, when he had the house. I take it that it arrived arm in arm with Mrs Cork.'

'Oh, I see what you mean. No, that isn't one of Mrs Cork's victims. It has been there ever since I was a child. My grandfather shot it.'

'Was he a hunter, too?'

'A mighty hunter. Very assiduous. No antelope was safe from him.'

'What hell life must be for antelopes,' said Jeff thoughtfully. 'Never a moment to themselves. One can imagine them consoling one another with the reflection that your grandfather, though a powerful pest, couldn't last for ever. And then, just as he hands in his dinner pail, along comes Mrs Cork.'

'Too true.'

'It makes you think a bit, doesn't it?'

'I think about it all the time.'

'It saddens you, I expect?'

'Terribly.'

'Me, too. Let's try to forget it. Where are my tablets? I must jot down a memorandum – Search antelope.'

'You wouldn't be scared to go into Mrs Cork's study and rout about inside antelopes?'

'Of course not.'

'Don't you Adairs know what fear is?' said Anne.

She was conscious of a sudden return of her dark mood. When she had made the suggestion to Lionel Green earlier in the day that he should perform this deed of derring-do, the latter had flatly declined to stir a step in the direction of his aunt's lair. Lionel knew all about the diamonds and was wholeheartedly in favour of their being found, for he shared the common taste of modern young men for marrying a wife with plenty of money, but there were risks which he refused to take, however admirable the end in view. And Anne, courageous herself, was inclined to deprecate pusillanimity in the opposite sex.

For an instant, she had asked herself whether her uncle might not be right about Lionel. And though she had dismissed the speculation instantly as disloyal, the after-effects lingered.

Jeff's cheerful readiness to undertake the perilous task forced her into an unwilling comparison of the two men, and left her, as has been said, depressed again. It is disturbing for a girl when the wrong man seems to have all the right qualities.

'Well, don't bother,' she said. 'I've done it.'

'You?'

'I did it just before I came out.'

Jeff felt entitled to be a little severe, as some knight of old might have been, who, preparing to save a damsel from a dragon, found that she had already knocked it cold with her distaff.

'Come, come,' he said. 'This is all wrong. You really must leave the rough work to me.'

'You weren't here.'

'But you knew I should be back. When the fields are white with daisies, you must have said to yourself, he will return. I assume, from your sober deportment, that you found nothing?'

'Only a lot of stuffing. And, unfortunately, just as I was peering into the thing, Mrs Cork came in.'

'My God! Had you your story ready?'

'Such as it was. I said I was looking to see if the moths had been at it.'

'Weak.'

'So I felt.'

'I should have done better than that.'

'No, you wouldn't.'

'Yes, I would.'

'Well, what would you have said?'

'I should have said – speaking with a light laugh – "Ah, Mrs Cork…"'

'Go on.'

'"Ah, Mrs Cork…" No,' said Jeff, on reflection, 'I don't know that I should have been so frightfully good, after all. Did she accept your explanation?'

'She appeared to. But I can't help feeling that I must have left her thinking that I had been bitten by Uncle George and infected with his particular form of eccentricity. I wonder she didn't dismiss me on the spot. It can't be pleasant for a woman to feel that her butler and her secretary are both off their heads.'

'Scarcely a matter for comment in a place like this, where the whole strength of the company are loopy to the eyebrows. A stranger, straying in while the boys and girls were doing one of those tribal dances, would be on the phone, telling the nearest alienist to drop everything and hurry round, before he had seen the first ten steps. Have you ever noticed that long, thin fellow in the pince-nez with the double-jointed hips?'

'Mr Shepperson? I dream of him sometimes.'

'So do I.'

'Mrs Barlow, too.'

'Which is she?'

'The stout woman with the chins.'

'I know the one you mean. What a jewel! What a gem! What a breath of air from the seaside! Yes, there's a lot of elevation and instruction, not to mention pity and terror, to be derived from observing the inmates of this amateur Colney Hatch. My only regret is that the butler does not participate in the rhythmic revels. It would be stimulating to watch him treading the measure. How those large, flat feet would spurn the antic hay!'

'That's right. Make fun of Uncle George's feet.'

'Thanks awfully. I'd love to. Let's both make fun of them. The old fathead, subjecting you to a fearful ordeal like that.'

'Do you feel you know me well enough to call my uncle an old fathead?'

'I feel as if I had known you all my life. I'm sure you will find, when you look into it, that we have been married for years, without knowing it.'

The operative word 'married' had a sobering effect on Anne. She had temporarily thrust from her mind Lord Uffenham's statement in the car that this agreeable young man was in love with her, and had given herself up wholeheartedly to the pleasant give and take of this conversation. It was not often nowadays that she was able to enjoy the lighter type of conversational exchange. The male residents of Shipley Hall were solid, earnest men, too conscious of their mission to allow themselves to indulge in badinage. And Lionel, though he looked like a Greek god, had always been a little heavy in hand.

It had been wrong of her, she now saw, to lower quite so completely the barriers between herself and Jeff. It was what censorious critics of an earlier age would have stigmatized as 'encouraging' one for whom there was, of course, no hope.

She gave a little shiver.

'Cold?' asked Jeff, as she had expected him to do.

'I am, rather.'

'Then let us go in. I can talk just as well indoors. Some people say better.'

They walked towards the sunken garden. Above the wall

which separated it from the lawn there were visible the head and shoulders of Mrs Molloy. She seemed to be engaged in toying with the tendrils of some trailing shrub which had been planted in a stone vase of antique appearance. And it occurred to Jeff that here was an excellent opportunity of delivering that veiled warning, which in his opinion was so highly necessary.

'There's Mrs Molloy.'

'Yes.'

'Don't look now,' said Jeff, 'but what do you think of her?'

'She seems quite nice.'

'She doesn't strike you as sinister?'

'Not a bit. Does she you?'

'Very much so.'

'I suppose almost everybody seems sinister to a detective.'

'Well, one's trained instinct enables one to probe beneath the surface, of course. There's not much you can hide from the bloodstain and magnifying-glass boys. I have a feeling that these Molloys will bear watching. They may be crooks.'

'That's what Mr Trumper thinks.'

'Does he, the shrewd little half-portion?'

'He came to me the other day, and asked me to use my influence with Mrs Cork to prevent her buying oil stock from Mr Molloy. Unfortunately, I have no influence with Mrs Cork. But go on. I don't see what harm they can do to us, even if they are as crooked as corkscrews.'

'How about those diamonds?'

'What do you mean?'

'Suppose they get after them?'

'But they don't know they exist.'

'They may get to know at any moment. Mrs Molloy often

goes and hobnobs with your uncle in his pantry. He might easily let slip something.'

'He wouldn't.'

'He might.'

'Of course, he wouldn't. He's not crazy.'

'Who told you that?'

It seemed to Anne that the moment had arrived to crush this young man. She liked him. Indeed, she could not remember ever having liked anyone so much, on such short acquaintance. But she felt that he needed the firm, repressive hand. She walked on a few paces, then stopped and, facing him coldly, prepared to speak.

It was at this point in the proceedings that the antique vase, suddenly becoming a thing of movement, fell with a crash on the pavement at her side, and she gave a little scream and postponed her observations.

Jeff was blaming himself bitterly. He should have known better, he was telling himself, than to have come within a hundred yards of Mrs Molloy and an antique vase, one of the most dangerous combinations in existence, especially when in the company of Anne Benedick. His sentiments towards Anne were now so clearly defined that he would have felt uneasy if he had seen a rose petal fluttering down upon her precious head. Her narrow escape from receiving an antique vase on the back of the neck shook him to his foundations, so that the world seemed to swim about him and he scarcely knew what he was doing.

A cold voice spoke through the mists.

'Would you mind letting me go, please?'

He discovered what he was doing. He was clasping Anne protectively to his bosom.

'Oh, sorry,' he said, and released her.

Anne, who had been white, was pink.

'Thank you,' she said.

A silence followed. Jeff was feeling oddly breathless. For the first time, he found himself swinging over towards the school of thought represented by Lord Uffenham, wondering whether, after all, there might not be something in the latter's crudely expressed but not unintelligent counsel. There had unquestionably been something about the feel of Anne's slender body in his arms that had seemed to satisfy some deep hunger in his soul.

Mrs Molloy came hurrying through the door in the wall, concern on every feature of her piquant face.

'Gee!' she cried. 'It didn't hit you, did it? I wouldn't have had a thing like that happen for a million dollars.'

Nothing could have been more admirably in keeping with the solemnity of the moment than her pretty solicitude, yet Jeff eyed her with something of the repulsion which he would have bestowed upon a cobra di capella, a reptile of which he had never been fond.

'I happened to kind of lean against it, and it suddenly sort of toppled over. Gosh, I am sorry!'

'It's quite all right,' said Anne. 'It only gave me rather a start.'

'I'll bet it did. It must have scared the daylights out of you.'

'Oh, no,' said Anne. 'It just made me jump. Please don't worry about it. I must go in. Mrs Cork may be wanting me.'

She disappeared abruptly, still pink, and Dolly, turning to Jeff, became aware of his stern, set face.

'Ha!' said Jeff.

Dolly laughed. She had rather an attractive laugh, lilting and musical, but Jeff found it lacking in appeal.

'You saffron-headed little blighter!' he said.

There was no mistaking the displeasure in his voice, but Dolly continued to seem amused.

'How's your packing coming along, big boy?' she enquired. 'Better get it started. I can't always miss, you know. Sooner or later, you're going to stop one.'

'Tchah!' said Jeff, and turned on his heel and left her. He was aware that the remark was far from being an adequate one, but he could think of nothing better on the spur of the moment. He was regretting that a gentle and chivalrous upbringing, with its insistence on the fact that the man who lays a hand upon a woman, save in the way of kindness, is a man who ought to be ashamed of himself, rendered it impossible for him to give this blot on the Kentish scene the slosh in the eye for which her whole scheme of behaviour seemed to clamour. In the life of every man there come times when he wishes he was James Cagney, and one of these had come to him now.

Dolly made her way back to the terrace. She had left her Soapy there, dozing over a detective story, and was surprised to find his chair empty. She applied for enlightenment to Mrs Barlow, the woman with the chins, who was doing deep breathing exercises on the lawn.

'Seen my husband anywheres, Mrs Barlow?'

'I think he was called to the telephone, Mrs Molloy.'

It was at this moment that the missing man appeared in the french window. There was agitation in his demeanour. He hurried to where Dolly stood, plainly disturbed.

'Honey!'

''Smatter, sweetness?'

Mr Molloy shot a glance at Mrs Barlow. She was once more doing deep breathing exercises, but even deep breathers have ears. He drew his wife aside to the far corner of the terrace.

'I've just been talking to Chimp on the phone.'

'Oh, was that who it was? I suppose he's been thinking it over and wants to put up a squawk about the terms?'

Mr Molloy shook his head. He paused for a moment. He hated to be the bearer of bad news.

'No, it isn't that,' he said. 'I'm afraid there's a nasty jolt coming to you, pettie. He's down here at the inn, and talks of clocking in at the house to-morrow morning.'

CHAPTER 14

Dolly gaped at her husband incredulously. As he had foretold, the news had shaken her severely. On the lawn, Mrs Barlow had begun to try out some steps of a tribal dance. It was a spectacle which at any other moment would have gripped and arrested, but now she lumbered to and fro disregarded.

'What!'

'That's right.'

'He's coming to the joint?'

'To-morrow, first thing.'

'But what about the hay-haired guy?'

Mr Molloy's gloom deepened.

'It begins to look like this isn't one of our lucky deals, sugar. We're standing behind the eight-ball. The hay-haired bozo means nothing in Chimp's life now. Of all the darned things that had to happen, he wrote Chimp a letter, and it seems Chimp was all wrong where he thought the bird had it in for him. It's a long story, and I couldn't follow all of it, but, according to Chimp, this bimbo didn't throw bricks at him – he threw some kind of cakes, which he wanted to get rid of on account he didn't like to hurt the cook's feelings by leaving them lay. And when Chimp saw him helling up the stairs, he was just coming to apologize. It sounds cock-eyed, but that's what he told Chimp in this letter.'

'Oh, gosh!'

'That's how I feel, too. It was bad enough being up against the straw-haired guy. If we've got to worry all the time about Chimp gumshoeing around and watching us to see we don't pull any quick stuff, I don't see as we can get anywheres. You know what Chimp's like. Eyes at the back of his head.'

Dolly mused. Her momentary weakness had passed. She had ceased to totter beneath the blows of Fate, and was looking to the future, framing schemes, formulating plans of action.

'We'll have to ease Chimp out, that's all.'

'Yes, but how?'

'I'll find a way. You go take a walk around the block, and leave me think a while.'

Mr Molloy did as he was bidden. From time to time, as he circled the lawn, he cast a hopeful glance at his pensive helpmeet, wondering how she was making out. It might be, he felt, that even this outstanding crisis in their affairs would find her equal to it. Dolly had always been the brains of the firm. He himself, he was aware, had his limitations. Give him a sympathetic listener, preferably one who in his formative years had been kicked on the head by a mule, a clear half-hour in which to talk Oil and plenty of room to wave his hands, and he could accomplish wonders. But apart from this one talent he was not a very gifted man, and he knew it.

It was as he was half-way through his sixth lap that he saw that Dolly had left the terrace and was crossing the lawn towards him. And his heart leaped up when he beheld the shining light of inspiration on that loved face. It told him that her brilliant intellect had found the way. And, as so often, he was conscious of a feeling almost of awe at the thought that it had been given to him to win the love of such a woman – a woman who with her educated fingers could keep herself in gloves, handkerchiefs, scent, vanity bags and even jewellery free of expense and, in addition, was able to solve all the vexing little domestic problems which came up from time to time in their lives.

'Don't tell me you've doped something out already?' he said, reverently.

'Sure. It just needed mulling over.'

'Honey,' said Mr Molloy, 'they don't make 'em like you nowadays. They've lost the secret. Spill it, pettie. I'm here to listen.'

A gratified flush crept into Dolly's cheek. She loved this man, and his words were music to her ears.

'Well, look,' she said. 'You say Chimp's at the inn?'

'Right there at the inn, sugar.'

'Then you go there and see him. You'll just have time. And when you see him, be all worked up, like as if you'd had a shock. Agitated, sort of. See? Can you make yourself tremble?'

'Like this?'

'No, not like that. You don't want to make him think you've got St Vitus's Dance or sump'n. Just be all of a doodah, like what you'd natch'ally be if you'd heard that old Lord Cakebread had located that ice and had gotten it in his room and was planning to hand in his portfolio to-morrow morning and mosey out of here with the stuff in his jeans.'

'Is that the spiel I'm to hand Chimp?'

'That's right.'

'But where does that get us, honeybunch?'

'Well, use your bean. If Lord Cakebread really had gotten the stuff and was aiming to quit the joint to-morrow, it would mean that we'd have to lay our hooks on it to-day, wouldn't it?'

'No argument about that.'

'And that would mean that one of us would have to sneak into his room and go through it.'

'Sure.'

'Well, it can't be you, because you're weak in the nerves and would be scared cross-eyed at the mere idea of doing such a thing.'

'What!'

'That's only what you say to Chimp.'

'Oh, it's part of the spiel?'

'That's right. Well, then, maybe, he wonders why I don't do it.'

'No use trying to kid him that you're weak in the nerves.'

'No. So you tell him you're planning to slip one over on me. You say that Lord Cakebread told me he'd got the stuff, and I told you, and you immediately seen where this was where you salted away a nice little private balance in the bank without me knowing nothing about it. Let's you and me, you say to Chimp, collect this ice and tell Dolly we couldn't find it.'

Mr Molloy nodded.

'Yes, he'd fall for that. If there's one thing Chimp'll always fall for, it's if he feels there's double-crossing going on. It's like catnip to a cat. And then what?'

'Why, then you tell him he's got to do it.'

'Bust into Lord Cakebread's room?'

'Yay. Only there won't be no question of busting. Tell him he can just walk in. Say there's a time, when it's getting along for dinner, when a butler's busy around the house, so there won't be no chance of Lord Cakebread muscling in and gumming the game. That's when he must sneak in, you tell him. And then you tell him where the room is.'

'But where is it?'

'On the ground floor, back of the joint, looking out on where the tradesmen's carts drive up and all like that. He can't miss it. There's a water barrel outside the window, tell him, and just to one side a tombstone with "To Ponto, Ever A Faithful Friend" on it. Where they buried a dog, I guess,' said Dolly, thinking it improbable that the remains of members of the family would be distributed about the grounds in this casual fashion.

Mr Molloy was surprised at this omniscience.

'How do you know all that?'

'I was up early a coupla days ago, you remember the morning, and I strolled around there, and I seen the old bird at the window, doing his daily dozen. He was in his pants, and nothing else except suspenders,' said Dolly, involuntarily dropping her voice to a whisper, for the spectacle of Lord Uffenham stripped to the waist, with a pair of mauve braces draped over his massive shoulders, had made a deep impression on her. 'He looked like King Kong. Well, that's the set-up. You tell Chimp the old bozo has gotten the ice somewheres in his room, you put him wise where the room is and when it's sure to be empty, and you tell him he's got to handle the searching of it because you haven't the nerve. All straight?'

Mr Molloy hesitated. He was reluctant to reply in the negative, for he felt that in some way not at the moment obvious to him it would place him in the unpleasant position of looking like a Dumb Isaac. He had had this experience before, on occasions when he had questioned the soundness of his wife's inspirations.

On the other hand, he could not see where the thing made sense.

'Well, I'll tell you, sugar,' he said. 'It's straight enough, far as that goes. But it seems to me as if nothing's going to happen. He sneaks in, hunts around, doesn't find the ice, because it's not there, and comes away. Where's the percentage? Aside from just making a monkey out of Chimp, of course. It don't seem to get us anywheres. I thought you were going to come across with something that would keep him from visiting at the house.'

'So I have.'

'I don't see it.'

It occurred to Dolly to reply that he wouldn't see the Woolworth Building if he was standing across the street with a telescope, but she refrained, partly because she loved her mate and shrank from paining him, and partly because this was no time for cracks.

'Well, look,' she said. 'What happens when Lord Cakebread comes in and catches him?'

'But he won't. You said he'd be busy around the joint.'

'I didn't say any such thing. I said that was what you was to tell Chimp. The moment you phone me that he's bit, I go to Lord Cakebread and warn him to watch out, because I happen to know there's a low-life coming to hunt around in his room this evening. So then what? He lies in wait, and catches Chimp. Maybe he beats him up. Maybe he just chases him out. But, anyway, whichever he does, Chimp'll have a swell chance of horning in next morning, saying he's a millionaire that's interested in these here new Ugubus and wants to join the gang. If he tries it, out steps Lord Cakebread and says to Mrs Cork "The hell he's a millionaire! He's just a porch climber," and Mrs Cork reaches for her gun and tells Chimp he's got two minutes to beat it away from here before he gets an ounce of lead in his pants and has the dogs set on him. Now, do you get it?'

Mr Molloy did not actually lay his head in the dust, but he felt a strong inclination to do so. Never again, he was telling himself, would he lack faith in this woman's schemes, even if their true worth was not immediately apparent to his slower masculine intelligence. His fine, candid eyes lit up.

'Honey, it's a pip!'

'I'll say it is.'

'It can't miss.'

'I'll say it can't.'

'You won't be able to see Chimp for dust.'

'I'll say you won't.'

'Then I'd best be getting along to the inn and contacting him.'

'Yay. And make it snappy. Call me from the post office, if everything's jake, and then I can go ahead. We don't want to lose no time.'

Mr Molloy set off at a capital pace, enthusiasm lending wings to a pair of legs not normally planned for swift pedestrianism. And so excellent were his speed and staying power that it was scarcely half an hour later that Dolly, having been informed over the telephone by her second in command that Mr Twist had swallowed the whole set-up, hook, line and sinker, and might be expected at the tryst any minute now, made her way to Lord Uffenham's pantry.

The glazed look in the latter's eyes – he had been giving his brain a rest at the moment of her entry – disappeared as he saw one whom, from her evident taste for his society, he had come to look upon as an old friend. He lumbered to his feet like a bison leaving a waterhole, and was about to offer her a courtly glass of port, when he saw that her fists were clenched and her eyes glittering. Plainly, something had occurred to disturb the dear little woman, and his generous heart ached for her. Dolly always aroused the protective instinct in him. She seemed so weak, so fragile, so unfitted to cope with the problems of life.

'Is something the matter, Madam?' he asked, solicitously, in his most artistic Cakebread manner.

Dolly gulped.

'You betcher. Am I mortified! I'm as mad as a wet hen.'

Such a statement, made to Lord Uffenham in other circumstances, would have plunged him into abstruse speculation as to how mad hens were, when wet – how you detected this dementia – and where such birds might be held to rank in eccentricity of outlook as compared, say, with hatters or the members of Mrs Cork's Ugubu colony. But now his only thought was for her distress.

'What's the trouble?' he asked, adding a rather un-Cakebreadian 'Hey?' It was not his practice, as we have seen, to step out of his role, but he was much moved.

'Listen while I tell you,' said Dolly, much moved herself. 'I've just heard they're sending a private dick this evening to search your room.'

'A private what?'

'Dick.'

'You mean a rozzer? A detective?'

'That's right. He's coming to search your room, on account they think you've got stolen property hid away there. That's what's made me so mad, feeling they're casting this what you might call slur on your honesty.'

As Lord Uffenham had been informed by Anne that it was Mrs Molloy who had been the first to cast this slur, and that it was she who was primarily responsible for the establishment of a detective on the premises of Shipley Hall, he might have replied with something calculated to reproach and wound. But he had long since forgiven his little friend for an action of which he was convinced that she would never have been guilty, had she had the privilege then of knowing him as well as she did now.

'You mean young Adair, as he calls himself?'

Dolly felt it advisable to start confusedly. She remembered that she was not supposed to know that her companion knew anything about the inwardness of young Adair.

'You know about that guy?'

Lord Uffenham chuckled fatly.

'Yes, I know all about him.'

'Well, aren't you smart!'

'People have said so,' said Lord Uffenham, though not naming them. 'Lord-love-a-duck, I don't mind young Adair searching my room.'

'Ah, but this isn't him,' said Dolly. 'This is another one. I've just been talking with that old bird, Trumper. It seems he isn't satisfied with Adair. Thinks him too young and frivolous. So, without saying a word to Mrs Cork, he's gone and hired a dick on his own account, and he's coming to search your room.'

Lord Uffenham's complacency had vanished.

'Is he, the rat? When?'

'I'm telling you. This evening. Any minute now. He chose this time on account he thought you'd be busy around the joint. What you'd ought to do, seems to me, is hide and pop out and paste him one.'

'I will, the slinking slug.'

'Is there somewheres in your room where you can hide?'

'Behind the screen.'

'At-a-baby!' cried Dolly, clapping her little hands with girlish enthusiasm. 'Park yourself there, and don't shoot till you see the whites of his eyes.'

It was some minutes later that Lord Uffenham, passing through the hall on his way back from the dining-room, whither he had been to see that everything was in order, so that he might go off duty for a while, encountered Mr Trumper, on his way to practise billiards in the billiard-room. He fixed him with a stare so cold and penetrating that the little man sagged beneath it like a bird *vis-à-vis* with a serpent. This butler always gave Eustace Trumper a scared, guilty feeling, as if he had been caught wearing a made-up tie or had used his fish fork for dealing with a *soufflé*.

CHAPTER 15

The hour of seven-fifteen found Chimp Twist at the main
gates of Shipley Hall, humming a gay air beneath his breath
and feeling that God was in His heaven and all right with
the world. He surveyed the rolling parkland, and admired it
enormously. He listened to the carolling of the birds, and
thought how sweet their music was. Even an insect, which got
entangled in his moustache, struck him as probably quite a
decent insect, if one had only got to know it. His mood, in
short, was one of saccharine benevolence. He was in the frame
of mind, when he would have patted a small boy on the head
and given him sixpence, though it is probable that a moment
later he would have tossed him for it and won it back again.

The letter which Jeff had sent round by district messenger
boy that morning had brought to this monkey-faced little
chevalier of industry a sensation of relief and *bien être* which
he could scarcely have obtained from a brimming beaker of the
most widely advertised nerve tonic on the market. Ever since
the Board Meeting which had ended in his being compelled to
entrust the executive end of their venture to the Molloys,
Chimp Twist had been tortured by the problem of how to
prevent these old friends double-crossing him, as he had no
doubt they would do, should the opportunity arise, with that
blithe alacrity which he had so often noted in them.

If, he had felt with a sinking heart, they succeeded in locating that ice, they would do it while he was far away, unable to keep an eye on them. And if ever a couple lived and breathed on whom it was advisable for a shareholder to keep an eye, and that a skinned one, it was the Molloys, Mr and Mrs. He trusted neither of them as far as he could spit, and he was a poor spitter, lacking both distance and control.

But now this letter had come, removing all obstacles in the way of a visit to Shipley Hall. And on top of that there had been his recent interview with Soapy.

The whole thing, he felt as he floated through the sunlit grounds, was going to be almost too easy to be interesting. And when he stood outside the window of Lord Uffenham's bedroom, and noted that it was open and presented no difficulties of access to even the least nimble of intruders, his confidence reached its peak.

Until this moment, burglary was a form of gainful occupation of which Chimp Twist had had no experience. He had always made his money by brain work. But now the circumstances had turned him temporarily into a manual labourer, there was no diffidence in his soul, no hesitation in his bearing. If, as he stood at journey's end, his heart beat a little faster, that was all.

Inside the room, his first act was to go to the door, open it and listen intently. Somewhere in the distance, a female voice was singing a hymn with a good deal of stomp in it, which would have indicated to the practised ear that Mrs Cork's cook had started to boil the spinach, but no other sound broke the silence. He left the door open, so that he might be warned, should feet come along the passage, and was pleased to see that the passage was a stone-flagged one. If such feet did approach, it would be to the accompaniment of a booming noise like the rolling of drums, and he would be enabled to withdraw well in advance of their arrival.

The room in which he stood, it seemed to him as his eye roamed about it, was a good deal more luxuriously furnished than one would have expected of a butler's bedroom. The explanation of this was that Lord Uffenham, in accepting employment at his old home, had made it clear to his niece that if he had to become a dashed Hey-You and cleaner of silver, he was blowed if he intended to live in absolute squalor; and he had collected from other parts of the establishment various pictures and ornaments, not to mention an easy chair, a carpet of the softest pile and even a chaise-longue, on which he could recline of an afternoon with his boots off. Thanks to this resolute scrounging, the place had become virtually a boudoir.

Nevertheless, there existed in Chimp's mind no doubt that he had come to the right spot. Immediately beneath the window was the water barrel of which Soapy had spoken, and beside it that touching memorial to the unidentified Ponto, stressing the deceased's fidelity and friendliness. All that remained for him to do, therefore, was to ransack the apartment and hope for the best.

He set to work swiftly and silently, like a New York Customs official dealing with the effects of a star of the musical comedy stage who has left her native America for a trip to Paris and, returning, has announced that she has nothing to declare. He looked in drawers, he searched cupboards, he hunted behind chairs and pictures. He even prodded the chaise-longue, to make sure that its stuffing was bona fide stuffing.

Activities like these, especially when the weather is sultry, take their toll of a man, and presently he was obliged to pause and mop his brow. And it was while he was so engaged that his glance happened to fall on a handsome lacquer screen which stood in the far corner. In the gap between its base and the carpet there was visible a colossal pair of boots.

They caught Chimp's eye, and astonished him by their dimensions, but they conveyed no sinister message to him. Just boots, he felt – his host's spare ones, presumably. It was only a moment later that, looking more closely, he noticed above them the southern end of a pair of trousers. And it was suddenly brought home to him, with a sickening shock which reduced his spinal column to the consistency of the spinach which was now boiling briskly on the kitchen stove, that inside these trousers were human limbs. It was, in short, no mere supplementary brace of beetle-crushers that stood there, but a pair in active use, with their proprietor in occupation.

He was still reeling bonelessly from the effects of this hideous discovery, when the screen was drawn aside by a powerful hand and there stood before him the largest man he had ever seen. To his excited senses, the newcomer seemed to fill the room from wall to wall, and even so to be a little cramped for space.

'Well, rat?' observed this eye-filling individual.

It had been Lord Uffenham's intention to intervene in the proceedings a good deal earlier than this. But, as always when he stood rooted to any given spot, he had allowed himself to float off on a train of thought. The stealthy movements without, announcing that his visitor had arrived, had set him musing on private detectives – what made them become private detectives, what they did in their spare time, about how much the income per annum of a fairly well-to-do investigator would amount to, and what had become of the one with the ginger moustache at whom he had thrown an umbrella in the year 1912.

He was now once more alert and the man of action.

The observation 'Well, rat?' is one to which it is not easy to find an immediate and satisfactory response. Chimp Twist did not even attempt one. He stood gaping pallidly at this large man, who seemed by some optical illusion to be expanding still further with every moment that went by, bestriding his narrow world like a Colossus. And, as so often happened when he was in thought or agitation, he automatically raised a hand to his waxed moustache and gave it a twiddle.

The action grated upon Lord Uffenham. Moustache-twiddling reminded him of Lionel Green, and he hated to be compelled to think about that rising young interior decorator.

'Stop it!' he said sternly.

'Sir?' said Chimp, all obsequiousness and anxiety to oblige.

'Leave that thing alone,' said Lord Uffenham. He eyed the unpleasant growth with increasing curiosity, for the sight of it had stimulated his always enquiring mind. 'That moustache. Had it long?' he asked, like a doctor making the preliminary inquisition concerning some rare type of disease. 'When did you first feel it coming on?'

Chimp, a little surprised, but extremely relieved at this unexpectedly pacific conversational opening, replied that the disfigurement in question was of fairly recent vintage. He had decided to grow it, he said, about a coupla years ago.

'What makes it stick out like that at the ends?' asked Lord Uffenham, going deeper and deeper into the subject.

Any topic other than that of his presence in the room would have been welcome to Chimp. He replied almost jauntily:

'Wax.'

'Yer put wax on it?'

'Yessir, wax.'

'What sort of wax?'

'Well, matter of fact, often as not I use soap.'

'What sort of soap?'

'Toilet soap. Or maybe shaving cream.'

'Then why did yer say wax?'

'Sometimes I use wax.'

'Beeswax?'

'Just ordinary wax.'

'And that's what makes it stick out?'

'Yessir, that's what makes it stick out.'

'Well, it looks bloody awful. If it was mine, I'd have it off at the roots. And now,' said Lord Uffenham, becoming the practical man of affairs and giving himself a shake to limber up his muscles and induce elasticity, 'and now to break every bone in your foul body, you ghastly-looking little half-pint of misery.'

In spite of the charming, comradely tone of the conversation up till now, with its underlying suggestion that he and Lord Uffenham were a couple of kindred spirits just lounging around and kidding back and forth, Chimp had never lost sight of the possibility that their chat might eventually work towards some such point. And even while answering his companion's questions in that almost fraternal spirit, he had been careful to keep well out of arm's reach and so to order his movements as always to be between the other and the door.

Lord Uffenham's words found him, accordingly, in an excellent strategic position to make the dash for life, and he made it without delay. In the days of his young manhood, when, as he had told Anne, he had been much followed by private detectives, Lord Uffenham had once waited round a corner for one who had been trailing him from St John's Wood to Berkeley

Square, and had made a sudden spring at him from a shadowy doorway. Except on that single occasion, he could not recall ever having seen an enquiry agent move more nimbly. It seemed to him that there was just a whirring noise and a puff of dust, and the fellow was gone.

He was deeply chagrined. He blamed himself for having allowed a thirst for information to divert him from the main issue at a moment when he should have been attending strictly to business. It was patent now that he had lost for ever the chance of taking this private investigator's greasy neck in his hands and tying it into a lovers' knot, a task to which he had been looking forward with bright enthusiasm. Opportunity knocks but once, and he had allowed it to knock in vain.

It seemed to Lord Uffenham, as it had seemed to the poet, that of all sad words of tongue or pen, the saddest are these – It might have been.

CHAPTER 16

It is never easy for a man in so delicate a situation as that in which Chimp Twist had found himself to preserve the *aequam mentem* recommended by the Roman writer as suitable in times of stress. Had he been calmer, he would on tearing himself away from Lord Uffenham's society have turned to the left along the passage, and thus have put himself in a position to effect a masterly withdrawal by the back entrance, which stood only a few short yards away.

As it was, losing his presence of mind in his intense desire to arrange for immediate absence of body, he turned to the right, setting a course which led directly towards the main portion of the house. And he had not proceeded far before he found his progress barred by a green baize door.

But only for an instant. He did not know what lay beyond this obstacle, but he had a lively sense of what was on his side of it, and he had no hesitation in charging at it like a footballer bucking the line. It gave way before him, swinging easily on its hinges, and he came into a spacious open space, dotted about with chairs, small tables and old oak settles, with a massive door at one end and to one side a broad flight of stairs. He was, in short, in the hall, and here for a moment he paused, wondering what to do for the best.

He was pleased to find that he had the leisure to do so, and even more surprised than pleased. It seemed inexplicable to him that there came to his ears no sound of following footsteps and that the green baize barrier did not swing violently open again, to reveal Lord Uffenham thundering in his wake. He wondered what had become of him.

As a matter of fact, Lord Uffenham had thundered in his wake for a few strides. But he was a man built more for statuesqueness than activity, the majestic glacier rather than racing whippet, and right from the start he had not had much hope of coming in anywhere but a bad second. When he had seen his quarry cutting out so excellent a pace, and had become aware of the creaking of his own joints, he had abandoned the pursuit. 'Easy come, easy go,' he had said to himself with the splendid Uffenhamian philosophy, and had gone off to his pantry for a glass of port.

Chimp stood holding his breath, his furtive little eyes darting about the handsomely appointed lounging place in which he stood. He was alone at last, but there was no saying how long this privacy would continue. There was a door to his left, and beyond it a passage, leading to the unknown. At any moment, some intruder might come through this door out along this passage. A little sleep, a little folding of the hands, may be all right for the man of leisure, but not for one who is virtually the hunted stag.

And now his eye was attracted by two small windows, with flower-pots on their sills. They stood one on either side of the massive door, and through them was visible blue sky and greenery. And he realized, though it had taken him some time to do so, that the massive door was Shipley Hall's front door, and that he had only to turn its handle to win through to the open air and freedom.

He darted towards it, but even as his fingers touched the latch there came from the other side the sound of voices. He leaped back, and the door near the passage began to open, and somebody within could be heard whistling. It was, to keep the record straight, Mr Trumper, who, greatly restored after his encounter with Lord Uffenham by some capital shooting on the billiard table, was about to go to his room to dress for dinner.

It seemed to Chimp that he was encompassed on every side, and for an instant he was about to resign himself to the inevitable. Then he saw that in this grossly over-populated house there was one vacant spot. There appeared to be no one on the stairs. He decided to fill this hiatus. He was up them like the monkey he so closely resembled in a series of rapid bounds, and Mr Trumper, emerging from the billiard-room, caught with the tail of his eye a flying form, the sight of which rendered him for a moment vaguely uneasy.

Thoughts of burglars flashed into Mr Trumper's mind. Then he dismissed the idea. Burglars, he reflected, were creatures of the night and would not be likely to put on what amounted to a matinée performance. Nor did they, it occurred to him, skim up stairs in this volatile fashion. They prowled and prowled around, like the hosts of Midian, but always, or so he had been given to understand, at a reasonable pace.

His fears allayed, he resumed his whistling, and after taking a glance at the hall table, to see if any letters had come for him by the evening post, turned to greet Mrs Cork, who had just entered through the front door accompanied by Mrs Barlow.

'Oh, Eustace,' said Mrs Cork, 'I wanted to see you. We have run out of ants' eggs for the goldfish. Will you go to the village first thing to-morrow and buy some? I think you can get them at the grocer's.'

'Of course, of course. Certainly, Clarissa, delighted,' said Mr Trumper.

Mrs Barlow said that she had often thought how curious it was that goldfish should ever have acquired a taste for ants' eggs, seeing that in their natural, wild state they could scarcely have moved in the same social sphere, so to speak, as ants. This led to Mrs Cork, who had a fund of good stories about the animal kingdom, telling of an emu she had known which ate aspirin tablets, and in the interest of these exchanges all thoughts of the mystery man with the indiarubber legs passed from Mr Trumper's mind.

Chimp, meanwhile, now arrived in the upper regions, had discovered that his spirited dash, though a sound tactical move and one which had saved him from having to plunge into Shipley Hall society and meet a lot of new people, which is always tedious, was not, as he had hoped, an end, but a beginning. Movements from the floor above indicated the presence there of yet another of the Hall's teeming millions, and to his agitated mind it seemed that this person was moving in his direction.

With people likely at any moment to come up, and other people likely at any moment to come down, it was plain to him that some haven of refuge in his immediate vicinity was essential, and the only one which presented itself was the bedroom outside which he was standing. Left to himself, he would have preferred not to go into any more strange bedrooms, for Lord Uffenham's had given him a feeling of satiety, but it appeared clear that he had no choice.

He crept to the door, and peered in. The room was empty. It seemed to him almost incredible that in a house like this there could be an unoccupied space, but so it was. He hurried in, and once more paused to listen.

It was at this point that he heard Mr Trumper coming up the stairs, and the paralysing thought crossed his mind that the latter might quite conceivably be making for this very room. And he was perfectly right. Mr Trumper, having heard all that there was to hear about emus and goldfish, had resumed his journey upstairs to dress for dinner. For an instant, Chimp stood transfixed, his beady little eyes flickering to and fro. Then, at the end of the room beside the fireplace, he saw that there stood a small wardrobe.

The sight of it affected him very much as that of a rainbow used to affect the poet Wordsworth. Wardrobes are practically the same thing as cupboards, and it has been shown that Chimp Twist was never really at his ease outside cupboards. A man either has or has not this cupboard complex implanted in him. Chimp had, and the wardrobe seemed to draw him like a magnet. He could see that it would be a snug fit, but he yearned for it as the hart yearns for the water-brooks. Not even on the occasion when he had beheld Jeff bounding up the staircase of Halsey Buildings had he experienced a stronger desire to put himself away in storage.

Thirty seconds later, he was inside. He could have made it in twenty-three flat, but he had paused to see if there was a key in the door, and this slowed him up. There was no key, so he went in without it, and was adjusting himself to his cramped surroundings, holding the inside of the door to prevent it falling open, when it was borne in upon him that he had done well to hurry. There was a sound of jocund whistling, and Mr Trumper entered the room.

Eustace Trumper was in excellent spirits. He had made two breaks of double figures in the billiard-room, always a sound reason for rejoicing, and in addition he had been asked by Mrs

Cork to go to the village and buy ants' eggs for her. It was this that so particularly exhilarated him.

Every lover likes to be called upon to perform deeds for his lady, and it seemed to Mr Trumper that this spirit of reliance on the part of the woman he loved – this leaning upon him, as it were, was promising. For twelve years, ever since the decease of her late husband, who had contracted pneumonia as the result of an injudicious dip in the Trafalgar Square fountain one chilly New Year's Eve, he had been wooing Mrs Cork in his timid way, and this sort of thing gave him hope. The woman who asks you to buy ants' eggs for her to-day is the woman who shyly whispers 'Yes' to-morrow. Or so it seemed to Mr Trumper.

It was to the accompaniment of further melodious whistling that he hopped out of his clothes, sluiced himself with hot water from the can in the basin and donned his shirt. Only when he was about to tie his tie, an act that called for care and concentration, did he become silent. And it was during this period of silence that Chimp Twist, who had been troubled for some little time with a bit of fluff up his nose, found himself unable to repress a violent sneeze. In the stillness of the room, it rang out like the hissing of a hundred soda-water syphons, and Mr Trumper rose six inches into the air and came down trembling in every limb, the tie falling from his nerveless hand.

Until this moment, as has been indicated, occupied with other and sweeter thoughts, Eustace Trumper had thrust into the background of his mind the mystery of that agile form which he had seen flitting up the stairs. It now came flooding back like a tidal wave, and he realized that his first suspicions had been correct. Irregular though it might be for burglars to start operating at an hour like this, the figure he had seen must have been that of a member of that unpleasant section of the community – some health-loving marauder, no doubt, who did not approve of late hours and liked to get his crib-cracking done in good time for the early bed and the long, refreshing sleep.

He based his reasoning on the fact that the noise, whatever it had been, had come from inside the wardrobe. Honest men, he felt, do not hide in wardrobes, and he was, of course, perfectly correct. The simple question 'Do you hide in wardrobes?' is a handy means of separating the sheep from the goats in this world. It is the acid test. At the man who answers 'Yes,' we look askance, and rightly.

On this point, Eustace Trumper was clear. It was when he started to try to decide what he was going to do about it that he found doubts and uncertainty creeping in.

Mankind may be divided roughly into two classes – those who, becoming aware of cracksmen in their wardrobe, fling open the door and confront them, and those who do not. It was to the latter group that Eustace Trumper belonged. What would have stimulated Lord Uffenham to instant action induced in him only profound thought.

The ideal procedure, of course, as he realized, would have been to steal softly to the wardrobe and turn the key in the door. Nothing makes a burglar feel so silly as being locked in a wardrobe. But even from where he stood he could see that there was no key in the door. This blocked the exploration of that avenue, and he found himself quite unable to think of an alternative scheme – one at least, which, while producing solid results, would avoid danger to the person.

And then, as he stood irresolute, there came floating into his mind like drifting thistledown the thought that there were other and younger men than he in the house, and that the risk of his becoming embroiled in unpleasantness could be avoided by handing over the whole conduct of the affair to one of these. Eustace Trumper had no objection to danger to the person, provided it was some other person. He was not familiar with the fine old slogan, Let George Do It, but if he had been, those were the words which would now have sprung to his lips, with the necessary substitution for 'George' of the name J. Sheringham Adair.

The great advantage of having a resident detective in the house is that, when anything like an incursion of burglars is bothering you, you can shove it off on to him, and tell him to deal with it and put it down on the bill. Jeff's bedroom, he believed, was on the floor above, and a housemaid, whom he met as he tiptoed out, verified this supposition. Third door along the passage, said the housemaid, and thither he repaired. He had considered for a moment the idea of taking the girl into his confidence regarding the contents of his wardrobe, but dismissed it. Housemaids, after all, are but broken reeds to lean upon in such an emergency. They lack stamina and the will to win.

But though he started out towards the third door along the passage, he did not reach his destination. The second door along the passage was the bathroom which served that part of the house, and as he came abreast of it there proceeded from within the sound of a voice raised in song. It was easily identifiable as that of the man he was seeking. On the previous morning, he had heard Jeff singing in the rhododendron walk, and it was not an experience one could forget. He halted, and placing his lips to the keyhole, said:

'Oh ... er ...'

The only response which greeted this effort was the sound

of splashing and a renewed burst of song. Mr Trumper, with some vague idea of not allowing himself to be overheard by the man in the wardrobe a floor below, had pitched his voice in an almost inaudible whisper. He was aware of this, but nevertheless found himself annoyed. He did not approve of hired investigators breaking into song. An old-fashioned man, with rigid views upon these things, there seemed to him something improper and disrespectful about such a procedure. You engage a detective, he felt, to detect, not to behave like a canary.

It was, accordingly, in a louder tone, with a note of asperity in it, that he spoke again.

'Mr Adair.'

Once more, all that came through was the whoosh of water and a repeated statement on the bather's part that some unidentified third party was the top.

'Mr Adair!'

This time he was more successful. A cheerful voice shouted 'Hullo?'

'This is Mr Trumper, Mr Adair.'

'I shan't be a minute.'

'I do not want a bath—'

'All right, I'll be out in a second. Excuse me a moment. I have to catch up with my singing.'

Mr Trumper felt discouraged. It occurred to him that even if the other could be induced to suspend his rendition of 'You're the Top', which he had now resumed, so that the position of affairs could be explained to him, it would be some considerable time before he could become dried and dressed and in a condition to deal with housebreakers. There is nothing, of course, that so brisks a young man up and puts him in shape for setting about the criminal classes as a good splash in the tub, but what Mr Trumper wanted was somebody already booted and spurred. On these occasions, time is of the essence.

It was at this moment that Lionel Green came out of the fourth door along the passage, clad in a futuristic dressing-gown and carrying sponge and loofah. He looked coldly at Mr Trumper, whom he disliked.

'Evening,' he said reservedly.

He tested the bathroom door, found it locked and clicked his tongue, annoyed. This meant that he would have to go to the floor below for his ablutions. With a distant nod at Mr Trumper, he was passing on, when the latter came trotting after him.

'Oh, Lionel,' bleated Mr Trumper. 'Just a minute, Lionel. I want to speak to you, Lionel.'

The reason Lionel Green disliked Mr Trumper was that he suspected the latter of being a spy in his aunt's service and the man who had told her that he, Lionel, sometimes looked in at the Stag and Antlers for a snack. He made no attempt to conceal his displeasure at being detained by such a one.

'Well?' he said, with much the same stiffness as had marked Lord Uffenham's manner, when using the same conversational gambit to Chimp Twist.

Mr Trumper sensed the hostility in his tone, but in view of the urgency of the crisis decided to ignore it.

'Lionel, a most disturbing thing has happened. There is a burglar in my wardrobe.'

Lionel Green's beautifully shaped eyebrows rose.

'A burglar?'

'A burglar.'

'A burglar in your wardrobe?'

'Yes.'

'There can't be.'

'There is.'

'Nonsense. You must have imagined it.'

That sense of discouragement, that feeling of not being *en rapport* with his audience, which had come to Mr Trumper during his talk with Jeff, began to afflict him once more. This was not the spirit of ready sympathy and selfless service for which he had hoped.

'I did not imagine it,' he said petulantly. 'I heard him.'

'Heard him what?'

'What do you mean, heard him what?'

'What did he do that you heard?'

'He made a noise.'

'What sort of noise?'

This caused Mr Trumper to search his memory and ponder. He had not made any attempt till now to analyse the extraordinary sound which had proceeded from the interior of the wardrobe. Thus taxed, he rather rashly tried to imitate it, and found his companion eyeing him with open incredulity.

'It couldn't have sounded like that,' said Lionel. 'There isn't such a noise.'

Mr Trumper in his exasperation broke into what looked like the opening steps of a tribal dance.

'Well, never mind what it sounded like,' he cried feverishly. 'What does it matter what it sounded like? The important thing is that there should have been anyone making noises in my wardrobe at all. The exact kind of noise he was making is wholly immaterial.'

'How do you know he was in your wardrobe?'

'I keep telling you the sound came from there.'

'Probably someone out in the corridor.'

'The sound came from my wardrobe, I tell you.'

'You thought it came from your wardrobe,' corrected Lionel Green. 'Did you look inside?'

'No.'

'Why not?'

'I – er – it was not my place to do so. It was young man's work.'

Again, Lionel Green's delicate eyebrows rose.

'You aren't suggesting that I should do it?'

'Yes, I am.'

'Well, I'm not going to. I haven't time. You know how annoyed Aunt Clarissa gets, if people are late for dinner. I shall only just be able to have my bath, as it is.'

'You're afraid,' cried Mr Trumper, forgetting all courtesy.

'Pooh,' said Lionel Green, and passed on, flicking a defiant loofah.

Mr Trumper remained where he was, seething. The abruptness of Lionel's manner would alone have been enough to wake the fiend that slept in him, and in addition to this he was feeling scornful and contemptuous. He was convinced that the explanation he had advanced of the other's reluctance to assist had been the correct one. Mrs Cork, he knew, admired her nephew, but to Mr Trumper there came the growing conviction that he had feet of clay, and cold ones, at that.

He was still fuming helplessly, when Anne came down the stairs. Secretary-companions have small rooms up near the roof.

'Why, hullo, Mr Trumper,' she said. 'You're looking rather lost. Is something the matter?'

To Mr Trumper, her advent had brought a marked improvement in the general outlook. It was not that he supposed that she could be of any practical assistance, for he classed secretary-companions with housemaids as among Nature's noncombatants, but she would listen and sympathize, and a sympathetic audience was what he most needed. So far, he had had the misfortune to draw either deaf adders who stopped their ears and sang 'You're the Top', or poltroons of distant and supercilious manner, who shirked their obvious duty on the thin plea that if they were late for dinner their aunts would be annoyed.

'Oh, Miss Benedick,' he squeaked, 'I hope you will not be alarmed, but there is a burglar in my wardrobe.'

He had not relied in vain on her womanly sympathy. Anne's eyes widened. Shipley Hall for excitement, she felt.

'A burglar?'

'Yes.'

'How do you know?'

'I heard him.'

'You couldn't have been mistaken?'

To a man who is telling a tale of burglars in wardrobes, there is a world of difference between such a query and the curt statement, chilled by an Oxford accent, that he must have imagined the whole thing.

'I assure you I was not mistaken. He made a noise.'

'What sort of noise?'

When Lionel Green had asked the same question, Mr Trumper had been exasperated, and possibly for that reason had failed to do himself justice as an imitator of sneezing burglars. His performance now was on a different plane altogether. It still did not come anywhere near suggesting what it was supposed to represent, but it lacked that element of unearthliness, of being something out of another and a horrible world, which had confirmed Lionel Green in his scepticism. You could not have said just what the noise was which he was supposed to be reproducing, but at least it sounded possible.

'Something like that,' he said.

Anne was looking thoughtful, as well she might.

'You don't think it could have been the cat?'

'What cat?'

'Any cat. Cats make a noise like that, if you step on them by accident. But, of course,' said Anne, for she was a kindhearted girl and saw that her companion could stand only just so much of this sort of thing, 'you didn't step on this cat.'

'Which cat?'

'The cat in the wardrobe, if it had been a cat, but of course it wasn't,' said Anne, making the thing clear to the meanest intelligence.

Mr Trumper clutched his forehead. For a moment he had had a nightmare feeling as if he had been about to plunge into an abyss, unable to stop himself though fully aware of the disadvantages of such an action. The Gadarene swine, rounding into the straight, must have experienced much the same uneasy sensation.

'Do you mind,' he said in a low voice, 'if we do not talk about cats? It merely clouds the issue. I am prepared to give you the most solemn assurance, Miss Benedick, that there was a man inside my wardrobe. As a matter of fact,' said Mr Trumper, suddenly brightening, for he realized that here was just the telling piece of evidence his story required, 'I saw him.'

'Oh, you looked in the wardrobe?'

Mr Trumper hastened to shake his head. The conversation, he perceived, was on the verge of slipping away from him again.

'No,' he replied. 'I am referring to an earlier occasion. I was coming out of the billiard-room, and I just caught a glimpse of a man running very rapidly up the stairs.'

'Golly!' said Anne, impressed. This looked like the real thing. 'What did you do?'

'I did nothing. He was gone like a flash, and I naturally supposed that he was one of the residents of the house. Now,

I am convinced that he was a burglar. Having run up the stairs, he must have concealed himself in my room.'

'Hid in the wardrobe.'

'Precisely.'

'What happened when he made the noise?'

'I was extremely taken aback.'

'I mean, you didn't go and investigate?'

Mr Trumper shuddered.

'No,' he said. 'I did not.'

'I wonder if he's still there.'

'Undoubtedly. If he had left the room, I should have seen him.'

'Then it seems to me,' said Anne, 'that the next move is to collect a gang.'

'I beg your pardon?'

'I mean, get reinforcements. What we want here is a horny-handed assistant or two. Why not try Mr Adair?'

'I did. But he was singing in his bath, and I was unable to make him understand. And when I approached Lionel Green for help, he affected to disbelieve my story. The truth was, of course,' said Mr Trumper vengefully, 'that he was afraid.'

Anne started.

'Oh, no!'

Mr Trumper was firm.

'Afraid,' he repeated. 'Terrified. He slunk away, and refused to have anything to do with the matter.'

Anne was biting her lip. It is not pleasant for a girl of spirit to be compelled to recognize in the man to whom she has pledged herself the absence of the quality she most admires in the male, and she would have given much to be able to dismiss the accusation as absurd. But she knew that it was not. She remembered the affair of the stuffed antelope. The man who refuses to go into his aunt's study and delve into stuffed antelopes is a man who, if he declines to apprehend burglars in wardrobes, does so from dastardly motives.

For an instant, as had happened before, there came to her the disagreeable suspicion that Lionel Green was not, as she had supposed, the top, but somewhere very low down on the list. She tried to scout the idea, but it would not be scouted. The poisoned barb remained.

'The man is a poltroon,' proceeded Mr Trumper, for the Trumpers did not lightly forgive. 'And he has left me in a most unpleasant quandary. I wish to finish dressing, and how can I, with burglars liable to come bursting out of wardrobes at any moment?'

Anne saw his point, and it seemed to her well taken. Under such conditions, the fastidious dresser cannot do himself justice. She reflected.

'You say Mr Adair was having a bath?'

'Yes. He assured me that he would only be a minute, but the impression I received was that he intended to remain wallowing in the water indefinitely. In any case, we cannot possibly delay until he is dried and dressed. I want something done about it immediately. My tie is in my bedroom. So is my coat. And I have not yet brushed my hair.'

Anne nodded, and fell again to thinking. Her brows were bent, and the tip of her nose wiggled.

'Do you know,' she said, 'I think our best plan is to go to Mrs Cork.'

The idea came as something quite new to Mr Trumper.

'Mrs Cork?' he echoed, turning it over in his mind. He believed in keeping the women out of these things.

'Yes, I know she is of the female sex,' said Anne, reading his thoughts. 'But does that matter – I mean, in the case of an exceptional woman like her? You wouldn't object to a spot of help from Boadicea, if she were handy?'

Mr Trumper admitted that the warlike queen of the Iceni might have been of considerable assistance in a crisis like the present one, and that he would have welcomed her co-operation.

'Mrs Cork,' said Anne, 'rather reminds one of Boadicea, don't you think?'

'There is a resemblance.'

'And after the sort of life she has led, this kind of thing will be right up her street. I mean, she has probably spent half her time these last years shooing lions and leopards and cannibal chiefs and things like that out of her tent.'

Mr Trumper endorsed this. Mrs Cork had often held him spellbound with tales of her adventures in the wilds, and he had been left with a confused impression that on most of these expeditions of hers her tent had been a sort of social centre for the wild life of the neighbourhood. 'Let's all go round to Cork's,' lions had said to one another, when they found time hanging a little heavy on their paws of an evening. And the same thing applied to cannibal chiefs and leopards.

'You are perfectly right,' he said, pleased at this happy solution of a problem which had threatened to become an *impasse*. 'Shall we go to her at once?'

'Tally ho!' said Anne.

CHAPTER 18

Mrs Cork's suite was on the first floor. It consisted of a vast bedroom and an almost equally large sitting-room, opening off it. Plain, even Spartan, though she might be in her mode of life when on shikarri, the great huntress was a woman who believed in doing herself well when the conditions were right. Established at Shipley Hall, she had striven to surround herself with an atmosphere of refinement and luxury, and she had succeeded. A leopard, calling upon her in these new quarters of hers, would have halted on the threshold and backed out with an awkward apology.

She had completed her simple toilet some time before Anne and Mr Trumper set out, for she was a swift dresser who did not bother much about primping. Off with the sporting tweeds and the sensible shoes, and into the tea-gown and the old pearl necklace, was her way. She was now reclining on a settee, reading *A Woman in the Wilds*, her favourite book. She was just feeling, as authors so often do about their own work, what capital stuff it was and how well written, when there was a knock at the door and Anne came in, followed by Mr Trumper in his shirt sleeves.

She eyed him in amazement. Mr Trumper was one of those correct, dapper little men, who always wear the right clothes on every occasion. Without a coat and tie, he was practically a nudist. He looked as if he had been surprised while bathing.

'Eustace!' she cried.

Mr Trumper reddened beneath the unspoken rebuke. She had no need to tell him that all this was highly irregular.

'I know, Clarissa, I know. But when you hear the circumstances—'

Anne helped him out.

'Mr Trumper has found a burglar in his wardrobe, Mrs Cork.'

'A burglar?'

'Yes,' said Mr Trumper, wondering if there was anybody in the world who, when informed that there was a burglar in his wardrobe, would not say 'A burglar?'

Mrs Cork was interested.

'Did you see him?'

'Well, yes and no.'

Mrs Cork began to wonder if there might not be some difficulty in getting at the facts.

'Tell me the whole story,' she said, 'from the beginning.'

'Omitting no detail, however slight,' said Anne. 'Don't forget the funny noise.'

Mr Trumper assured her that he would not forget the funny noise. It seemed to him that he would never forget it, but that it would haunt him in his dreams for the rest of his life, getting louder and funnier as the years went by.

'He made a funny noise, did he?' said Mrs Cork, as if this had caused her to take a more serious view of the affair. 'What sort of noise?'

Practice makes perfect. This time, Mr Trumper put up such a realistic performance that both his hearers found themselves convinced that the sound, bizarre though it was, had proceeded from human lips.

'H'm,' said Mrs Cork, having pondered on it. 'I think the man must have been having some kind of a fit. It startled you, I expect?'

'Very much, Clarissa. I nearly jumped out of my skin.'

Mrs Cork was conscious of a stir of protective pity. Hers was a heart toughened over a long period of time by the constant necessity of being on the alert to see that native bearers did not start any oompus-boompus, but it had remained soft in spots, and it was these spots that Eustace Trumper always touched so unerringly. He seemed to her, as Dolly Molloy seemed to Lord Uffenham, so weak and fragile. A rush of resentment against this marauder, who had frightened him, filled her bosom. She went to a writing desk in the corner of the room, and took from a drawer an automatic pistol, the woman in the wilds' best friend.

'And the noise came from the wardrobe?' she asked, having examined the weapon and satisfied herself that it did not lack ammunition.

'The wardrobe, Clarissa.'

'Mr Trumper thinks the man must have hidden there after he ran up the stairs,' said Anne. 'You had seen someone sprinting upstairs a bit earlier but thought no more of it, hadn't you, Mr Trumper?'

'Quite. That was why, when you asked me if I had seen the man, I replied, "Yes and no." I am still not sure that it was the same man, but I think it must have been.'

'Mr Trumper was coming out of the billiard-room—'

'Exactly. And a man went whizzing up the stairs. It was just before you came in at the front door with Mrs Barlow.'

'You didn't see who it was?'

'It was nobody I knew. So far, of course, as I was able to ascertain from a quick glance.'

Mrs Cork reflected.

'Could it have been Mr Adair? He runs up stairs,' she said, speaking with a certain disapproval. Like Mr Trumper, she held strict views on deportment for detectives. Mr Trumper thought they ought not to sing in their baths. Mrs Cork liked them to observe the speed limit in built-up areas.

'No, it was not Mr Adair.'

'Perhaps it was Cakebread.'

'I doubt if he could run upstairs.'

'That is true. Then it certainly seems as if it must have been a burglar. Though what a burglar can be doing in the house at this hour is more than I can understand.'

She spoke disapprovingly, as was natural in a woman of her regular views. Even in the wildest parts of Africa, she had always been able to count on having her tent to herself till sundown. No leopard, however lacking in the social sense, would have dreamed of dropping in before lights-out.

'We had better go and see. Keep behind me, Eustace.'

'I will, Clarissa.'

'It is all most annoying,' said Mrs Cork. 'One did expect that one would be free from this sort of thing in Kent.'

A frown was still darkening her forehead, as she led the procession along the corridor. Anne, watching her rigid back and noting the firmness of the hand which held the automatic pistol, could not repress a pang of commiseration for the unknown malefactor.

Already, she felt, if not a very dull man, he must have begun to suspect that this was not his lucky evening, but he little knew what dark forces he had unchained. In spite of a healthy liking for excitement and the feeling that, if he had done so, the anticlimax would be a jarring one, she found herself hoping that the man had had the sense to escape.

But Chimp Twist had not escaped. He was still crouching in the wardrobe like a weevil nestling in a biscuit. The disadvantage of hiding in wardrobes, even if you enjoy doing that sort of thing, is that it is not easy, once you are stowed away, to ascertain just what is going on outside. The fact that his sneeze had produced no immediate opening of the door, and that for quite a while now silence had been reigning in the room beyond, had suggested to Chimp, as the only explanation that would cover the facts, that he had had the good fortune to seek refuge in the bedroom of a deaf man. Only one so afflicted could have failed to hear the sneeze, and it never occurred to him that anyone who had heard it would have been so lacking in natural curiosity as not to try to track it to its source.

As to what had been happening since the explosion, one could only suppose that the fellow was still dressing. Presently, no doubt, he would complete his toilet and go down to dinner. Meanwhile, there was nothing to be done but wait patiently till the gong sounded the signal of release. To pass the time, he fell to meditating, and his meditations, as was only to be expected, were bitter ones.

To an intelligent man like himself, there could be no doubt by now that the story which Mr Molloy had told him at the inn had been an essential part of a deliberate trap laid for his undoing. The fact that Lord Uffenham had obviously been advised of his coming, and warned to lie in wait, removed all uncertainty on that point. It was not long before he was able to see the whole mechanism of the plot as clearly as if he had been present at the Molloy family conference, and it is not too much to say that he burned with indignation and resentment.

To a little mild double-crossing among friends Chimp Twist had no objection whatever. It was only natural in any business venture involving large sums of money that investors should wish to protect their interests. But luring a man on into a position where he would encounter somebody like Lord Uffenham in a small bedroom was a very different matter.

It was against Dolly that most of his pique was directed. It was plain to him that it was in her ingenious brain that the dastardly scheme must have germinated. He yielded to no one in his respect for Soapy's ability to sell valueless oil stock to the most difficult prospects, but Soapy, he knew, would not have been capable of organizing anything like this in a million years. Every detail of the plot betrayed the woman's touch and, never a great admirer of the sex, he found himself taking one more step in the direction of becoming the complete misogynist.

He was just feeling what a Paradise the world would be without women, and hoping that he would never have to speak to one again, unless perhaps an occasional barmaid, when these dreams of an Eveless Eden were shattered with an abruptness which caused him to bump his head on a projecting hook.

'Come out of it!' said a voice and, deep though it was in tone, he had no difficulty in recognizing that the lips from which it proceeded were feminine lips.

CHAPTER 19

A silence followed the words, broken only by the tumultuous beating of Mr Trumper's heart. It was partly apprehension that was causing it to imitate a motor-cycle, but principally the sudden gush of adoration which he felt for the intrepid woman behind whom he was standing. This was the first time he had seen Mrs Cork in action, and while tales of female heroism may impress us, they can never do so as completely as the actual sight of their heroine doing her stuff.

Only now did Eustace Trumper realize the full splendour of Clarissa Cork. She was, he felt, correctly, magnificent, and he awaited with interest the unseen miscreant's response.

This did not come immediately. Chimp Twist was human, though most of his acquaintances would have liked to have this proved to them, and it is a human trait to keep on hoping, however sticky the outlook. There was, he felt, just the barest possibility that the words had not been addressed to him. Dogs, he reminded himself, sometimes get into bedrooms, and when this happens, women tell them to come out of it. He remained where he was, silent and trying not to breathe.

Mrs Cork did not imitate his reserve. Hers was an impatient nature that chafed at delays.

'You inside that wardrobe,' she said. 'I am Mrs Cork, the

owner of this house. Unless you come out of it in three seconds, I shall start shooting.'

Her manner was rather formal, but a certain stiffness is unavoidable on these occasions. The important thing, as far as Chimp was concerned, was that her meaning was clear. She had purposely stripped her words of all ambiguity and they left him in no doubt as to the advisability of quick action. Three seconds is not a very liberal margin to allow for getting out of a wardrobe, but it was ample for Chimp. A stop-watch would probably have clocked him at about one and a tenth. He poured into the room as if he had been liquid, and Mrs Cork eyed him austerely over the automatic pistol.

'That's better,' she said. 'Now, then, what's it all about?'

When she had asked the same question – in native dialect, of course – of cannibal chiefs discovered hiding in her tent, the latter had almost always been frankly tongue-tied and embarrassed. They had not known which way to look. But she was dealing now with a man of ready resource and swift intelligence. Chimp Twist had been in too many delicate situations in his life to allow himself easily to be disconcerted. Brief though the interval was which had been granted him for reflection, he had already discovered the way out of this unpleasantness.

'Pleased to meet you, Mrs Cork,' he said, with easy polish. 'Hope I didn't startle you and the folks.'

Such airy geniality on the part of detected housebreakers is not usual, and Mrs Cork's hard stare showed her appreciation of this fact. A forceful reply was on her lips, when Chimp went on speaking.

'Should have told you I was coming, but I wanted to have a word with that fellow first.'

'Me?' said Mr Trumper, surprised.

'Not you, sir,' said Chimp, still with that strange affability. 'With the guy that's in this joint, impersonating me. I am J. Sheringham Adair, Mrs Cork. I understand you wished to engage my professional services. I ran into our mutual friend, Mr Molloy, a coupla days back, and he happened to mention it. And then he told me something that surprised me. He said there was a fellow here already, calling himself Sheringham Adair and claiming to have bought the business off me. Well, naturally I said to myself "Hullo, hullo, hullo!"'

To Mr Trumper it seemed that such a piece of information might well have provoked these hunting cries. In him, Chimp had found a credulous and uncritical hearer.

'Who the guy can be, and what his game is, I don't know. According to Molloy, he was engaged by a Miss Benedick, that you sent along to my office. I should like to have a talk with her later on.'

'Here she is,' said Mr Trumper, obligingly indicating Anne, in whom a close observer during these last few minutes would have noted signs of anxiety and concern. 'Miss Benedick, Mr Adair.'

'Good evening, Miss.'

'Good evening.'

'Nice weather.'

'Very.'

'Only hope it holds up,' said Chimp. 'And now, Miss Benedick, what happened when you called at my office? You found this guy there, I take it? What was he doing?'

'Sitting at the desk.'

'Some birds have got a nerve. He told you he was me?'

'Yes.'

'And then what?'

'I explained why I had called.'

'Well, there you are, Mrs Cork. That's how it was, and that's how I come to be here. I wanted to see this bozo and get the lowdown on him. Maybe he's a crook, planning to clean out the joint, or maybe he's some young fellow impersonating me just for the hell of the thing. I don't know. If he's one of these bright young cut-ups doing it simply for a gag, I wouldn't want to be too hard on him,' said Chimp magnanimously. 'We'll have to push him out, of course, but, far as I'm concerned, there won't be no hard feelings.'

He eyed Mrs Cork beamingly, and was pained to observe that her stony face showed no signs of softening.

'All this,' she said coldly, giving the automatic pistol a twirl, to show that it was still there, 'does not explain why you were prowling about my house and hiding in Mr Trumper's wardrobe. You gave him a most unpleasant fright.'

'He did, indeed,' assented Mr Trumper.

Chimp was amazed.

'Is this *your* room, sir? Well, I'll be darned! I thought it was the impostor's.'

Mrs Cork continued stony.

'Why?'

'Pardon?'

'What gave you the impression that this room belonged to the impostor, as you call him?'

'I asked around. Made guarded enquiries, like we detectives do. I was planning to jump out and confront him. But it seems I was given a wrong steer. Well, well, well! Sorry I threw a scare into you, Mr Trumper.'

'Not at all.'

'Last thing I'd have wanted to happen.'

'Don't mention it,' begged Mr Trumper, charmed by his consideration. Unlike Mrs Cork, he had taken Mr Twist's story in through the pores, and was remorseful that he should ever have misjudged this blameless investigator.

'Trumper?' said Chimp, musing. 'There was a guy called Trumper I once recovered a lot of important papers for. Some relation, maybe?'

'Hardly likely, I think. I have very few relatives living. Just some cousins at Oxford.'

'Swell little town, Oxford.'

'Very nice.'

'All those old colleges.'

'Quite. I am a Balliol man.'

'Is that so? I was educated in the States myself.'

'Really? I have never been in the United States.'

'You should certainly go.'

'I have often meant to.'

'Don't put it off,' urged Chimp.

The frown on Mrs Cork's face had deepened during these polite exchanges. The atmosphere of camaraderie jarred upon her. Eustace, she felt, was treating this man's irruption far too much as if it had been an ordinary afternoon call. To him, it was plain, the occasion seemed a purely social one. She herself was by no means satisfied that this was the moment for chatting of the past and making plans for the future.

'I still fail to understand,' she said frigidly, 'why you could not have come to the front door to see this man who you say is impersonating you.'

'And have him take a run-out powder? Be yourself, lady.'

'I should be glad if you would not tell me to be myself. And may I point out that, while your story may be perfectly true, we have only your word for it.'

'Is that so? How about my old friend Molloy?'

'I beg your pardon?'

'Granted.'

'What he means, I think, Clarissa,' interpreted Mr Trumper, 'is that Mr Molloy will vouch for him.'

He spoke with a slight diminution of his former cordiality. As has been stated, he was not without his dark suspicions of that big-hearted pusher of oil shares, and it detracted from Chimp's charm, in his opinion, that he should be a friend of such a man.

'I see,' said Mrs Cork. 'Yes, that would settle the point. Then we had better go to Mr Molloy. His room is down the passage.'

The Molloys, when the expedition arrived, had finished dressing and were playing solitaire. That is to say, Dolly was playing solitaire, while Soapy, in the role of kibitzer, leaned over her shoulder and told her to put that black ten on that red jack. A charming domestic picture, which broke up abruptly as Mrs Cork entered, shepherding Chimp before her.

'Sorry to disturb you, Mr Molloy,' she said. 'I have just found this man—'

'This gentleman,' Chimp ventured deferentially to suggest.

'—in Mr Trumper's wardrobe,' concluded Mrs Cork, ignoring the proposed emendation. 'He says he is a friend of yours.'

This, to both Soapy and Dolly, seemed to call for but one answer. They had opened their mouths simultaneously to assure their hostess that they had never seen Chimp before in their lives, when they caught the latter's eye. The glance which he was directing at them was keen and full of meaning.

'And so I am. Known him for years. In fact,' said Chimp, laughing as if some thought had amused him, 'I could tell you a lot about my old side-kick, Molloy. Yessir, a whole lot that would interest you.'

He underlined the words with another significant look, but it was not really needed. Both Soapy and Dolly, though the former was not always very quick at the uptake, understood him without the slightest difficulty. Dolly looked at Soapy, and her eye said 'Watch your step, baby. A wrong play here, and the little insect'll be spilling the beans about that Silver River stock of yours,' and Soapy looked at Dolly, and his eye said 'You betcher.'

He did the only possible thing, and he did it without delay.

'Sure!' he cried heartily, advancing with outstretched hand. 'Sure he's a friend of mine. How are you, old pal?'

Chimp, though ignoring the hand, for the Twists resembled the Trumpers in that they did not easily forgive, replied that he was swell. He said Soapy was looking swell, and Soapy said he was feeling swell. Soapy said it was swell to see Chimp, and Chimp said it was swell to see Soapy. In short, to Mrs Cork, who was not a mind-reader, the whole thing was so suggestive of an unexpected encounter between Damon and Pythias that it seemed no longer possible to doubt the authenticity of the story to which she had been listening.

'This *is* Mr Adair, the private detective?' she asked, just to get the thing straight.

'That's who it is. J. Sheringham Adair, the smartest man in the business.'

'Then who is the other one?'

'Ah,' said Soapy. 'That's what we'd all like to know.'

'You was telling Mrs Cork, I suppose,' said Dolly, addressing

Chimp, 'how he strung the beads to I and Soapy about having bought the business.'

'Sure.'

'And we believed him,' said Soapy. 'Can you beat it!'

Dolly said that anyone would have been took in, and Soapy agreed that the impostor was a smooth performer, as artful as a wagon-load of monkeys and cooler than a fish on a cake of ice.

Mrs Cork's manner was now grimmer than ever.

'I shall go and see that young man,' she said. 'As for you, Mr Adair, I hope that from now on you will refrain from hiding in wardrobes, however excellent your motives. You will, of course, take up your residence here. Where are you now? At the inn? Then you had better remain here, and I will have your things sent for. You will be just in time for a lecture on the Ugubu outlook, which I am giving in the drawing-room after dinner.'

'If it's going to be any trouble,' said Chimp, who had started slightly at this information, 'I could easy string along at the inn till to-morrow.'

'I will have arrangements made for giving you a room,' continued Mrs Cork, who was never a good listener. 'Miss Benedick—'

She had been about to instruct Anne to see to it, but no charming voice replied 'Yes, Mrs Cork?' Anne had disappeared. She was at this moment hurrying up the stairs in quest of Jeff. Those words of her employer about going and seeing that young man had seemed to her charged with a fearful menace. What Mrs Cork did when she went and saw young men who had got into her house pretending to be private detectives, she did not know, but she felt very strongly that he must be found and warned – possibly urged to escape down a water-pipe without his luggage while there was yet time.

Mrs Cork clicked her tongue, annoyed, and strode out, Mr Trumper trotting in her wake.

Only a very dull observer, entering the room on her departure and seeing Chimp Twist staring bleakly at Soapy Molloy, would have supposed himself in the presence of a modern Damon and Pythias. And, if he had, the impression would have vanished when the former started to give utterance to his thoughts, cleansing his bosom of the perilous stuff that weighed upon his soul. Chimp's opening speech touched a high level of eloquence, the passage in which he gave a character sketch of Mrs Molloy, as seen through his eyes, being a singularly powerful one.

To Soapy and Dolly, however, the important section of his address was not this purple patch, but the more pedestrian sentences where, descending to the practical, he announced his intention of severing his connection with the Syndicate and opening up a rival business of his own.

'I wouldn't, Chimpie,' urged Mr Molloy. Such a move, he felt, could not but complicate further an already difficult position of affairs.

'Well, I'm going to,' shrilled the injured man, his moustache quivering at the ends at the thought of his wrongs. 'I'm in, aren't I? Then what do I want to go stringing along with you chisellers for?'

Mr Molloy shook his head, plainly deploring this spirit.

'I wouldn't do nothing hasty, Chimpie. No sense in flying off the handle. That yarn I told you may not have been on the up-and-up from start to finish, but it's a fact that the madam has been getting mighty friendly with Lord Cakebread these last days. Aren't I right, sweetie?'

'I'll say you're right,' said Dolly. 'Him and me's just like that.'

'Any minute now, he's liable to remember where he parked that ice, and when he does, I'm betting he'll spill the info' to the little woman. So, if I was you, Chimpie,' said Mr Molloy, 'I wouldn't go and do nothing mutton-headed like what you say. Stick round and play ball. We're all working for the good of the show. And, as for handing you a raw deal, well, you know how these things happen. The madam's impulsive, and she gets carried away at times. But there's no sense in being sore and putting a crimp in your business prospects. That don't pay no dividends.'

He had struck the right note. Those few manly, straight-from-the-shoulder words were just what the situation called for. Business to Chimp Twist was always business, and he rarely allowed sentiment to interfere with it. If Dolly really was likely to be the recipient of Lord Uffenham's confidences, and he wouldn't put it past her to be able to soften up the big stiff and get him talking, he wanted to be in on the ground floor.

'I guess you're about right,' he said, after a pause for reflection. 'Yes, there's sense in that. But, listen, lemme tell ya sump'n. From this on, no more of Dolly's cute cutting up. Tie a can to the funny stuff, see? If I want to laugh, I'll read the comic strip.'

'Sure,' said Mr Molloy.

'Sure,' said Mrs Molloy, with equal heartiness.

'Okay, then,' said Chimp.

The Syndicate was in being again – a little shaky about the foundations, perhaps, but once more a going concern.

CHAPTER 20

Anne, meanwhile, had reached Jeff's room and found it empty. Jeff, like Mrs Cork, was a quick dresser and had long since dried and clothed himself and gone out into the garden to enjoy what to the connoisseur is the best part of a fine summer day. Purified by his great love, he had grown very fond of the twilight of late.

Anne, crediting him with less soulfulness, had the idea that he might have gone to her uncle's pantry for a quick port, to enable him to face with greater fortitude the dinner and lecture which lay before him. It was thither that she now hastened.

She found Lord Uffenham standing motionless in the middle of the floor. His eyes were closed, and he was holding between his hands a small forked stick.

'Hullo, my dear,' he said. 'I came on this in the hall the other day. Must have been there fifty years, I should think. It belonged to my old father. It's a thing water-diviners use. You hold it like this, and if there's water anywhere, twists like a serpent. I remember experimenting with it as a boy, but whether it worked or not, I couldn't tell yer.'

Anne was not interested in finding water. She wanted to find Jeff.

'Have you seen Mr Adair?' she asked, breathlessly.

'No,' said Lord Uffenham. 'But if you run across him, send him to me. I've got a job for him. It's an odd thing, but as I was standing here just now with my eyes shut, thinking of water and waiting for this apparatus to wriggle, the word "pond" suddenly flashed into my mind. The word "pond",' said Lord Uffenham, impressively. 'I consider that dashed significant.'

'Angel, I must find Mr Adair.'

'His name's not Adair.'

'I know it isn't.'

'It's ... No,' said Lord Uffenham, after a pause, 'I thought I had it, but I haven't. If you had asked me a minute ago, I could have told you. It's some name like Willard or Tiller. But I was saying about this word "pond" suddenly flashing into my mind. There's only one pond at Shipley, as far as I know, and that's the one by the sunken garden. Nothing is more likely than that I put those dashed diamonds – in a biscuit tin or something, no doubt, with a string tied to it – in that. It's just the sort of place that might have suggested itself, because I was rather using them up towards the end. And I used to wander round there quite a lot in the old days. Sort of a favourite spot of mine. I consider this one of the most promising ideas I've had. Get hold of young Tiller and tell him to go and wade about there to-morrow morning, early. Save him having a bath.'

'But he won't be here to-morrow morning.'

'Hey?'

'A frightful thing has happened, darling. That's why I'm trying to find him. The real one has turned up.'

'What d'yer mean, the real one?'

'The real Sheringham Adair. Mr Trumper found him in his wardrobe. An awful little man with a waxed moustache.'

'Good Lord! Is that who the rat was?'

'You haven't met him?'

'Of course, I've met him. Had a long talk with him about his moustache. You know how he gets the ends to stick up like that? Smears 'em with soap. Told me so himself. "What d'yer put on the filthy thing?" I asked him. "Beeswax?" And he said No, just ordinary wax or toilet soap or shaving cream. "Lord-love-a-duck!" I said, thinking to myself that it takes all sorts to make a world, and then, just as I was going to break his neck, he skipped away like a cat on hot bricks. So he got into Trumper's wardrobe, did he? Wish I'd known.'

'But how did you come to meet him?'

'That sweet little woman, Mrs Molloy, told me he was going to search my room, of all dashed impertinence, so I lay in wait for him and pounced out at him, and he told me all about his moustache. He's a spy in the pay of Trumper.'

'He's got nothing to do with Mr Trumper.'

'Yes, he has. Trumper has bought him with his gold. She told me so. Mrs Molloy.'

'Well, never mind. I haven't time to argue about it. I must find Jeff. Where can he have got to?'

'Jeff?'

'Mr Willard or Tiller, or whatever his name is.'

'It might be Spiller.'

'It might be anything. The point is that I've got to find him. I can't let him receive the full impact of Mrs Cork without warning. It would be too awful.'

Lord Uffenham appeared to be musing.

'His name's Jeff, is it?'

'So he told me.'

'Do you call him Jeff?'

'When I call him anything.'

'It hasn't taken you long to get to Christian names. Just as I foresaw. You've fallen in love with the feller.'

'Oh, angel, don't gibber. Not now. Things are too tense. You should have seen Mrs Cork. Boadicea, bristling with pistols. I must tell Jeff to fly before she gets hold of him. Where do you think he can be?'

Lord Uffenham was a difficult man to sidetrack, once he had embarked on a train of thought.

'Christian names,' he said musingly. 'The infallible test. If it happens soon enough, of course. I remember when I was a young man, noticing that if a woman called me "George" after we'd had a couple of lunches and a spin in a hansom cab together, it was always the beginning of the end. You call him "Jeff", do yer? And all this fuss and bustle and running around wringing your hands and crying "Oh, where is he? I must save him, I must save him!" You're potty about the chap.'

'I'm not!'

'And a very good thing, too. I'm delighted. Just the right young feller for you. He'll keep yer bright and interested. That plumber of yours would have bored you stiff in a week. It's going to be embarrassing for you, by the way, having to tell him you've changed your mind.'

'I haven't changed my mind.'

'But you've only yourself to blame,' said Lord Uffenham, more in sorrow than anger. 'Did I or did I not repeatedly warn yer that you were crazy to suppose for an instant that you could marry that perisher? But you would stick to it that he was the blue-eyed boy. That,' he concluded, becoming profound, 'is the whole trouble with fellers like Lionel Green. If you see one without actually wanting to kick him, you think, "This must be love."'

'Darling, will you stop!'

'Stop what?'

'Talking this absolute nonsense. I do love Lionel.'

'What, still? Even though this splendid young Spiller has come along? I don't understand it,' said Lord Uffenham, wagging his ponderous head. 'He can't have been playing his cards right. In spite of what I told him. "The obvious course for you to pursue, Spiller," I said to him, "is to reach out and grab her and fold her in a dashed close embrace. That'll work it." I don't see how I could have put it plainer.'

Anne was conscious of a warmth about the cheeks. Only an hour or two had elapsed since Jeff actually had folded her in an embrace almost close enough to satisfy even her uncle's exacting standards. And though she had comported herself on that occasion with a maidenly dignity which would have pleased Emily Post, she was guiltily aware of not having been as shocked and repelled as she should have been. For an instant, indeed, until she had thought of Lionel Green and how devoted she was to him, she had had a distinct illusion that she was passing through an experience not wholly without its pleasurable aspect.

Lord Uffenham had fallen into a silence. He had the air of a man who is trying to probe a mystery to its depths. He came out of his thoughts, to put a question.

'Has he kissed yer yet?'

'No, he has not.'

'Well, I'm dashed.'

'Did you tell him to?'

'Of course I did. I look on that young feller as a son – don't know when I've met a young feller I've taken more of a fancy to – and I considered it my duty to promote his interests.'

Anne drew a deep breath. She regarded her uncle fixedly. A weaker uncle might have wilted beneath the look.

'I see. So if I suddenly find Mr Spiller treating me as if I were a sack of coals, I shall have you to thank for it.'

'I don't want any thanks. Only too glad to help. Bring the young folks together, that's what I say. My knowledge of life told me what ought to be done, and I handed the tip on to young Miller.'

'Is his name Miller or Spiller?'

'Miller. I've just remembered.'

'But how do you know?'

'I found out.'

'Why didn't you tell me?'

'I forgot.'

'How did you find out?'

'It was the day he arrived here. I was taking a look round his room, just to see if they had made him comfortable, and there was a book on the table by the bed, with his name written in the fly leaf. Oddly enough, it was a name I had an idea I'd heard somewhere. J. G. Miller.'

'What!'

Anne was aware of something that felt like a powerful electric shock passing through her.

'Yerss. J. G. Miller.'

Anne was still tingling. J. G. Miller! ... It was possible, of course, that this was another and a blameless J. G. Miller, but it seemed to her highly improbable. The surname Miller is not an uncommon one, but the juxtaposition of the initials was surely damning.

'Are you certain?'

'Of course, I'm certain. Why the name should have seemed

familiar, I can't tell you. I've a memory like a steel trap, but it doesn't always work as it should. Now that I think back, I believe it was the cook who was saying something about a feller called J. G. Miller, who had done something or other. And I seem to recollect a conversation on the same subject with that little squirt, Trumper.'

'Oh!'

Anne had given a little jump. Her memory, working with more accuracy than her uncle's, had told her where it was that she had seen Jeff before. And now she knew, beyond further possibility of doubt, that he was the man whom Mrs Cork wanted to strangle with her bare hands, and for whom she herself, ever since she had read of Lionel Green's dark hour in the witness box, had been feeling so violent an animosity.

Her eyes flashed. Her teeth clenched. She quivered from head to foot. Mrs Molloy, had she been present, would have had no hesitation in describing her as mad as a wet hen. She was asking herself how she could ever have been deceived by his superficial charm into imagining for an instant that she had liked Jeff. She strode to the door, a figure of almost Cork-like menace.

'You off?' said Lord Uffenham.

'Yes. I want a word with Mr J. G. Miller.'

'Of course. Going to tell him Mrs Cork is after him with her hatchet.'

'That and other things.'

'Well, don't forget about the pond.'

'I'll get Lionel to look there to-morrow.'

'Lionel?' said Lord Uffenham, aghast. 'What's the use of Lionel? He'd be afraid to get his feet wet. For God's sake, don't put your trust in that poop. If you want my frank opinion of Lionel Green—'

It appeared that Anne did not. She went out without waiting for it. It had just occurred to her as a possibility that Jeff might be in the garden.

Lord Uffenham stared at her in his solid, unblinking way. Then, feeling that he had done his duty as an uncle, he took up the forked stick and closed his eyes again.

CHAPTER 21

It been Jeff's original intention, on leaving his room, to go and smoke a cigarette on the lawn. But the sudden appearance there of Mr Shepperson, the man with the double-jointed hips, had caused him to alter his plans. It might be, of course, that Mr Shepperson would not say 'Nice evening' and engage him in conversation, but the risk was a grave one and not to be taken by a lover who wished to be alone with his thoughts. He sheered away, accordingly, like an antelope that had caught sight of Mrs Cork, and was enabled by this prompt action to nip the menace in the bud. For some minutes, he had been strolling up and down the rhododendron walk in a deep reverie.

The solitary meditations of the Jeff Miller of pre-Anne days would have had to do with far different themes than those which now engrossed him. Love had tapped a deep vein of poetry in him and he was trying to remember how that 'Come into the garden, Maud' thing went. Not a thought of mysterious Malays, screams in lonely houses and Inspector Purvis drawing in his breath sharply and saying 'This is human blood!' had so much as entered his mind.

He was still in difficulties with the second and fourth lines, when Anne came out of the house, breathing flame softly through the nose and looking to left and right like a lioness seeking her prey. In her passage from Lord Uffenham's pantry to the lawn, she had lost none of her desire to have a word with Mr J. G. Miller.

She was aware of Mr Shepperson ambling up.

'Nice evening,' said Mr Shepperson.

'Yes,' said Anne. 'I'm looking for Mr Adair.'

'I think you will find him in the rhododendron walk. He was on the lawn when I came out, but he hurried off. A pity,' said Mr Shepperson. 'I should have liked a chat. A charming chap, don't you think?'

Anne gulped. At such a moment, this sort of thing was not easy to bear.

'Very,' she contrived to say.

'Most attractive. Dinner is late, is it not?'

'I'm afraid there has been a sort of upset.'

'Dear, dear,' said Mr Shepperson, who wanted his spinach, and Anne resumed her purposeful prowl.

The light in the rhododendron walk was dim. Steep bastions of flowered bushes shut out the afterglow, leaving only above the mossy path a canopy of spangled blue. But the visibility was good enough to enable Jeff to identify Anne, as she entered it, and all unconscious of the impending doom he hastened to meet her, scarcely able to believe that such good fortune had been vouchsafed him. His spirits soared, and he immediately started to buzz.

'What an extraordinary thing,' he said. 'I was just saying "Come into the garden, Maud," and here you are. Some people would call that a coincidence, but I should put it down to will power. You don't know how the rest of it goes, do you?'

'The rest of what?'

'"Come into the garden, Maud."'

'No, I don't.'

'I thought everybody knew "Come into the garden, Maud." When they educated you privately, I'm afraid they scamped their work. You should have gone to Roedean, where you would have been filled right up to the brim.'

Anne was conscious of a feeling that the scene was developing along the wrong lines.

'I didn't come to talk about poetry.'

'Never mind why you came. You're here. That's the great thing.'

'I have something to say to you.'

'And I have all sorts of things to say to you. We'll have one of our long, cosy chats.'

Anne tried again.

'My uncle—'

'God bless him!'

'—was talking to me just now, and he said something which came as a great shock.'

Jeff nodded sympathetically

'He has his coarse moments. But a fine old English gentleman, none the less.'

'Will you listen!'

'I'm listening.'

'He told me he had been in your room—'

'Quite all right. Tell him to treat it just as if it were his own.'

'He looked round.'

'I should have said pear-shaped.'

Anne's foot began to tap on the mossy path. She was wishing the light had been better, so that he could have seen her face.

Its expression, of a malevolence calculated, she felt, to excite remark and questioning, would have enabled her to get down to essentials more rapidly than she appeared to be doing.

'If you would not mind letting me finish—'

'Of course, of course. Go ahead.'

'Thank you. My uncle happened to be in your room the day you arrived here. There was a book on the table by the bed. He picked it up, and looked at the fly leaf.'

Jeff's exuberance waned a little. He regretted the carelessness which had led him to leave a book, which was evidently going to turn out to have had his name in it, within arm's reach of a Parker so notoriously nosey as the sixth Viscount Uffenham. He began to understand what had given him the impression at certain points of this conversation that Anne was not her usual cheery self.

'Oh, yes?' he said warily.

'It had the name "J. G. Miller" in it.'

'Oh, that one?'

'What do you mean?'

'It was that book I borrowed from Miller, was it? I must remember to return it. Thanks for reminding me.'

'Not at all.' Anne's voice was very soft and gentle, the voice of a girl who is amused at an absurd misunderstanding. Her fury had given way to a strange calm, like that of a boiling kettle which has come to the height of its fever. 'So it was just a book you had borrowed? I thought for a moment that you might be J. G. Miller.'

'No, no. My name is Dalrymple. Geoffrey Dalrymple. Adair is, of course, only a trade name.'

'I see.'

Anne was silent for a moment. She glanced up at the sky, as

if wondering why lightning did not proceed from it and scorch this man to a cinder.

'So your name is Dalrymple?'

'Dalrymple, yes. But keep on calling me Jeff.'

'And Mr Miller is a friend of yours?'

'Oh, rather. Known him for years. A splendid chap.'

'Really?'

'But I'll tell you something about him. He's a buzzer. What I mean is, he talks a lot. And you mustn't judge him by what he says. If he loved a girl, for instance, she might be misled into thinking his heart wasn't really in the thing. She might imagine he was just kidding, because he prattles away in a buzzing sort of spirit, saying this and that but never really getting down to brass tacks. She might even think he was a bit too pleased with himself. But it's really shyness.'

'Shyness!'

'You wouldn't think it, but I'm very shy.'

'I thought you were talking about J. G. Miller.'

'So I was. One gets confused. But he and I are very much alike.'

'You have my sympathy.'

'Eh?'

'Because I think J. G. Miller is the most detestable man in existence.'

'Oh, come! There is no vice in J. G. Miller. His heart is the heart of a little child.'

'Indeed? How about the way he behaved to Mrs Cork's nephew? Perhaps he told you about that?'

'You mean that case? Pennefather versus Tarvin? Yes, I seem to remember him mentioning it.'

'I thought you might. So your name is Dalrymple?'

'Didn't you say that before?'

'It seems so odd.'

'Odd?'

'Yes. There must have been a misprint in the programme.'

'Programme?'

'Of the England and Scotland football match at Twickenham last March.'

Jeff started.

'You weren't there?'

'Yes, I was. That was where I saw you before. You were playing for England, and the programme said your name was J. G. Miller.'

Jeff was obliged to devote a moment or two to reflection.

'I see what you mean,' he said, at length. 'This rather explodes the Dalrymple theory.'

'It does, doesn't it?'

'Perhaps I had better come clean.'

'If you think it necessary.'

'I am J. G. Miller.'

'Yes.'

'Yes. Fancy you being at Twickenham that day.'

'Yes.'

'Good game, didn't you think? We were lucky not to lose. Tough eggs, those Scottish forwards. I was sore for weeks afterwards. I don't know why it is, but education at Merchiston, Loretto, Fettes and such establishments seems to bring out all that a man has of boniness of knee and the ability to kick cavities in the rib structure of the opposition talent. I don't know how well you understand Rugby football, but I was what is known as a scrum-half. It fell to me to fling myself on the ball when the blighters wheeled and came away with it at their toes. In future, I shall collect old china.'

Anne's foot was tapping the moss again.

'I wish those Scotsmen had killed you,' she said, speaking between clenched teeth in a way which would have extorted the admiration of Mrs Molloy, who was a specialist.

Jeff had begun to recover some of the old Troubadour ease of manner. He was telling himself that, while the outlook was beyond a question unsettled, all might yet be well. Men, he reminded himself, had gone through worse than this and come out on the other side. An instance of this had occurred in his first thriller. There, the heroine had broken off all relations with Inspector Purvis because she had been told by a one-eyed Chinaman that it was he who had murdered her brother. She had stated in an impressive scene that she would never speak to him again or, for the matter of that, even think of him without a shudder of abhorrence. Yet all had come right in the last chapter.

'Perhaps my uncle told you that I am engaged to Lionel Green?'

'He did, yes. I was appalled.'

'Indeed?'

'Utterly appalled. If you read the reports of the case of Pennefather versus Tarvin, and studied my remorseless *exposé* at all carefully, you will know by now the sort of chap Stinker Green is.'

'How dare you call him that?'

'Everybody did at school. And not without reason. I tell you, there was many a sensitive lad at the old Alma Mater who wished that Lionel Green had been educated privately.'

The things which Anne wanted to say in response to this outrageous statement were so numerous that she found it difficult to sift and select. The one she chose was not too good.

'Don't be idiotic! Lionel is always taking baths.'

'He has a lot of leeway to make up.'

There came to Anne the feeling, which had so depressed Mr Molloy, of being in the presence of one who knew all the answers. If the path on which she stood had been harder, promising more impressive results from such a gesture, she would have stamped her foot again.

'No, no,' said Jeff. 'You mustn't dream of marrying Stinker Green. We shall find you someone better than that.'

Anne decided to be cold and biting.

'You, perhaps?'

'You take the words out of my mouth. How about it? I love you. I loved you the moment I saw you. But, of course, you know that. Your uncle told you.'

'Yes, he told me.'

'I don't know what he said, but however strongly he put it he didn't exaggerate. Nobody has ever loved anyone as much as I love you. It couldn't be done.'

Anne thought it would be better to be brisk and practical. She had just remembered that there was another message which she had come to deliver.

'I haven't time to stand here, talking nonsense,' she said. 'I only came to say I knew who you were and to tell you that you had better leave as quickly as you can.'

'Leave?' Jeff's voice was plaintive. 'People are always telling me to leave. I don't want to leave.'

'Well, you'd better. The real Sheringham Adair is here. I left him with Mrs Cork. He had just finished explaining who he was. She is looking for you.'

Jeff was silent for a space. He seemed to be turning this over in his mind, as indeed he was. Even a calmly resourceful young man like himself could see that it had complicated matters. The situation thus created was unquestionably of the type which Mrs Molloy would have recommended him to try on his pianola.

'I thought I had better warn you.'

'It was a kindly impulse.'

'Have you ever seen Mrs Cork on the war-path?'

'Not yet.'

'You soon will.'

'She is annoyed?'

'A little.'

'She resents my having deceived her?'

'She does.'

'I shall have to explain.'

'How?'

'I shall tell her the truth.'

'Can you tell the truth?'

'I did, when I said I loved you. "Ah, Mrs Cork," I shall say—'

'With a light laugh?'

'With a fairly light laugh. "Ah, Mrs Cork"—'

'You got as far as that last time.'

'"Ah, Mrs Cork, I am told that you are a little steamed up about my coming here with my papers not quite in order. But I feel sure that you will understand and sympathize when you know the facts. I love Anne Benedick, Mrs Cork, and I had to come because I couldn't stay away from her."'

'You think that will soothe her?'

'It should. All the world loves a lover. And there's another point you must not overlook. She has this ridiculous idea that you are infatuated with Lionel Green. When she finds you're not, she'll be so delighted that she will forgive all.'

'Is it any use my keeping on telling you that I do love Lionel?'

'Not the slightest.'

'Then I may as well go.'

'But you haven't answered my question.'

'What question?'

'My proposal, rather. I asked you to marry me.'

'Did you? I don't remember.'

'Tut, tut. The subject of your future husband came up, and you suggested that I might apply for the position. I then said "How about it?" '

'Oh? That was a proposal of marriage, was it?'

'It was.'

'Well, the answer is in the negative.'

'But why? Can't you see that we're affinities?'

'I hadn't noticed it.'

'Then you should have done. Look at the way we hit it off right from the start. No awkwardness, no stiffness, just a couple of soulmates getting together and picking up the threads after their previous existence. We agreed, if you remember, that we must have met in some previous existence.'

'When you were a king in Babylon.'

'And what a king! With my pipe and my bowl and my fiddlers three. You were ready enough to marry me then.'

'I wasn't.'

'You were. It all comes back to me. So why you won't do it now is more than I can understand.'

Anne came to herself sharply. She saw that she had been taking the wrong attitude, and that if the conversation were allowed to proceed along these lines, she was in danger, after having come in like a lioness, of going out like a lamb.

Her plan of action at the outset had been simple. She had proposed to reduce this young man to pulp with a few incisive words, and then to sweep haughtily away and leave him writhing in shame. And she now perceived that she had allowed him to lure her into one of those light chats which had been such a feature of their association, and which she was compelled to admit that she had always enjoyed. Worse, she was compelled to admit that she was enjoying this one. Revolted to discover that she was smiling, she hardened her face and infused a stiffness into her manner.

'Well, good-bye,' she said.

This struck Jeff as a little sudden.

'You aren't going?'

'I merely came to warn you that Mrs Cork was looking for you. It's for you to decide what you want to do about it.'

'I told you. I shall explain the circumstances.'

'If you've time.'

'You think she may be too quick on the trigger to allow of reasoned explanations?'

'You'll be lucky if you're able to say "The rest is silence."'

'The rest is what?'

'Silence.'

'But why should I want to?'

'I thought you might need a dying speech. That was Hamlet's – a character in a play of that name by William Shakespeare,' said Anne, and was once more aware that this was becoming a light chat. 'Good-bye,' she said, calling herself to order again.

'No, don't go,' said Jeff. 'I want to talk to you about this private education of yours. It strikes me as having been very spotty. You confess to being unfamiliar with "Come into the garden, Maud," and yet you seem to have chased Shakespeare up a tree, where you can get him any time you want him. I must probe into this. What are the principal rivers of England? And it's no good saying "Hides, tallow and hemp," because that's not the answer.'

'Good-bye.'

'I wish you wouldn't keep saying "Good-bye." Did you have governesses? Or were you educated by your uncle?'

'I am not going to stay here talking to you. I don't want to talk to you. I'm furious with you. After the abominable way you behaved to Lionel—'

'I did put it across him, didn't I? How he wriggled and twisted beneath my piercing glance! If it hadn't been for the referee blowing his whistle all the time and putting me off my stroke, there would have been no Lionel Green left in that witness box – just a small spot of grease. And serve him right for telling people I wore bed socks.'

'What?'

'That was the loathsome story he spread about me, when we were boys together. It took me years to live it down and become the hero of the school. By the way, did I ever tell you how I became the hero of the school?'

'No. And I don't want you to.'

'It was during the great football match of the season against St Ethelberta's, a girls' school in the neighbourhood who were our deadly rivals. It was nearly the end of the game, and we were leading by the narrowest of margins. Then all of a sudden their captain broke loose with the ball under her arm, a large, spectacled girl called Flossie, and no one between her and the goal line but me. The question naturally arose "Will J. G. Miller prove equal to this emergency?" and all through the crowd it was recognized as a very moot point. Well, to cut a long story short I didn't. I let her through, and she crossed the line and we lost. I shall never forget that day.'

'And that made you the hero of the school?'

'Of the other school. Of St Ethelberta's. But let's get back to your private education. Did your uncle attend to it?'

'No.'

'A pity. He has some good ideas.'

Anne gave a sudden start. She was facing the entrance of the rhododendron walk, and in it, silhouetted against the evening sky, there had just appeared a large woman, accompanied by a small man. The light, though dim, was good enough to enable her to identify them, respectively, as her employer and Mr Trumper.

'He told me I ought to kiss you,' said Jeff.

His voice shook a little. He was conscious of a strange breathlessness. All through this conversation, he had found himself becoming more and more attracted by the elder man's views on the way in which a woman should be wooed. It needed but the merest trifle to turn him into a wholehearted convert.

'Oh!' cried Anne. 'Here she comes!'

Jeff looked over his shoulder, and saw what she had seen.

'Yes,' he said. 'There she spouts.'

He drew in his breath sharply, like Inspector Purvis. His mind was made up. Mrs Cork's arrival, he saw, had simplified everything. He had been planning to explain to her that it was his love for Anne that had brought him to Shipley Hall, and now there was no need for tedious verbal explanations. She should witness an ocular demonstration which would convince her of the position of affairs.

Anne uttered a wordless cry. She recoiled, but not far enough.

To a man trained in boyhood to make flying tackles against the finest talent of St Ethelberta's, she was still within easy reach. The next moment, Mrs Cork, sailing up like a great galleon moving into the battle line, halted abruptly, wondering if she could believe her eyes. Then a squeak from behind her told her that Mr Trumper was believing his.

Anne came hurrying past her, and vanished into the shadows.

'Well!' said Mrs Cork.

'Bless my soul!' said Mr Trumper.

They were aware of Jeff approaching them. It was plain to see that he was bathed in modest confusion.

'I really must apologize, Mrs Cork,' he said. 'I thought we were alone.'

It was not often that Mrs Cork found herself at a loss for words, but this strange experience happened to her now, and Jeff went on, speaking with a persuasive charm which Mr Trumper, for one, found touching and full of appeal.

'Miss Benedick had just been telling me that you were aware that I had accepted your hospitality under what I suppose one must call false pretences. She was very upset about it, and I was trying to comfort her. I told her that, when you knew the true facts and realized that I had come here simply because the strain of separation from her was too great, you would understand and sympathize. It was wrong of us, I know, to deceive you, so that we could be together, but love is love, Mrs Cork.'

'Ah!' breathed Mr Trumper.

Mrs Cork's stormy brow cleared. Jeff's manly explanation had not been in vain. She decided to take what Mr Molloy would have called the big, broad view. The discovery that her apprehensions regarding Anne and her nephew Lionel were groundless had filled her with a relief that left no room for hostile feelings.

'I ought to be very angry with you,' she said, still rumbling a little, like a partially extinct volcano.

'You ought, indeed.'

'You have behaved very badly.'

'Abominably. Nobody could blame you if you ordered me out of the house.'

'I had intended to.'

'But you won't? Not now that you know the facts?'

'No. You may stay.'

'Thank you,' said Jeff. 'Thank you.'

He disappeared and Mrs Cork stood for a moment in thought.

'A curious young man,' she said.

'Most extraordinary,' said Mr Trumper.

'Well,' said Mrs Cork, 'this has certainly taken a great weight off my mind. I was so sure that there was something between Miss Benedick and Lionel. I shall now let Lionel have that money he wants for that partnership of his. I will go and tell him at once. I know the dear boy has been worrying about it.'

Mr Trumper accompanied her to the house in silence. There had been no melting of his animosity towards the man who had failed him in his hour of need, and he resented this showering of happy endings on so undeserving an object.

CHAPTER 22

Lionel Green was in his bedroom, completing his preparations for dinner by sprinkling brilliantine on his hair, when Mrs Cork came to inform him of her decision. His joy, as he heard the good news, was so intense that he nearly dropped the bottle. Not even the discovery that his benefactress believed in strict business between relations, and that he would be expected to pay a stiffish rate of interest and eventually refund the capital, was able to diminish his ecstasy.

'You can rely on me absolutely as regards all that part of it, Aunt Clarissa,' he assured her fervently. 'Tarvin's shop is a gold mine. You will have your money back in a couple of years. How can I thank you enough? Such a wonderful surprise. From what you were saying the other day, I rather got the impression—'

'At that time I had not made up my mind. I don't see any reason why I should not tell you, Lionel,' said Mrs Cork, deciding to be frank. 'Until this evening I had an idea that there was something between you and Miss Benedick, and I wouldn't have permitted any nonsense of that sort for an instant.'

Lionel Green laughed gaily.

'What an extraordinary notion, Aunt Clarissa!'

'Yes, I realize that now. It has taken a great weight off my mind. I was not going to have you getting entangled with a penniless girl, no matter how good her family might be. But now that I know that she is in love with that young man who calls himself Adair—'

'What!'

'I found him kissing her just now in the rhododendron walk, and of course it altered everything. I have no longer any hesitation in letting you have this money. It is a very large sum, but, as you say, Mr Tarvin's is a prosperous business, and I have no doubt that you will be able to repay me quite soon. We will go into Tunbridge Wells to-morrow and have the papers drawn up at my lawyer's. Well, I must hurry off now. I have to see Mrs Cleghorn, to tell her to keep dinner back.'

She left the room abruptly, glad to escape from what might have developed into an emotional scene, and Lionel, absently sprinkling more brilliantine on his already well-moistened scalp, gave himself up to a survey of the situation.

His feelings were mixed. He resented, and rightly, the fact of his betrothed being kissed by other men in rhododendron walks, but at the same time he could see that it was a very fortunate thing that this had happened. His aunt's words had left no room for doubt that it had just done the trick as regarded the flotation of that loan.

It was not long, therefore, before he had reached the comforting conclusion that all things had worked together for good, and he was humming lightheartedly and considering the question of putting some brilliantine on his moustache, when the door opened and Anne came in.

For the last quarter of an hour, Anne had been walking up and down beside the pond, always her refuge in times of stress, in the grip, like Lionel, of mixed feelings. But, unlike him, she had not found the blue bird. Nothing was further from her mind than to hum lightheartedly.

Reflecting on Jeff and the horror in the rhododendron walk, she vibrated with outraged fury. If she had been the heroine of the thriller to which allusion had been made, she could not have been firmer in her resolve never to speak to him again. She would also have been glad to have the opportunity of hitting him with a brick. But at the same time, oddly enough, quite a good deal of her resentment had spilled over and was directing itself against Lionel Green. In moods of strong emotion, when things have been happening to upset and disturb them, women, endeavouring to fix the responsibility and assign the blame, are inclined to scatter their shots and take in a wide target.

But for Lionel's policy of caution and concealment, she was feeling, all this would never have occurred. Her frank and open nature had long chafed at the degrading tactics which had been forced upon her, and this evening her distaste for Safety First methods seemed to have come to a head. If Mrs Cork's objections to her as a niece by marriage were so strong as to lead her, if defied, to cut off supplies, then let her cut off supplies. Anything was better than the shifts and subterfuges of a secret engagement.

That was how Anne felt, and she had come to Lionel's room now resolved to have a straight talk and to insist upon his doing the square and intrepid thing, regardless of the consequences. She was alive to the fact that his Aunt Clarissa was a tough egg – prolonged association with her in the capacity of secretary-companion had left her as clear on that point as any native bearer or half-caste trader – but she was feeling militant and reckless, in the mood when women urge their men to desperate deeds.

In the demeanour of Lionel Green, as she entered, there was none of the elation of the ardent lover at the sight of his lady. All the joy which had been thrilling him, as he thought of that visit to Tunbridge Wells on the morrow, was swept away as by a squeegee, to be replaced by dismay and panic. He did not say 'She is coming, my own, my sweet,' but leaped like a pea on a hot shovel, spraying brilliantine in all directions.

'Good Lord!' he cried, appalled. 'What on earth are you doing here?'

If he had studied for weeks, testing and examining every possible conversational opening, he could scarcely have found one less calculated to remove from Anne's mind that feeling of being out of sympathy with him. She started violently, as if she had been stung by a wasp or kissed by a scrum-half in a rhododendron walk, and for an instant stood staring incredulously. Then there fell upon her an ominous calm.

'I do wish you would be more careful. You might have run into Aunt Clarissa. She has only just left.'

'I see,' said Anne. 'I'm sorry.'

She spoke so quietly, so meekly, her whole air so like that of a good little girl remorseful for having been naughty, that a wiser and more experienced man than Lionel Green would have climbed the wall and pulled it up after him. But, incredible as it may seem, he sensed no peril. He continued to speak, his always high voice rising higher, as was its wont when he ventilated a grievance.

'I've told you over and over again that we simply must not be seen together. Over and over again. And it's more vital now than ever. Aunt Clarissa has promised me that money. That was what she came to see me about. But I haven't got it yet, and she might easily change her mind. It's too bad of you, risking ruining everything like this. It's not as if I hadn't told you.'

'Over and over again?'

'Yes,' said Lionel Green, struck by this neat way of putting it. 'Over and over again.'

Once more, a tremor passed through Anne, as if the wasp had played a return date or the scrum-half kissed her twice.

'I see,' she said, still quietly, still meekly, still with that intensely unpleasant suggestion of being Mother's little helper conscious of having fallen short of her duty. 'I'm sorry.'

Lionel Green pointed out the discrepancy between her words and her actions.

'You keep saying you're sorry, but you still go on standing there. Suppose she came back?'

'Couldn't I say I had come to borrow your brilliantine?'

Lionel became aware that he was still holding the bottle. He walked to the wash-hand stand and relieved himself of it.

'It's no joking matter,' he said, stiffly.

'I was only trying to be helpful.'

'It wouldn't take much to make her change her mind.'

'Or me mine.'

'What do you mean?'

'I mean that all this secret, snaky stuff has begun to get on my nerves. It makes me feel a worm. What exactly is your idea about that money? To get it and then for us to go ahead and get married?'

'Of course.'

'Would you call that playing the game?'

'Eh?'

'I was only wondering if it was quite fair to deceive the poor lady.'

'I've got to, or I shan't get the money.'

'Money isn't everything.'

The revolutionary idea contained in these words startled Lionel Green. He decided, rather belatedly, to be soothing.

'You mustn't talk like that, darling. I know how you're feeling. It's a strain, having to keep things dark, but we've no choice. Aunt Clarissa told me in so many words that she would never give her consent to our marriage.'

'And what did you tell her?'

'How do you mean?'

'I should have thought you would have told her to go to the devil, because you loved me and weren't going to have anybody dictating to you about it.'

Lionel Green stared.

'Tell Aunt Clarissa that?'

An unwilling tribute forced itself from Anne. No one-eyed Chinaman could have made her feel more hostile towards J. G. Miller, but she was fair.

'Jeff would have done it.'

'Jeff?'

'I mean Mr Adair, though his name is really Miller. But you knew that, of course. By the way, he kissed me just now.'

'Er – yes. Aunt Clarissa told me.'

'It doesn't seem to have upset you much. I suppose you felt that it was the luckiest thing that could have happened.'

This was so exactly what Lionel had been feeling that he found himself unable to reply, and a silence fell.

On Lionel's part, it was an uneasy silence. It had taken him some time to make the discovery, but he had suddenly become conscious that there was an oddness about this girl's manner. She put him in mind of a bomb on the point of exploding, and it disturbed him.

In the relations of Lionel Green and Anne Benedick, there had always been on the part of the former something a little superior, a shade condescending. A charming girl, he had felt, but one who required moulding. He had looked on himself as the wise instructor with the promising pupil. And now, all of a sudden, she had changed into something formidable and intimidating.

Anne, on her side, had become aware that strange things were happening to her this evening, constituting something that amounted to a complete mental and spiritual upheaval. It was as if she had been a Sleeping Beauty, and Jeff's the kiss which had awakened her. She seemed to herself to have come out of some sort of trance, and to have come out of it in a critical and dissatisfied frame of mind.

Until this moment, she had always accepted Lionel Green on his face value – and that, though Jeff would have denied it hotly, was value of a high order. Lionel Green was a handsome, almost a beautiful, young man. Few women had seen him for the first time without a flutter of the heart, and Anne had been convinced, almost from their initial meeting, that in him she had found her ideal.

But now, in this novel mood of criticism and analysis, she had begun to doubt. Her uncle's odious words insisted on coming into her mind. 'You wouldn't give that poop, Lionel Green, a second thought,' Lord Uffenham had said in that crude, uncouth way of his, 'if he hadn't the sort of tailor's dummy good looks that women seem to be incapable of seeing through,' and had gone on to add, if she remembered correctly, that he was capable of making a better man than Lionel Green, any time he saw fit, though handicapped by such limited materials as two lumps of coal and a bit of putty.

At the time, she had scoffed at the possibility of such a feat, but now she was asking herself if it might not be within the scope of an ingenious man, clever with his fingers. Still criticizing and analysing, she found herself definitely dissatisfied with Lionel. Had he nothing, she wondered, except those beautifully regular features? In a flash of humiliating clear thinking, she suddenly saw herself as the sort of girl who falls in love with film stars.

The silence continued. Lionel Green had begun to shift uneasily from foot to foot. His agony of spirit was growing with every moment that passed. Anne, he noted wanly, appeared to be as firmly rooted to the spot on which she stood as if she had been her Uncle George in one of his most contemplative moods. It was difficult to see how he could find the eloquence and clarity of reasoning to shift her, seeing that all his efforts up to the present to do so had failed, though nobody could have argued more lucidly or pointed out with a more persuasive force the peril which her presence involved.

Seeing cooks about putting dinner off is not a lengthy task, and who knew but that his Aunt Clarissa, her mission concluded, might not take it into her head to come back and resume their conversation?

Anne spoke. Her mind had returned to the last remark she had made before the great silence.

'I suppose it was that that made her decide to give you the money?'

'Eh?'

'Seeing Jeff kiss me.'

'I wish you wouldn't call him Jeff.'

'I'm sorry. But was it?'

'Yes, it was.'

'I was wondering why she had made up her mind so suddenly.'

'Yes.'

'And another thing I have been wondering is this. Why didn't you tell Mrs Cork about Mr Miller? You knew perfectly well who he was. You knew you had only to tell Mrs Cork, and she would turn him out of the house. You must dislike him very much. So why—'

Throughout this questioning, Lionel Green had betrayed a certain nervousness, but it was as nothing compared with the almost epileptic spasm of panic which afflicted him now, as he saw the door begin to open.

The next moment, he saw that the ultimate disaster had not occurred. It was not Mrs Cork who was entering, but Jeff.

It was pure kindness of heart that had brought Jeff at this critical moment to the apartment of Lionel Green. As has been made clear, he was not fond of Lionel, but he had promised, while at Shipley Hall, to watch over his interests, and the word of the Millers was their bond.

He had bought Anne's chocolates that morning at the famous Regent Street establishment of Duff and Trotter, and it was while he was passing from the confectionery department into that devoted to what the firm described as Picnic Goods that his eye had fallen on a large, and quite evidently succulent, pork pie. With a considerateness which did him credit, he had purchased it for Lionel. It was just these little acts of kindness, he had reflected, that raised Man, the Boy Scout, above the beasts that perish.

In the rather hectic rush of recent events, this delicacy had faded from his mind, and he had only just remembered it. He was here now to make delivery.

The sight of Anne in the Green G.H.Q. surprised and disconcerted him a good deal. His position, he realized, was about what that of a Troubadour would have been, who had allowed his lower nature to get the better of him for a moment and had behaved towards some fair lady more like a Robber Baron than a guitar player, and he had devoted no little thought to wondering what would be the correct attitude for him to adopt at their next meeting.

And, as such a Troubadour would probably have done, he grinned sheepishly and said: 'Oh, hullo!'

'So there you are,' he said. 'I was wondering where you were. I – er – wanted to see you.'

Anne did not reply, unless a cold and haughty look can be counted as a response.

'To tell you that I am not leaving. Mrs Cork is very kindly allowing me to stay on.'

'Oh?'

'Yes. She says I can stay on.'

Lionel Green broke in upon this one-sided duologue. Reaction from panic had left him irritable. Jeff's intrusion infuriated him. He did not like Jeff, and in any case would have resented the way his bedroom was filling up.

'What do you want?' he demanded, curtly.

His tone was offensive, and in any other circumstances Jeff would have pointed this out to him. But Anne's attitude, so patently lacking in the let-bygones-be-bygones spirit, had reduced him to a mere shivering shadow of his former self. He was feeling chilled and unhappy, as if he had been snubbed by a Snow Queen.

'In pursuance of our gentleman's agreement,' he said brokenly, 'I have brought you a pork pie.' He looked pleadingly at Anne, but failed to catch her eye. 'Well,' he said, having stood on one leg for a moment, 'I'll be getting along.'

He shambled out, leaving behind him a throbbing silence. Anne was staring at Lionel. Lionel was staring at the pork pie.

Anne's gaze was alive with incredulous horror. Standing there with taut lips and bent brows, she enveloped Lionel and the pork pie in one comprehensive look of amazement and disgust. Those words of Jeff's about the gentleman's agreement, taken in conjunction with the gift he had brought, had told her the whole sordid story. She knew now the answer to the question she had been asking.

The scales had fallen from her eyes. For the first time since his fatal beauty had ensnared her, she was seeing Lionel Green steadily and seeing him whole. And as she realized what manner of man he was, her soul seethed in a turmoil of revolt, and love fell from her like a garment.

For if we look askance at the wretch who sells himself for gold, how much more do we recoil from him who allows himself to be bought with pork pies. Remembering her uncle's estimate of the material required for making a man like Lionel Green, there came to her the thought that his specifications had erred on the side of extravagance. The bit of putty, she felt, would be ample, without the lumps of coal.

'So that was why!' she said.

The fact that in her emotion she had sunk her voice to a whisper, added to the fact that Lionel Green's attention was so urgently engaged elsewhere, caused the words to fall unheeded. Lionel was still staring at the pork pie, absorbed. No Israelite, contemplating a wholly unforeseen consignment of manna, could have been less in touch for the time being with extraneous things.

Lionel Green's was a stomach of the peevish, impatient type. For nearly an hour it had been sending out messages couched in a more and more querulous strain, putting in rush orders for something solid and making a fuss when service was denied it. And now it had received official information that something solid would shortly be on the way.

'I say!' he exclaimed, his voice quivering. 'This is all right, what? Sit down and have a slice,' he said hospitably, quite forgetting that a short while before he had been urging his visitor to leave. A Duff and Trotter pork pie permits of no divided thoughts. 'I've got a knife in the drawer. You'll have to use your fingers, I'm afraid.'

Anne found herself choking, partly at the very thought of sharing this pie of shame, partly because emotion was still interfering with the smooth working of her vocal cords.

'Lionel!'

'And there's no salt, of course.'

'Lionel!'

'Or mustard.'

'Lionel, I'm not going to marry you.'

'What?'

'Not.'

'Not what?'

The facilities for stamping the foot were not perfect in Lionel Green's bedroom, for the carpet was a thick and expensive one, but they were superior to those of the rhododendron walk, and the impact of Anne's foot made quite a satisfactory bang.

'I am not going to marry you!'

For the first time in the history of that illustrious firm, a Duff and Trotter pork pie failed to retain its possessor's undivided attention. Lionel Green was listening now, and at these words, so definite in their import, so impossible to misunderstand, he started visibly, displacing a flake of crust, which fell silently to the carpet. The fact that he did not stoop to retrieve it, though there was quite a bit of jelly adhering to its inner surface, showed how deeply her statement had affected him.

'What!'

'No.'

'You're not going to marry me?'

'No.'

'Don't be absurd.'

'I mean it.'

'But why?'

'Think it over.'

There was a pause. A dark flush crept into Lionel Green's face.

'Think it over?' He laughed a bitter, sardonic laugh, and put the pork pie on the chest of drawers. He nodded his head, causing the scent of brilliantine to float about the room like an unseen presence. 'I don't need to think it over. I see it all.'

'I thought you would.'

'You're in love with that fellow Miller.'

This monstrous charge, so totally unexpected, deprived Anne completely of the power of utterance. She stared dumbly, and Lionel proceeded to develop his theme. His manner was stern, his eye hard. Anyone who had been present at the trying of the case of Pennefather *v.* Tarvin would have been irresistibly reminded of plaintiff's counsel cross-examining witness for the defence.

'I've suspected it for days. You're always together. You don't seem happy out of his company. He's always kissing you—'

'He isn't always kissing me. He kissed me once.'

'So you say!' said Lionel Green, and emitting another of those sardonic laughs, he turned to the mirror to arrange his moustache. He had a feeling that it needed attention, and what he had to say could be said just as well, perhaps even better, with his back turned.

'Well, if you think I'm going to sit meekly by and put up with that sort of thing, you're very much mistaken. I shall go at once to Aunt Clarissa and tell her who he is. That'll settle his hash pretty quick. He'll be out of the house to-night.'

His moustache was all right now. He turned, to find that any further remarks he might have to make would be addressed to an absent audience. Anne had gone.

CHAPTER 23

Jeff's tottering feet, having borne him out of Lionel Green's bedroom, had taken him down the stairs, across the hall and through the green baize door which led to the quarters of the domestic staff. His objective was the butler's pantry. After that interview with Anne, he wanted sympathy and something to keep the cold out, and it had occurred to him that Lord Uffenham would provide both.

Lord Uffenham, by the time he arrived, had wearied of trying to find water with the diviner's rod and was shaking pennies in a bowl to see how many came out heads and how many tails. From this intellectual pursuit he looked up and greeted Jeff with his customary affability.

'Hullo, young feller.'

'Hullo,' said Jeff, hollowly.

'Anne was looking for you.'

'She found me. May I have a slight glass of port?'

'Help yourself.'

'Thank you,' said Jeff.

He drained the beaker, and felt better. Life seemed to return to the frozen limbs. It would be too much to say that he had thawed out, but he thought he might if he had another. He had another, and Lord Uffenham remembered that Anne was not the only person who had been looking for his young friend.

'Lord-love-a-duck!' he exclaimed. 'I'd clean forgotten. Mrs Cork!'

Jeff nodded.

'She found me, too.'

'Has she booted yer out?'

'No. As far as the Cork angle is concerned, all is well. I had a chat with her, and she is letting me stay on.'

'In spite of your not being the real I-forget-the-feller's dam-name?'

'J. Sheringham Adair.'

'That's right. In spite of your not being the real J. Sheringham Adair?'

'Yes.'

'Extraordinary.'

'Not so very. A fair-minded, clear-thinking woman, she realizes what a venial offence it is not to be J. Sheringham Adair. As she pointed out, she is not J. Sheringham Adair herself, nor are many of her best friends. Could I borrow another drop of the old and fruity?'

'Have all yer want. That's what it's there for,' said Lord Uffenham, and feeling that he had now done all that could be expected of him in the way of playing the genial host and seeing to his guest's comfort, unbuttoned his waistcoat and prepared to strike a sterner note.

Anne's revelations in this pantry so short a while before had shaken the altruistic peer a good deal. A kindly elder, anxious to bring the young folks together, does not like to learn that his advice, based on the experience of a lifetime, has been neglected by the man whose happiness it was intended to promote.

He spoke now, accordingly, with a grave reproach in his voice, the loving father rebuking the erring son.

'Spiller.'

'Miller.'

'Are you sure?'

'Quite sure.'

'I'm bad at names,' admitted Lord Uffenham. 'Always was. I remember a girl called Kate, back in the year 1912, giving me the push because I wrote to her as Mabel. It might be simpler if I called you Walter.'

'It would be the ideal solution,' Jeff agreed, 'if it were my name.'

'Isn't it?'

'No.'

'Then what is your dashed name?'

'Geoffrey.'

'Of course. Anne calls you Jeff.'

Jeff winced.

'She used to call me Jeff.'

Lord Uffenham mused.

'I knew a girl in 1907 that they used to call Jeff. Her name was Jefferson.'

'And did you alienate her affections by sending her a telegram addressed to Smith?'

The conversation had worked round to just the point where Lord Uffenham wanted it. The sternness of his manner became more marked.

'No, young feller, I did not. If you wish to know, I alienated her affections by treating her with the distant respect of a man brushing flies off a sleeping Venus. I was a mere callow youth at the time, and I had the insane idea that what women appreciated was being looked up to as if they were goddesses. This Jefferson was in the chorus at the Gaiety, and she didn't understand that sort of thing. Shortly after I had taken her out in a punt on the river one summer afternoon, it was brought to my attention that she was going about London saying I was a muff.'

'A what?'

'A muff. An expression of that period signifying a young feller deficient in spirit and enterprise. What Mrs Molloy would describe as a boob, a sap, or possibly a wet smack.'

This implied intimacy with the most dangerous of her sex startled Jeff.

'Are you seeing much of Mrs Molloy these days?'

'Quite a good deal.'

'I wouldn't confide in her too extensively.'

'How d'yer mean?'

'Well, about those diamonds, for instance.'

'My dear feller! Of course not. As if I should dream of doing such a thing. When it comes to keeping a secret, I'm like the silent tomb. Yes,' said Lord Uffenham, resuming his reminiscences, 'she was going about telling everybody I was a muff. It appeared that she had been expecting something radically different from my scrupulously correct behaviour. That episode taught me a lesson which I have never forgotten. It is a lesson which I have striven to pass on to you. But have you learned it? No. After all I said, in spite of the fact that I pleaded with you – yes, dash it, with tears in my eyes – to grab Anne and hug her till her ribs squeaked, you appear to have been muddling along with that idiotic Troubadour stuff of yours and, as I foresaw, getting nowhere. She was in here just now reiterating that she loved Lionel Green. Disheartening, I call it. Enough to make a man feel he'll never lend anyone a helping hand again.'

Jeff smiled wanly.

'You are not quite up to the minute with your information. Since you saw her, there has been a rather abrupt change in the position of affairs. Troubadour Ordinaries have taken a sharp drop, and there has been a corresponding rise in Catch-As-Catch-Can Preferred.'

'Hey?'

'I took your advice.'

'You kissed her?'

'I did.'

'Splendid. So everything's all right?'

'Terrific. Except that she won't speak to me.'

'It worked out like that, did it?'

'That was how it worked out.'

Lord Uffenham laid a soothing hand on Jeff's knee. At least, though it nearly broke the bone, Jeff assumed that it was intended to soothe.

'Don't you worry, my boy. She'll come round.'

'You think so?'

'Sure of it.'

'No need for me to commit suicide?'

'Not the slightest.'

'Fine,' said Jeff. 'I was just going to ask if you could lend me half a brick and a bit of string, so that I could drown myself in the pond.'

The sudden jerking of Lord Uffenham's glass, nearly spilling some of its precious contents, showed that the word had touched a chord.

'Pond! That reminds me. Did she tell you about the pond?'

'No, she did not tell me about the pond. Even now,' said Jeff, 'you appear not to have grasped the inwardness of what I have been saying. You seem to be under the impression that she and I are on excellent terms and conduct long conversations on any subject that happens to crop up – as it might be ponds. This is quite erroneous. Such talking as takes place between us is done almost exclusively by me. I occasionally extract an "Oh?" from her, and glad to get it, but for the most part she confines herself to freezing looks. Just try to form in your mind the picture of a female Trappist monk on one of her more taciturn mornings, and you won't waste valuable time enquiring if she has been telling me about the pond. Arising from this, why should she tell me about the pond? Assuming that our relations were such as to permit her to bring herself to tell me about the pond, what would she have told me about it? And what pond?'

Lord Uffenham had made a discovery which others had made before him. He imparted it to his companion.

'Young man, you talk too bloody much.'

Jeff was wounded.

'It's all very well to say that, but when I substitute action for words, look where it gets me. I think I'll borrow that brick, after all, just to be on the safe side.'

'If you'll let me get a word in edgeways—'

'Certainly, certainly. You would speak of ponds?'

'You know the pond here?'

'Of course. One of Nature's beauty spots. What with its sloping banks, carpeted with verdure, its lily pads—'

'Walter!'

'Jeff.'

'I mean Jeff, dammit. May I ask you one simple question?'

'Proceed.'

'That mouth of yours. Does it shut? It does? Then shut it, blast yer. Lord-love-a-duck, anyone would think you were one of those ghastly fellers in Shakespeare that do soliloquies. About this pond. I was telling Anne it was quite possible that I might have hidden the diamonds in it. And do you know what she said?'

'Did she say anything?'

'Of course she did.'

'This must have been a long time ago.'

'She said she would get Lionel Green to look there.'

'Absurd.'

'So I told her.'

'Lionel Green may possibly have improved in his habits since the days of school to the extent of going into the bathroom and locking the door and splashing the water about with his hand, or more probably the bath brush, but you would never get him into a pond. And, if by some miracle you did, he would never find anything. Though, mind you, I would love to see him paddling in a pond – standing, as it were, with reluctant feet where the brook and river meet. My idea would be to loll on the bank and make funny cracks about September morn.'

'Walter!'

'Hullo?'

'You're talking again.'

'I'm sorry.'

'You say Anne won't speak to you. I don't suppose you give her a chance. Of all the garrulous, gabby ... However, I won't go into that now. You must search that pond.'

'I'll do it to-night.'

'In the dark?'

'There's a moon. Can you lend me a bathing costume?'

'Haven't got one.'

'I'll borrow Shepperson's. I know he has one, because I've seen him dancing in it before breakfast. You're sure the stuff is there?'

'Not sure, no. I've had too many disappointments to be sure of anything nowadays. But, as I was telling Anne, the word "pond" suddenly came flashing into my mind. I thought it significant. It means something.'

'For one thing, a cold in the head for me.'

'Don't falter, Walter.'

'Who's faltering? And my name isn't Walter. I'm up and doing, with a heart for any fate. As a matter of fact, the whole scheme fits in perfectly with my plans. If I find the diamonds, I'll throw them ashore to you, and then I can just go ahead and be drowning myself.'

'I don't like to hear you talk like that.'

'You don't like to hear me talk at all.'

'I've already told you that she'll come round.'

'She won't.'

'She will.'

'She won't. You're basing your theory on your own experience, and it doesn't apply to the case in hand. I dare say girls used to come round in 1911, and possibly even in 1912, but Anne is different.'

'No girl is different.'

'Yes, she is, if she isn't the same. I offended her past forgiveness. I shocked her to the foundations of her being.'

'You didn't.'

'I did, I tell you. I was there.'

Lord Uffenham bestowed another bone-crushing buffet on his young friend's knee.

'Don't you worry, my boy. I know Anne, and I assure you she will come round. Lord-love-a-duck, don't you think girls like being kissed?'

'By the right man.'

'Well, that's what you are. You're just the chap I'd have picked for her. Don't have a moment's uneasiness. I'm the one that ought to be feeling uneasy.'

'You? Why?'

A solemn look had come into Lord Uffenham's face.

'Because, if we don't find those diamonds, I shall have to make the supreme sacrifice.'

'What do you mean?'

'Perfectly simple. Anne's little bit of money was my sacred trust, wasn't it? If I've gone and lost it, I shall have to do something about it, shan't I? See that she's all right, and all that sort of thing? Of course, I shall. As a man of honour, I have no alternative. But I don't mind telling you that I shudder at the prospect.'

'The prospect of what?'

'Marrying Mrs Cork.'

His association with George, Viscount Uffenham, brief though it had been, had left Jeff with the feeling that nothing the latter could say or do would be able to surprise him, but at these words he saw that he had been mistaken. He stared blankly. Lord Uffenham was sitting bolt upright, looking noble.

'What was that you said? You're going to marry Mrs Cork?'

'If we don't find the diamonds. Can't let Anne lose by my well-meaning, but possibly mistaken, handling of her money. It's a case of . . . dash it, what's that expression? It's on the tip of my tongue.'

'*Noblesse oblige*?'

'That's right. *Noblesse oblige.* Thank you, Jeff.'

'Not at all.'

'Yerss, that's how matters stand. So when you search that pond, my boy, search it well. Leave no stone unturned.'

'But do you think Mrs Cork would marry you?'

Lord Uffenham raised his eyebrows. The question seemed to amuse him.

'Go and see about that bathing suit,' he said.

For some moments after Jeff had left him, Lord Uffenham continued to sit motionless, still with that look of nobility on his face. Gradually, however, this faded away, and became replaced by one of nervousness and apprehension. He was envisaging Mrs Cork in the role of a life-partner, and the picture which rose before his eyes was not one that exhilarated him.

By the end of five minutes, his thoughts had become so sombre that it was a relief to him when the door opened and he was no longer alone with them. Expecting Jeff, he found that his visitor was Anne. She came in with flushed face and gleaming eyes, leading him to hope that Jeff had met her in the passage and kissed her again. It was a thing which he felt could not be done too often.

Apparently, however, it was not this that had provoked that flush and caused her eyes to gleam. She delivered her news without delay.

'Uncle George.'

'Hullo, my dear?'

'I've broken my engagement.'

'Hey?'

'I've broken my engagement. I'm not going to marry Lionel. I suppose you're pleased.'

Nothing, not even tidings of the gladdest joy, could have

made a man of Lord Uffenham's build leap from his chair, but he rose with what for him was an almost unexampled celerity, holding out his arms like the good old father in a melodrama welcoming his long-lost daughter.

'Pleased? I'm delighted. When did this happen?'

'Just now.'

'You've really handed him the mitten, have yer? Come to yer senses at last, hey? Well, well, well, well, well! Splendid. Capital. Excellent. Jeff,' cried Lord Uffenham, as the door opened once more. 'Great news, my dear feller! News that'll send yer singing about the house. She's broken her dashed engagement to that herring-gutted window-cleaner of hers.'

Jeff halted abruptly, tingling from head to foot.

'What!'

'Yerss.'

'Is this true?'

'Just told me so herself. Isn't it wonderful?'

'Terrific.'

'Now what about that advice I gave yer?'

'I take back all my criticisms.'

'Didn't I tell yer—'

'You certainly did.'

'And wasn't I right?'

'You definitely were.'

'I'm always right about women.'

'You've studied them.'

'Since early manhood.'

'Now we know why that Jefferson tragedy in 1907 was sent. It was to enable you in your declining years—'

'What d'yer mean, declining years?'

'I should have said in the prime of your life. It was to enable you in the prime of your life to bring aid and comfort to a deserving junior. We learn in suffering what we teach in song.'

'Jeff!'

'Hello?'

'You're talking too much again.'

'I'm sorry.'

'Fight against this tendency, my boy. It's your only fault.'

'Would you say that?'

'I would. Except for that disposition of yours to collar the conversation and not give anyone else the chance to say a dashed word, you're a very fine young feller and there's nobody I'd sooner see my niece married to.'

'It's awfully good of you to say so.'

'Not at all. The thought of her wasting herself on a chap who goes about with his head on one side and his hand on his hip, telling people to take the table out of the dining-room because it doesn't harmonize with the wallpaper, was agony to me. She'll be all right now. You're just the husband for her.'

'I'll try to make her happy.'

'She'll be as happy as the day is long.'

'And I can't tell you how grateful I am to you. But for you ...'

Anne had been listening with set, haughty face to the proceedings of this mutual admiration society. She had not spoken before, because it had been difficult to find a point at which to cut in on the spate of verbiage, but at the word 'you' Jeff had paused and was regarding his friend and helper with a worshipping eye, as if searching for phrases which would express the emotions surging in his bosom. She took advantage of the lull.

'May I say something?'

'Do,' said Lord Uffenham cordially.

'Do,' said Jeff, even more cordially.

'It's just this,' said Anne, ignoring him and addressing her uncle. 'I wouldn't marry Mr Miller, if he was the last man on earth.'

It was a line on which many a heroine of many a play had taken her exit, laughing hysterically. Anne did not laugh hysterically, but she left the room, and closed the door behind her with a bang.

CHAPTER 24

It was Lord Uffenham who broke the silence which followed her departure. He had been sitting for some moments with wrinkled brow, in his eyes that thoughtful look which was always a sign that his great brain had found something to engage it.

'"Were", surely?' he said.

Jeff shook off that numbed feeling, so apt to come to young men on hearing loved lips utter words like those to which he had just been listening. That odd, dreamlike sensation of having been hit on the base of the skull with half a yard of lead piping slowly left him.

'"Were"?'

'Not "was". "I wouldn't marry Mr Miller if he were the last man on earth." Dash it,' said Lord Uffenham, driving home his point, 'the thing's a conditional clause.'

Not since the November afternoon at school when, in the course of a heated house-match, the opposition scrum-half had sprung upon him and twisted his neck into a spiral, when he was nowhere near the ball, had Jeff experienced so strong and sudden an urge to break the sixth commandment. Then he reminded himself that this man loved him like a son and meant well.

'Postponing the lesson in Syntax for just half a minute,' he said, almost gently, 'what do I do about this?'

'Hey?'

'What would you do, if you were the last man on earth and the girl you loved wouldn't marry you?'

Lord Uffenham dismissed the thing with a jerk of the hand, as if brushing away a fly.

'No need to worry, my boy—'

'Don't tell me. Let me guess. Because she'll come round?'

'Exactly.'

'You still feel that she will?'

'Of course.'

'I had an idea that that last crack of hers sounded a bit final.'

'Nothing of the kind. Girls never mean ten per cent of what they say. Go after her, and talk to her.'

'And when she merely looks at me as if I were – not was – something the carrion crow had brought in? I did mention, didn't I, that she was inclined to be a little on the silent side with me just now?'

'Laugh her out of it.'

'I see. Laugh her out of it.'

'You can do it, if you try. Got a very keen sense of humour, that girl. Chaff her. Jolly her along, as Mrs Molloy would say. I know what you're thinking. You're saying to yourself "What would a Troubadour do in my place?" and you've got an idea that you ought to grovel. I do beg and beseech you, my dear feller, to forget all that Troubadour nonsense. Be gay. Be airy. You've got the gift of the gab. I've had to complain about it. Use it. Don't crawl up to her, looking crushed and tragic like a dashed black-beetle that's just had insect powder sprinkled over it by the cook. Shove your chin out and stick your thumbs in your waistcoat. It's obvious that she's crazy about you. If she isn't, why did she give that lavatory inspector the push? I told you kissing her would do the trick, and it did. You fold her in a close embrace, and – *bingo* – off she rushes and breaks her engagement. What more do you want?'

A little breathless after this powerful exordium, Lord Uffenham paused and refilled his glass. He was pleased to observe that his words had caused his young friend to brighten considerably.

And, indeed, it did seem to Jeff that they had been such as to encourage hope. Plainly, something had influenced Anne to break her engagement. It could scarcely be mere coincidence that the change of heart should have occurred right on top of his activities in the rhododendron walk. Pleasanter to believe that Lord Uffenham's advice on tactics had proved itself sound.

And if the old maestro had been right then, there was every reason to hope that he was right now.

'Well, I'll go and see what happens,' he said. 'I'm bound to say I feel a little as Commander Peary must have felt on approaching the North Pole, but I will go and see what happens.'

'That's the spirit,' said Lord Uffenham, sipping port at him encouragingly. 'I shall expect yer back in ten minutes, to tell me that everything is hunky-dory.'

'I beg your pardon?'

'Another of Mrs Molloy's expressions,' explained Lord Uffenham. 'Sweet little woman.'

It is proof, if proof were needed, of the wholeheartedness of Jeff's great love that, as he went in quest of Anne, his mind did not occupy itself with this further evidence of the intimacy which existed between the susceptible peer and a woman whose every move he had come to view with alarm. He was thinking of what Lord Uffenham had said about the small importance to be attached to the utterance of girls in moments of wrath.

If girls really never meant ten per cent of what they said on such occasions, it might be that they meant only – say fifteen per cent of what they looked – in which case, it seemed to him that there were grounds for optimism.

Nevertheless, when, passing through the green baize door, he heard someone playing the piano and recognized Anne's touch and made his way to the drawing-room, whence the sounds were proceeding, he was aware of a definite sinking of the heart. If Commander Peary had come along at that moment, he would have shaken him by the hand and told him he knew just how he had felt.

It was in the hope of soothing her ruffled nerve centres that Anne, on sweeping from the pantry, had hurried to the drawing-room piano. Most girls, who can play the piano at all, like to play it at times of spiritual storm and stress, and recent events, culminating in that meeting of the mutual admiration society, had left her feeling as if her soul had been passed through the wringer.

She had been relieved to find that the beauty of the evening was keeping Mrs Cork's guests out of doors and that she had the drawing-room to herself. If she had known that this solitude was shortly to become a *tête-à-tête*, her relief would have been less pronounced. But she did not know it. She sat down at the piano, and healing music began to pour from her fingertips.

It may seem strange, considering the testing experiences through which she had passed this evening, but what had upset her most had been those last words of hers in the pantry. She was, as Lord Uffenham had said, a girl with a keen sense of humour, and girls with a keen sense of humour do not like to think that they have been guilty of trite and pompous *clichés*. If there was anything more banal, she felt as her fingers strayed over the keys, than saying that you would not marry a man, if he were the last man on earth, she did not know what it was.

And yet, hackneyed though the words were, she told herself that they had exactly expressed her meaning. As far as actual lucidity was concerned, she had no complaints to make. It was only that she wished that she could have hit on something which, while making her attitude equally clear, would have been fresher and more original. And the reflection that, even if inspiration were now vouchsafed to her and she thought of the ideal phrase, it was too late to say it, was a bitter one.

The result of these meditations was to leave her more coldly hostile to Jeff than ever, and the latter could hardly have selected a less fortunate moment for entering the room. The look which she flashed over her shoulder gave him some inkling of this. Even if you wrote off eighty-five per cent of its austerity on the Uffenham system of book-keeping, it was not an inviting look, and it was only by a strong exercise of will power that he was enabled to continue his advance across the floor.

He came to a halt at her side, looking down at her with eyes in whose intent gaze, he hoped, devotion and remorse were neatly blended.

'Hullo,' he said. 'Playing the piano?' and was immediately conscious of not having found the ideal conversational opening. It was not gay. It was not airy. It was not even reasonably intelligent. He would, he realized, have to do much better than this.

Anne made no reply. The question which he had propounded was one which could have been answered with a verbal affirmative, but it is much simpler if, when you are playing the piano, a man you dislike extremely asks you if you are playing the piano, to go on playing the piano, so that he can see for himself. She did so, and as Jeff had not yet thought of the bright remark which the situation demanded, the conversation waned.

It was still flagging, when Mrs Cork came into the room.

Mrs Cork had been looking for Jeff, for she had just met Lionel Green in the hall and heard his momentous news. And now, as her eyes fell on him, drooping beside the piano, there sprang into them that stern gleam which so many a giraffe and antelope had seen there just before qualifying for the obituary column.

In the statement of Lionel Green, made under the stress of strong emotion, there had been much which Mrs Cork had found confused and rambling, and she was still at a loss to understand the motives which had led him to preserve silence until now on a subject calling, one would have supposed, for instant ventilation. But the main point or gist of it had got across nicely, and there was in her voice, as she spoke, a throaty growl which any leopard would have been proud to include in its repertoire.

'Your name is J. G. Miller,' she said, with that avoidance of polite preliminaries which was so characteristic of her direct nature.

A certain something in her manner, as she bore down upon him, had warned Jeff that for some reason his charm had become diminished in his hostess's eyes: and her words, though they came as a shock, did not come with all the shock of the unexpected. Mindful of Lord Uffenham's excellent advice, he thrust his thumbs into the armholes of his waistcoat. He also smiled a pleasant and, he hoped, ingratiating smile.

'That's right,' he said. 'J. G. Miller. I had been meaning to tell you.'

'You will leave this house immediately,' said Mrs Cork.

The words, though powerful and forcefully delivered, caused her a passing sensation of dissatisfaction. She did not feel, like Anne in the pantry and Jeff in this drawing-room, that she could have put what she had to say better. What irked her was being compelled to confine herself to mere words. A woman who has toyed with the idea of strangling a man with her bare hands does not like to have to modify the programme to the extent of simply telling him to leave the house.

But the taboos of civilization are rigid. Conduct, which in Africa is normal and ordinary, provokes in Kent the pursed lip and the raised eyebrow. A woman who wishes to settle in Kent is faced by two alternatives. Either she must refrain from strangling people, or she must go somewhere else.

Jeff bowed his head. He had removed his thumbs from the armholes of his waistcoat, and his manner was now meek and conciliatory, like that of a black-beetle which sees the cook reaching for the insect powder and does its best to show her that it fully realizes that it has brought this on itself.

'I quite understand,' he said. 'After my behaviour in court that day you naturally wish me to leave. I suppose it is no good telling you that I am gnawed by remorse for what I did?'

'There is a train in half an hour.'

'And that if I had had the slightest idea that Lionel Green was Mrs Cork's nephew, my line of cross-examination would have been very different?'

'I have told my butler to pack your things.'

'I feared as much.' Jeff turned to Anne. 'Good-bye,' he said.

'Good-bye,' said Anne.

'I shall be gone in half an hour.'

'Half an hour soon passes,' said Anne.

'But before I go,' said Jeff, once more enveloping Mrs Cork in that winning smile, 'I have a favour to ask. Will you autograph my copy of *A Woman in the Wilds*? It has always been one of my treasures, but it lacks that final touch.'

In the greatest men and women there is almost invariably one weak spot. Achilles had his heel. Mrs Cork had her *Woman in the Wilds*. Approach Clarissa Cork with the statement that you had purchased her brain-child, and you had found the talking point. It would be too much to say that at these words she turned instantly into a thing of sweetness and light, but she unquestionably went off the boil. Her gaze, which had been one of loathing, as if Jeff had been a caterpillar which she had discovered in her bowl of native maize, softened visibly.

It is the secret sorrow of authors that they too seldom come into direct contact with their public. Her publisher's statement had told Mrs Cork that two hundred and six splendid men and women had bought *A Woman in the Wilds*, but never till now had she stood face to face with anyone on the roll of honour. She had had to satisfy herself with the thought that the *Peebles Advertiser* considered the book bright and interesting and the more reserved verdict of the *Times Literary Supplement* that it contained three hundred and fifteen pages.

True, she had seen visitors at Shipley Hall leave the house with their copy tucked under their arm, but only after she had forced it on them, in Lord Uffenham's powerful phrase, like a nurse making a child take liquorice powder. And to her sporting mind there was something about this strong-arm form of circulation building that smacked of not playing the game. She had done it, but it had given her a guilty feeling, as if she had shot a sitting hippopotamus.

'That chapter about the crocodile,' said Jeff. 'I don't know if you remember it. That impressed me enormously. I had always been uneasily conscious that if I saw a crocodile lying on a sand bank, I should not know what to do, and I was rather ashamed of myself, because it is a thing which every young man ought to know. You really swam across and shot it?'

'In the eye.'

'That is the best place?'

'The only place.'

'I must bear that in mind. And that story of the witch-doctor who swallowed the snake. Enthralling.'

Mrs Cork was now giggling almost girlishly.

'You seem to know the book very well.'

'Practically by heart.'

'Fancy that!'

'It has been an inspiration to me. It has made me so eager to go to Africa that I shall probably start directly I leave here.'

'I have been—'

'Let me see. Allowing two days for buying my outfit—'

'I have been thinking it over—'

'What should I need? Guns, summer clothing, a solar topee, stout boots, some form of ointment for leopard bites—'

'I have been thinking it over, Mr Miller,' said Mrs Cork, 'and it seems to me that there is really no reason why you should leave Shipley Hall. I still feel that your behaviour in court was most extraordinary—'

'Unpardonable. I regret it all the more because, since I came here, I have had the opportunity of seeing something of your nephew, and his quiet charm has impressed itself upon me very much. I shall be particularly sorry to go, knowing that in another week or so we should have become firm friends. But don't think I don't see how right you are.'

'I shall be delighted, if you will remain here.'

'You mean that? Well, this is simply too kind of you, Mrs Cork. I can hardly believe it.'

'Miss Benedick, will you go and tell Cakebread not to pack Mr Miller's things.'

'Yes, Mrs Cork.'

'I'll go with you,' said Jeff.

'Don't trouble,' said Anne.

'No trouble at all,' said Jeff.

Out in the corridor, Anne turned. Her face was hard.

'Stop it!' she hissed.

'Stop what?'

'Smirking like that and saying "Genius, genius!" '

'But it was genius,' protested Jeff. 'Genius of a high order.'

'Good-bye!'

'But half a minute—'

Anne had turned, and had started for the butler's pantry, moving well. Myrtle Shoesmith had made good time down the stairs of Halsey Chambers, but it seemed to Jeff, as he followed, that any handicapper who knew his business would have felt obliged to give her a liberal start in any hundred-yard dash for which Anne also had entered.

'But listen—' he said.

Few things are more difficult than to pour out your heart to a girl who is racing along a corridor ahead of you. By the time they reached the green baize door, Jeff had merely touched the fringe of his subject, and his case was still only partially stated when they entered Lord Uffenham's presence and roused him from what appeared to be a trance of more than ordinary cataleptic quality.

'Uncle George,' said Anne.

'Hey?' said Lord Uffenham, coming slowly to the surface. 'Oh, it's you? I wanted to see you, my dear, and you, Jeff. That pond thing is off. I did drop the stuff in the dashed water, attached to a stout string, but I remember now that I took it out again next day.'

'Uncle George, Mrs Cork says you're not to pack Mr Miller's things.'

'Hey? Not pack 'em?'

'No.'

'Isn't he leaving?'

'No.'

'Splendid,' said Lord Uffenham. 'Capital. I see what happened. You pleaded for him. Good girl, good girl.'

'I did not plead for him!' said Anne, and was out of the door like a fish darting through water. Jeff, blinking as she flashed by, thought he saw now where she had the edge on Myrtle Shoesmith. She was a quicker starter.

Lord Uffenham, too, had been impressed by her mobility. He had seen girls leave rooms like that in the early nineteen hundreds. He nodded sagely.

'She's still ratty.'

Jeff shuddered at the adjective, but he could not but admit that, though revolting, it covered the facts.

'Still ratty,' he assented.

'Not come round.'

'No, not come round.'

Lord Uffenham pondered.

'Have you kissed her again?'

'No, I have not.'

'Then go and do it.'

'I won't.'

'It might just turn the scale.'

'Listen,' said Jeff, patiently. 'I told you she spoke to me either not at all or very sparsely. You have now seen for yourself that she has developed a tendency to shoot out of my presence as if released by a spring. This renders it difficult for me to follow your advice.'

'Yerss. You'd want her to stay put, of course.'

'Exactly.'

'Is she always as nippy as that?'

'Sometimes even nippier.'

Lord Uffenham pondered once more. It was some moments before he spoke again. When he did, it was to throw out an observation which, while not perhaps of any great help as regarded the matter in hand, was fraught with interest.

'Did you know that ants run faster in warm weather?' he asked.

'Ants?'

'Yerss.'

'I thought for a moment you said Anne.'

'No, not Anne. Ants. When the weather's warm, they run faster.'

For an instant, Jeff eyed the erudite old gentleman fixedly.

'This is wonderful news,' he said. 'Thank you for telling me. And now shall we return to Anne for a while?'

'You want to know what you ought to do next?'

'Exactly. The situation seems to be at a deadlock, and I should be glad to find a formula.'

'Yerss. Yerss, I see. What happened when you saw her after you left me?'

'I tracked her to the drawing-room and tried to start a conversation, but she simply sat and played the piano at me.'

'Is that so? Girls are odd.'

'Very.'

'I knew a girl in—'

Jeff raised a hand.

'Not now.'

'Hey?'

'Some other time. Later.'

'I was only going to say—'

'I know. But don't.'

'It was simply that, when she got ratty, she used to play the trombone,' said Lord Uffenham, and relapsed into silence.

It was the silence, Jeff could see, of deep thought, and in the hope of stimulating the other's mental processes he drew out his cigarette-case and offered it.

Lord Uffenham shook his head.

'Never smoke now. Gave it up.'

'You found it stunted your growth?'

'No. No, didn't stunt my growth. Feller staying here happened to say to me one evening that I hadn't the will power to do it, so I just took the pipe out of my mouth – we were in my study at the time – laid it down – took up the tobacco jar – new half-pound of Pond's Prime Honeysweet – put it away in the cupboard – put the pipe in the cupboard – and turned the key. And from that day to this I've never touched the stuff.'

'That showed great strength of mind.'

'Enormous.'

'And made your friend look silly, no doubt.'

'He looked silly already.'

'Sillier than usual, I should have said.'

'Yerss,' agreed Lord Uffenham. 'Yerss.'

He seemed about to pass into a coma again, but suddenly

just as his eyes had begun to glaze, he sat up with a startled 'Lord-love-a-duck!'

'Jeff!'

'Hullo?'

'Well, dash my wig and buttons!' exclaimed Lord Uffenham, looking like a sibyl about to prophesy. It was plain that his brain had received some abrupt stimulus. You could almost hear the popping. 'Jeff, we've come to the end of the long, long trail.'

'What do you mean?'

'I'll tell yer what I mean. Pond's Prime Honeysweet! Now I see why the word "pond" seemed so dashed significant. I put those diamonds at the bottom of that tobacco jar!'

'No!'

'I did. I remember doing it.'

Jeff had sprung to his feet. News like this was not to be taken sitting down.

'Is this official?'

'Absolutely official. The whole scene rises before my mind's eye. There was I, and there was the tobacco jar, and I put the package in it, underneath the dashed tobacco.'

'Golly!'

'Yerss.'

'We can get it after dinner.'

'We'll have to be careful. That Cork woman's always popping in and out of the study.'

'But she's giving a lecture on the Ugubus in the drawing-room after dinner.'

'She is.'

'The coast will be clear.'

'Absolutely clear.'

'A child could get the stuff.'

'A child of ten.'

'A child of six.'

'A child of four,' boomed Lord Uffenham, now completely infected with his junior's enthusiasm. 'Any dashed child, in fact, that wasn't crippled in both legs and both arms and could walk in and turn a key in a door.'

'Have you the key?'

'Certainly I have.'

The mental vista down which he was looking became more and more beautiful to Jeff.

'And here's another thing,' he said. 'Once we have those diamonds, Anne will be so thankful and overjoyed and delighted that we shall have no more of this Trappist monk and professional sprinter stuff.'

'You mean she'll come round.'

'That's what I mean. She'll come round.'

'You're right, Jeff! She won't be able to help herself. Three hearty cheers!' said Lord Uffenham.

There was a tap at the door. Dolly Molloy entered.

'Hello, big boy,' she said, in her genial way. 'Hello, Pop. Got a drop of that port of yours to give a fellow?'

'Certainly, certainly, certainly,' said Lord Uffenham, beaming freely. 'Sit down, dear lady, and take the weight off yer feet, ha, ha, ha. That's one of her expressions,' he explained to Jeff, and noting that the latter was making preparations for departure added: 'You off?'

'Yes,' said Jeff.

He fixed his old friend with a meaning glance.

'Careful!' his eye said.

'The silent tomb!' replied Lord Uffenham's.

CHAPTER 25

Soapy Molloy, when his wife had suggested to him that he accompany her to Lord Cakebread's pantry and get a quick snootful before the evening meal, had reluctantly declined the invitation. He liked port, but he had to think about his figure. He had remained in their mutual bedroom, taking his ease in a chair with his feet on the window-sill, a mild cigar between his lips.

Fanned by the gentle breeze which stole in from the darkening garden and played about his lofty forehead with a soft caress, he would have been feeling completely happy, but for one crumpled rose leaf. Chimp Twist, although a bedroom of his own had now been assigned to him, had elected to come and keep him company, and Soapy found his presence embarrassing.

True, the little tiff which had resulted from Dolly's impulsiveness had been adjusted by those well-expressed arguments of his, but it had not been adjusted quite enough. On Chimp's side, it was plain, a coolness still existed. This was made evident by the fact that, almost from the moment he entered the room, he had started to speak to himself in an undertone, as if he had been one of those soliloquizing characters in Shakespeare whom Lord Uffenham disliked so much, about low-down double-crossers and people with whom skunks would blush to associate. He did not mention names, but Soapy had no difficulty in identifying the persons whom he had in mind, and his cigar, as he listened, lost much of its power to soothe.

It was a relief to him when the door opened, and Dolly re-entered.

Dolly's vivid face was alive and her eyes sparkling, and it seemed to Soapy, as he gazed on those loved features, that that port of old Cakebread's must be considerable port, to have produced this uplift in such quick time. For an instant, remembering his refusal to sit in at the orgy, he was tortured by the thought of what might have been.

'You seem kind of pepped up, sugar,' he said, and Chimp Twist felt the same. Suspending his soliloquy, he eyed Dolly sourly. It offended him to behold such radiance in a woman through whose machinations he had gone through so much. He would have preferred not to see Dolly at all, but if he had to see her he would have liked to do so when she had toothache or had recently been run over by a truck.

Dolly, observing Chimp's presence, for a moment found it, as Soapy had done, unwelcome. She had that to say which she would have preferred to impart to her husband's ear alone. Then it occurred to her that in the enterprise, with the outlines of which her agile brain had been busy since she had left Lord Uffenham's pantry, there would be a part for him to play, and she checked the impulse to ask him why the heck he was sitting there like a bump on a log.

'I'll say I'm pepped up,' she cried. 'Guess what, pettie. Give you three guesses.'

Her words were cryptic, but, taking them in conjunction with the strange, almost febrile vivacity of her demeanour, the two men found them pregnant with meaning. Chimp, sitting with his elbows on his knees and his chin cupped in his hands, straightened sharply, quivering like a blancmange. Soapy, who had been tilting his chair back, tilted it too far and had the misfortune to sustain a nasty blow on the back of the head.

But at a moment like this he could ignore physical pain. He did not even bother to rub the place. Sprawling on the carpet, he gazed up at his wife with bulging eyes.

'You don't mean—'

'Yessir. I've gotten the whole dope.'

'From Lord Cakebread?'

'From his own personal lips.'

'He told you where the ice was?'

'Just that little thing.'

'Well!'

'You may well say "Well!"'

'I'll tell the world I may well say "Well!"' said Soapy, rising and clasping her fondly to his bosom. 'Honey, you're terrific.'

'Well, I'll admit I don't think I'm so bad myself,' said Dolly, producing her lipstick and restoring the mouth which her mate's caresses had temporarily obliterated.

There is an unpleasant type of man on whom the spectacle of married love jars. Chimp Twist was such a man. It was with a celibate's moroseness that he surveyed the affectionate couple. Soapy was standing with his arm about Dolly's slim waist, while Dolly, busy with the lipstick, rested her head on his shirt front, and he made it clear that the sight nauseated him.

'Ah, cut it out,' he said, peevishly.

A change had taken place in Chimp Twist's manner since Dolly had begun to speak. What had been joyous animation had become the coldness of the sceptic. Second thoughts had warned him that all this was probably just another of those things. Briefly, he feared a trap.

'So he told you where the ice was, did he?'

'I said he did.'

'I heard you. And I suppose,' said Chimp, giving his moustache a sardonic twirl, 'it turns out that it's in his bedroom, after all, and you want me to go there again and have another look around?'

It was only too plain that he spoke satirically, and this reopening of old sores pained Soapy. He was a man who liked the dead past to bury its dead.

'Now, Chimpie,' he protested, 'is that the way to talk?'

'I only wanted to know.'

Dolly was more offended than pained. She replaced the lipstick and, raising her head, glared balefully.

'One of these days,' she said, 'I'm going to bean you, Chimp Twist, and bean you good!'

'Now, honey,' pleaded the pacific Mr Molloy.

'Well, what does he want to sit there making cracks like that for, when he ought to be thanking me on his bended knees?'

The reproach had little effect on Mr Twist. The blush of shame did not mantle his cheek.

'I don't believe the old guy told you a darned thing about where the stuff was.'

All the woman in Dolly flashed from her eyes.

'He did, too, tell me where the stuff was. At least—'

Chimp Twist uttered a short laugh, and repeated the last two words in a dry, unpleasant voice. And even Soapy's confidence seemed shaken.

'How do you mean, "at least", honey?' he asked anxiously.

'Well, natch'lly he wouldn't come straight out with it. He'd be too cagey for that. Here's what happens. I go in, see, and he's sitting there, chinning with the straw-haired guy. The straw-haired guy fades out soon as he seen me, on account of course he's sore at me for trying to crown him this afternoon with a antique vase, and Lord Cakebread sets 'em up and we both has a glass of port. And pretty soon I seen where he's grinning all over his pan, so I say "Hello," I say, "you're looking mighty peart. Somebody been leaving you money?" And he says, "It amounts to that, dear lady, it amounts to that." And then he says he had some little savings, the fruit of years of being a butler, and he stowed them away somewheres and forgot where, and now he remembers they're in Mrs Cork's study. And he's going to get them d'rectly after dinner, he says, soon as this lecture on the Ugubus gets started. Well, I don't know how you feel, but that was good enough for me.'

The anxious expression faded from Soapy's face.

'He must have meant the ice.'

'Sure, he meant the ice. What else could he have meant?'

Mr Twist, the heckler, had another question to ask.

'Whereabouts in the study?'

Dolly made no attempt to disguise her exasperation.

'Say, listen,' she cried, 'if you're wanting to know did he give me full written instructions and a map marked with a cross and a team of bloodhounds and a valise to fetch the stuff away in, he didn't. But if it's in the study, and he's going there soon as this lecture starts, there's nothing to it. It's in the bag. All we have to do is you lurk around in the garden, Soapy, outside the window till you see him come in, and when he's gone to the place where the stuff's hid and dug it out, you sim'ly step forward and stick him up.'

No instructions from a commander-in-chief could have been

simpler or more clearly set forth. It was not lack of comprehension that caused Mr Molloy's fine forehead to wrinkle.

'Me?'

'Sure, you. I and Chimp'll be busy somewheres else.'

Mr Molloy continued to brood doubtfully. In his distaste for the more spirited forms of action, he resembled Lionel Green.

'Stick him up?'

'Yay.'

'What with?'

Dolly crossed the room, and took from the drawer of the dressing-table a serviceable-looking pistol.

'Here you are. Here's the old equalizer.'

In her husband's gaze, as it lingered on the lethal object, there was both horror and astonishment. He looked at it not only as if it had been a poisonous snake but a poisonous snake which he had not expected to be called upon to meet.

'I didn't know you had a gun, pettie.'

'Sure, honeybunch. I always carry it around. You never know when it mayn't come in useful. Put it in your pocket.'

Mr Molloy did so, but with that same brooding expression on his face. He admitted frankly that he did not like guns, and Dolly, ever practical, said that there was no necessity for any such affection on his part.

'All you got to do,' she explained, 'is push it in the old bimbo's stomach. That's not difficult.'

Soapy was obliged to concede that the operation she had outlined was in essence a simple one. Lord Uffenham's stomach was a target which one could scarcely miss. Nevertheless, his objections were not yet satisfied.

'But what do I say?'

'You say "Stick 'em up!"'

'But I can't.'

'Why not?'

'It sounds so silly.'

'Then just point it at him. He'll understand.'

'Well, all right, sugar,' said Soapy, still plainly unhappy. 'Okay, if that's the way you see it. But I'd a lot rather you'd ask me to sell him oil stock. What's Chimp doing all this while?'

'Chimp's holding up the gang in the drawing-room, so's they don't come busting out and muscling in on you.'

It seemed that there was better, braver stuff in Mr Twist than in Mr Molloy. He advanced no far-fetched objections to this scheme, but was on his feet in an instant with out-stretched hand.

'Swell,' he said. 'Gimme a gun.'

'That's the only one I got,' said Dolly. 'What do you think I'm doing – running a shooting gallery?'

'Then what do I use?'

'You don't use nothing. Just stick your finger in your coat pocket, so's they'll think you've gotten a Roscoe there. What you looking like that for?'

Chimp Twist was looking like that because the plan, as outlined, seemed to him fundamentally unsound.

'That's the idea, is it?'

'What's wrong with it?'

'It's cuckoo.'

'It isn't, too, cuckoo. A bunch of prunes like that isn't going to try and rush you.'

'And how about the Cork dame?'

'Are you scared of a woman?'

'You betcher I'm scared of that woman,' said Chimp, with decision. What little he had seen of Mrs Cork had impressed him enormously. 'And lemme tell ya sump'n. If I've got to stick up an eat-'em-alive baby like her with nothing but a finger in my pocket, I want an extra cut. Yes ma'am,' he proceeded firmly, ignoring Dolly's stricken cry and her husband's gasp of pain, 'you can forget that fifty-fifty stuff. Either I have a rod, or it's seventy-five-twenty-five.'

A lesser woman than Dolly Molloy might well have been nonplussed. But this sudden crisis, threatening a deadlock at the eleventh hour, found her equal to it. A few moments of thoughtful silence, punctuated by little moans from Mr Molloy, and she had found the solution.

'Well, listen,' she said, holding up a hand to check her husband, who was asking Mr Twist if this was nice. 'Here's what, then. I'll lock her in the cellar before you start your act. I guess that'll satisfy you?'

'How you going to do that?'

'I can swipe the key. It's hanging on a nail in Lord Cakebread's pantry.'

'But how you going to get her to the cellar?'

'Tell her Lord Cakebread's inside, raising Cain. That'll make her come running.'

Dolly turned to her husband, silently seeking his applause, and he gave it without stint. Even Chimp Twist was forced to admit that the scheme was pretty much of a ball of fire. At the prospect of not having to cope with his formidable hostess, he had brightened noticeably.

'All straight now? You've got the set-up? Soapy sticks up Lord Cakebread. You stick up the prunes. I ease the Corko into the cellar and lock her in, and then I go to the garage and get a car out and have it waiting on the drive, all ready for the getaway. Anybody anything to say?'

Both men had. Mr Molloy said:

'Pettie, they ought to make you a General in the United States Army.'

Chimp Twist said:

'Juss a minute, juss a minute, juss a minute!'

The other members of the Syndicate looked at him apprehensively. His tone had had that flat note which they had observed in it on a previous occasion when he had made use of the same expression, and it seemed plain that he was about to go on to say something which would mar the harmony and interfere with the pull-together spirit.

'Eh?' said Mr Molloy.

'Now what?' said Dolly.

Chimp made himself clear.

'What happens then?' he asked. 'Here's the scenario, as I see it. Soapy'll have the ice. You'll be outside with the car. I'll be in the drawing-room with the prunes. How do I contact you? I wouldn't want you,' said Chimp, that flat note still in his voice, 'to drive away with the stuff, and then look at each other after you'd gone fifty miles and say "Why, hello! Where's Chimp? I clean forgot about him!"'

Dolly sighed.

'We won't forget about you.'

'Oh, no?'

'I'll fire off the gun, when we're set to start. Then you take it on the lam and join us. Oke?'

'Oke,' said Chimp, though a little dubiously. 'You won't let it slip your mind?'

'You can trust the madam,' said Mr Molloy coldly.

'Oh, yeah?' said Chimp, and on these always unpleasant words took his departure.

As the door closed, Dolly drew a deep breath.

'If I don't bean that little cheese mite before I'm much older,' she said, 'something'll crack. My constitution won't stand it.'

CHAPTER 26

These bi-weekly lectures of Mrs Cork's, the eleventh of which she was to deliver this evening, were among the most delightful features of life at Shipley Hall. Their range was wide. One night you might find yourself assisting from a distance at a native wedding; three days later enthralled by a Walter Winchell peep at the home life of the rhinoceros. And their appeal was not only to the ear, but also, for they were accompanied by the exhibition of home-made cinematograph films, to the eye.

It was with the gratifying feeling, accordingly, that she was about to give pleasure that she always approached her task, and it never failed to wound and exasperate her when she discovered that members of her flock, who did not know what was good for them, had sneaked off while her eye was elsewhere.

This very seldom happened, for the strength of personality which enabled her to get rid of copies of *A Woman in the Wilds* served also to intimidate would-be backsliders, but it was not absolutely unknown, and to-night provided the worst case on record. Counting heads before settling down to business, she was shocked to note that no fewer than three of her audience were missing. Mr Molloy was not there. Nor was Mrs Molloy. And the keenest scrutiny failed to reveal J. G. Miller. It topped the black evening when Mr Wix and Mr Henderson, absent from parade without leave, had been found in the latter's bedroom, drinking whisky and discussing the future of dog-racing.

Mrs Cork was not the woman to remain supine under this sort of thing.

'Miss Benedick?'

'Yes, Mrs Cork?'

'I do not see Mr and Mrs Molloy, nor Mr Miller. They may be out in the garden. Go and find them and tell them that we are waiting to begin.'

Anne hurried out, and Mr Trumper, hovering at the lecturer's side, clicked his tongue.

'Most annoying, Clarissa.'

'Most.'

'People should be here at the proper time.'

'Yes.'

'I always am.'

A tender look crept into Mrs Cork's eyes. Her frown vanished. For the hundredth time, she was thinking that Eustace was wonderful. Standing by, switching on the lights, switching off the lights, leading the applause, keeping her glass of water filled, picking up her wand if she dropped it ... whatever the demand made upon him, Eustace Trumper was equal to it.

'You are exceptional,' she said. 'I often feel that I don't know how I could get along without you.'

Something seemed to go off like a spring in Eustace Trumper. It was as if a voice had whispered to him that now was the time to put his fate to the test, to win or lose it all. They were standing outside the drawing-room, well removed from earshot of the docile disciples settling themselves in their seats, so that conditions could not have been better. And, as he quite rightly felt, if you have worshipped a woman for twelve years, you cannot be condemned as precipitate if at the end of that period you mention it.

Left to himself, his instinct would have been to edge into his theme with a cough or two and perhaps half a dozen assorted squeaks and bleats, but he saw that these bronchial preliminaries were out of the question now. Footsteps could be heard approaching along the corridor, and at any moment the owner of these feet would be coming into view.

'Clarissa,' he said, 'I love you. Will you be my wife?'

The words were crisp and to the point. He could hardly have made them crisper and still kept his meaning clear. But, even so, he had cut it too fine. Before Mrs Cork could reply, Dolly Molloy appeared. It was she whose footsteps had obliged Mr Trumper to speed up his declaration, and he eyed her, as she drew up beside them, with no little annoyance.

'Golly!' said Dolly.

She spoke breathlessly. It was evident that the even tenor of her life had been interrupted by some untoward happening. Mr Trumper's annoyance gave way to curiosity.

'Is something the matter, Mrs Molloy?' he asked.

To Mrs Cork, this agitation seemed only natural. She took it for the decent remorse of a woman who has suddenly realized that she is late for a lecture and has been keeping everybody waiting.

'It is quite all right, Mrs Molloy,' she said graciously, 'I have not started.'

'Then that's where you're different from me,' said Dolly. 'I started plenty. Gee! I jumped six feet.'

Mrs Cork froze a little.

'I beg your pardon?'

'When that bottle came whizzing past my bean.'

'Bottle?'

Dolly laughed – hysterically, it seemed to Mr Trumper.

'I'm starting the story at the wrong end,' she said. 'Here's how it was. I'm on my way here, see, and I'm going through the hall, when one of the help comes up and tells me Cakebread's acting sort of peculiar, and they don't like to disturb you, so would I step along and see could I do anything about it.'

Mrs Cork's eyes hardened.

'Cakebread?'

She spoke grimly. Her views on her eccentric employee had come of late to resemble those entertained by King Henry the Second towards Thomas à Becket. The words 'Will no one rid me of this turbulent butler?' seemed to be trembling on her lips.

'Cakebread? What has he been doing now?'

'Getting pie-eyed.'

'Pie-eyed?'

'Sozzled.'

'Sozzled?'

'Fried. Plastered. Ossified. Oh, hell,' said Dolly, impatient, as so many of her compatriots had found themselves when in England, at the slowness of comprehension of the aborigines. 'Drunk.'

'Drunk!'

'He's got a load on that would sink an ocean liner.'

Mr Trumper squeaked amazedly.

'Bless my soul! Are you sure?'

'Sure?' repeated Dolly, weighing the question. 'Well, no, I'm not sure. I'm only guessing. The bozo may be a strict teetotaller, for all I know. I'm just going by the fact that he's in the cellar, singing comic songs and breaking bottles.'

'Breaking bottles?'

'Yay. He seemed to be using a hatchet on them. All except one. That was the one he loosed off at me when I poked my head in at the door and said "Hello, what goes on?" It missed my perm by an inch, and I backed out, sort of feeling that I'd best not get mixed up in what begun to look like a vulgar brawl. I reckoned the thing to do was to come and hand in my report to you.'

'You did quite rightly. I will attend to this.'

Mr Trumper was squeaking incredulously.

'This is most extraordinary. He seemed perfectly normal at dinner.'

'No,' said Mrs Cork. 'I remember now noticing that there was a wild gleam in his eyes. No doubt he had been drinking like a fish all the afternoon.'

There was disapproval in her voice, but mingled with it a certain note of satisfaction, even of relief. Except in print where it can be investigated by Inspector Purvis and his like, everybody hates a mystery, and the enigma of Cakebread had been vexing her intensely. Dolly's story had made everything clear. All that was wrong with Cakebread, it now appeared, was that he was a secret dipsomaniac. She knew where she was with dipsomaniacs. Many of her most intimate acquaintances in Africa had been native chiefs who could never say No when the Cape gin was circulating.

'He is in the cellar, you say? I will go and see him at once.'

'Better take a battle-axe or sump'n.'

Mr Trumper again proved how invaluable he was when there was any job to be done, any little thing to be fetched. He galloped into the drawing-room and came back with the poker.

'Take this, Clarissa.'

'Thank you, Eustace.'

'I will come with you.'

'There is no necessity.'

'I would prefer it,' said Mr Trumper, with quiet decision, and Dolly, too, announced her intention of making one of the party.

The procession passed through the green baize door, and by stone-flagged passages and worn stone steps came to the cellar. Its door stood open, but no sounds of revelry proceeded from beyond it.

Mrs Cork peered in. Mr Trumper and Dolly exchanged whispers in her rear.

'He seems very quiet,' said Mr Trumper.

'Just biding his time,' said Dolly.

Mrs Cork gave tongue, speaking with a sharp imperiousness. Her nerves were of chilled steel, but this uncanny silence was having its effect on them. When a butler has received wide publicity as a bottle-breaker, you expect to find him breaking bottles. If he merely lurks, you are disconcerted.

'Cakebread!'

The silence continued.

'Cakebread!'

More silence. It was as if this butler were crouching for the spring.

'Perhaps he has gone,' suggested Mr Trumper hopefully.

'No,' said Dolly. 'I can see his eyes gleaming over there at the back.'

The statement was like a bugle call to Mrs Cork. It was never her way to stand bandying words when there was a possibility of action. Grasping the poker, she strode into the darkness, and Eustace Trumper, with only the merest suspicion of a pause, strode in after her.

He had scarcely crossed the threshold, a little weak about the knees but conscious that this was a far, far better thing that he did than he had ever done, when the door slammed behind him and he heard the key turn in the lock.

Anne, meanwhile, on her way to the garden to round up stragglers, had reached the terrace. About to cross it, she halted abruptly. Out of the corner of her eye, she had seen that the lights were on in Mrs Cork's study. And the sudden thought came to her that she had been the last person in it. Her employer had sent her there only a quarter of an hour before to fetch a copy of *A Woman in the Wilds*, extracts from which she wished to incorporate in her lecture.

Bowed down with the sense of guilt which weighs on those who leave lights on in unoccupied rooms, she hurried in through the french windows to repair her negligence, and found that the room was far from being unoccupied. The first thing she saw in it was England's least likeable scrum-half, J. G. Miller. His back was towards her, and he was making encouraging noises to something on the floor, at the moment obscured from her view by the desk. Moving closer, she found that this something was a substantial trouser-seat. It was jutting out from the interior of a cupboard, and the eye of love told her that it was a trouser-seat she knew – that of her uncle, George, sixth Viscount Uffenham.

An intelligent girl, she should have realized that if her uncle's rear elevation was sticking out of cupboards, it was because he was prospecting for diamonds there. But the strenuous day through which she had passed must have dulled her senses, for the spectacle surprised her.

'What—' she began, and Jeff soared into the air like a man

practising for the Standing High Jump. And simultaneously what Inspector Purvis would have recognized as a dull, sickening thud told that the last of the Uffenhams had bumped his head on the roof of the cupboard.

Jeff, turning in mid-air, had been enabled to identify this addition to their little gathering.

'Oh, hullo,' he said, cordially. 'Come on in. You're just in time.'

It was open to Anne to draw herself to her full height and stare coldly at him without speaking. But no red-blooded girl, agog with inquisitiveness, can pursue a settled policy of aloof silence even towards the dregs of the human species, when such dregs seem to be in a position to provide first-hand information on the point which is perplexing her.

'What on earth are you doing?' she cried.

Jeff was brief and to the point. Good news need not be broken gently.

'We've found 'em!'

Anne gasped.

'The diamonds?'

'Yes. All over but the cheering.'

Lord Uffenham backed out of the cupboard like a performing elephant entering an arena the wrong way round. With one hand he was rubbing his head, with the other he clutched a large tobacco jar.

'Here they are, my dear. But I wish you wouldn't speak suddenly like that. Not at such a moment.'

Jeff could not subscribe to this view. The long, enthralling conversation he had just had with this girl had refreshed him as rain refreshes the parched earth. It was true that the shock her voice had given him had turned his hair white and probably

affected his heart permanently, but if she liked to speak suddenly, he felt, by all means let her speak suddenly. The great
thing was to get her speaking.

'Yerss,' said Lord Uffenham. 'Here they are.'

'Then stick 'em up!' said a strong, firm, manly voice, and Mr
Molloy walked jauntily in, preceded by the pistol.

CHAPTER 27

At his last appearance in this chronicle, it may be remembered, Soapy Molloy was far from being in debonair mood. Introduced to the pistol which he was now bearing with such a flourish, like a carefree waiter carrying an order of chipped potatoes, he had quailed visibly, as if he had found himself fondling a scorpion. Nobody, seeing him then, could possibly have mistaken him for the Happy Warrior, and a word or two will be necessary to explain why he now walked jauntily and spoke in a strong, firm, manly voice.

It was to the thoughtfulness and tact of his wife that this altered deportment was due. His perturbation had not gone unnoticed by Dolly, and her first act after Chimp Twist had left the room had been to give him a couple of shots from a bottle of brandy which she had begged from Lord Uffenham and kept stowed away, ready for emergencies, in a drawer underneath her step-ins.

Brandy, like port, has the disadvantage that it is not good for the figure, but Mr Molloy, though a man whose constant aim it was to preserve the streamlined body, was prepared in consideration of the special circumstances to disregard this. He had his couple, and they acted like magic. By the time he had finished, he was throwing the pistol in the air and catching it by the barrel. The suggestion he conveyed was that just one more whack at the life-giving fluid would have had him balancing the weapon on the tip of his nose.

It was with a hearty intrepidity, accordingly, that he advanced into the room. There were three persons present, and he had expected only one, but this in no way disconcerted him. The more, he felt, the merrier. And as for experiencing any shyness or embarrassment at being obliged to say 'Stick 'em up!' he thought it just the thing one would naturally say at such a moment.

His abrupt entry had produced a silence, but it was not in Lord Uffenham to abstain for long from probing and questioning.

'Stick what up?' he enquired, with his usual thirst for information.

Soapy explained that he had referred to the hands of those present, and Lord Uffenham wanted to know why.

'What's all this about?' he said, turning to Jeff. 'Is the blighter tight?'

Soapy made his position clear.

'I want that tobacco jar.'

Anne uttered a cry.

'Oh, no! Don't give it him, darling!'

'Give it him?' said Lord Uffenham, surprised. 'When it's full of my dashed diamonds? Of course, I won't give it him.'

Soapy, who had been led to expect that if he said 'Stick 'em up!' his public would do the rest, might have been taken aback by this attitude, had it not been for the beneficent effect of the two brandies. 'Get tough,' they whispered to him, so he got tough.

'Slip it across, or I'll blow a hole in you!'

Lord Uffenham ignored this observation. Ever since the interview had begun, he had been staring at Soapy in his unblinking way, and he now recognized him. He was also reminded of something he wanted to say to him.

'You're Mrs Molloy's husband, aren't yer?'

It was a description which some men might have resented, but Soapy was proud to be so labelled.

'That's me, brother.'

'Thought so. I've noticed the back of your head, when I've been waiting at dinner. I don't know if you know it, but you've got a bald spot coming.'

Soapy's jaw fell.

'You don't mean that?'

'I do. If you aren't careful, you'll be getting as bald as a toad's stomach. Try Scalpo. Excellent stuff.'

'I will,' said Soapy, fervently. 'Thanks for telling me.'

He raised a hand to feel the back of his head, and found that it was holding a pistol. The discovery recalled him sharply to his duty.

'Well, to hell with all that,' he said, blushing as he thought what his wife would have felt, had she been there to witness his neglect of the vital issue. 'Gimme that jar.'

His insistence annoyed Lord Uffenham.

'But I keep telling yer it's got my diamonds in it.'

'I think that's why he wants it,' said Jeff. 'I ought to have mentioned it to you before, but he's a crook.'

'A crook? You mean one of these foul gangsters?'

'Something on those lines. That was why I wanted you to be careful what you said to Mrs Molloy.'

'Is that sweet little woman a crook, too?'

'More deadly than the male.'

'Lord-love-a-duck!' said Lord Uffenham, pained and disillusioned. 'I must think this over.'

'Gimme that jar,' said Soapy, but he might have saved his breath. Lord Uffenham was in a trance.

There was a silence. Soapy was uncertain as to what his wife would wish him to do next. Anne was looking at Jeff reproachfully. He was standing with his hands in the air, and this meek acceptance of the position came as a shock to her. She disliked him, but she had supposed him a man of spirit.

'Can't you do something?' she demanded.

Before he could reply, Lord Uffenham had come to life, and it was evident that his meditations had been fruitful. There was a sort of phosphorescent glow in his eyes which looked like the light of inspiration.

'Leave this to me, my dear feller,' he said, buoyantly. 'I can handle this. I've suddenly remembered something.'

He advanced on Soapy, waggling the tobacco jar sternly.

'You can't point that gun,' he said. 'You can't pull the trigger. You can't even hold the gun!'

Soapy could not follow this.

'Why not?' he asked, surprised.

Lord Uffenham, as he turned to Jeff, was plainly disappointed.

'Odd. It doesn't seem to work. I heard a feller in a play in New York say that to a feller with a pistol, and the other feller, the feller with the pistol, just dropped the dashed thing and burst into tears. Perhaps I didn't say it right.'

'It sounded fine,' Jeff assured him. 'But I doubt if mere words are what you need here. Excuse me a moment.'

With a sudden dive, he launched himself at Soapy's knees, and Soapy, who, though he had seen him coming, had expected him to arrive a good deal higher up, crumpled beneath the onslaught. Jeff's arms were round him before he could step aside, and he staggered and fell. There was a sharp report, as the pistol exploded, and then the confused noise of two strong men face to face, rolling about on the carpet.

Every drop of fighting blood in Lord Uffenham's veins stirred at the sight. He started like a war horse. A good many years had passed since he, too, had rolled about on carpets in this manner, but the old spirit still lingered and he itched to join in the fray.

Pawing the air and snorting valiantly, he found himself hampered by the tobacco jar. A man cannot give of his best in a rough and tumble unless his hands are free. And he was wondering where to put the thing so that it would be safe for a minute or two, when he was aware of a sylph-like form at his elbow and gratefully enlisted its services.

'Just catch hold of this, will yer, my dear,' he said.

It was only after he had handed over the encumbrance that he made the discovery that his female assistant was not, as he had supposed, his niece Anne, but that ex-sweet little woman, Dolly Molloy.

The report of the pistol was what had brought Dolly to the study. After locking the cellar door on Mrs Cork, she had hurried to the garage, started up her hostess's two-seater and steered it out into the drive, and it had been her intention to remain seated at the wheel till Soapy joined her. But shots in the night alter everything. They always caused Inspector Purvis to break into a sharp run, and they had the same effect on Dolly.

She had not liked the sound of that shot. It seemed to suggest that her mate had struck a sticky patch, and, like a good wife, she flew to his assistance. A glance told her that she had done well to make it snappy.

At the moment when she entered the room, Soapy had contrived with a lucky kick to free himself for an instant from his adversary's clutching hands, and he was now on his feet. But he was in poor shape. Selling shares in non-existent oil wells is profitable, but it does not develop the thews and sinews, and only the two brandies had enabled Soapy to put up the admirable fight he had been doing. He had the air of a man who would crumble at the next onslaught.

And it was plain this onslaught was in the very process of developing. Jeff, too, had risen, and his whole demeanour was so patently that of one who is measuring his distance preparatory to swinging the right to the button that Dolly did not hesitate, but acted at once like the resourceful little woman she was. She raised the tobacco jar in both hands and brought it down with a bump on the back of his head.

The tobacco jar was one of those large, thick, bulging tobacco jars, constructed apparently of some sort of stone and ornamented with a college coat of arms. Lord Uffenham had bought it in his freshman year at Cambridge, and the fact that in all this time it had not managed to get itself broken testifies to its rugged strength.

Dolly, moreover, though of apparently frail physique, was stronger than she looked. She possessed good, muscular wrists and had a nice sense of timing. The result was that one blow or buffet, as Ernest Pennefather would have termed it, was amply sufficient. Jeff's eyes rolled heavenwards, his knees buckled beneath him, and he sagged to the floor.

And, as he did so, Anne sprang forward with an anguished scream and flung herself on the remains.

'Jeff!' she cried. 'Oh, Jeff, darling!'

Considering her views, strongly held and freely expressed,

regarding this young man, such agitation may appear strange. One would have expected a 'Bravo!' or possibly a round of applause. But it is a well-known fact, to which any authority on psychology can testify, that at times like this the feminine outlook tends to extreme and sudden alteration.

A girl may scorn and loathe the scrum-half who leaps at her in rhododendron walks, but let her behold that scrum-half weltering in his blood after being rapped over the head with a tobacco jar, and hate becomes pity, pity forgiveness, and forgiveness love.

It is true that Jeff was not weltering in a great deal of blood, for all that had happened was that the ragged edge of the arms of Lord Uffenham's Alma Mater had scratched his scalp, but he was weltering in quite enough to make Anne realize that she loved him, that she would always love him and that, so far from being the dregs of the human species, he was the finest flower that species had produced to date.

'Oh, Jeff!' she wailed.

'His name's Walter,' corrected Lord Uffenham, who, tense though the situation was, could not let this pass. 'No, by Jove, you're right,' he added. 'Forget my own name next.'

He turned to stare reproachfully at Dolly, who was picking up the pistol.

'Hey!' he said.

Dolly was busy with Soapy, who was leaning against the desk, slowly recovering.

'Feeling okay, honey?'

'Shall be in a minute, sweetness.'

'At-a-boy. Did you get the ice?'

'It's in the jar.'

'In the jar?'

'Sure, in the jar. The old egg said so.'

'If by "the old egg" you mean me,' said Lord Uffenham, offended, 'let me tell you, you greasy Tishbite—'

Dolly raised a hand.

'Just a minute, Pop. Be with you in a second.' She turned back to Soapy. 'Get to the car, pettie, quick, and start her up. We want to be on our way before Chimp comes horning in. It's just along the drive. Turn to the right as you go out. Take the jar.'

'Okay, honeybunch,' said Mr Molloy dutifully, and disappeared.

'Now, Pop,' said Dolly briskly, 'I'm with you. What's on your mind?'

Lord Uffenham stared.

'What's on my mind? What's on my dashed mind? D'yer realize that every penny of my capital is in that tobacco jar that your blasted husband's gone off with?'

'Is that a fact?'

'Every ruddy penny.'

Dolly chewed her lip. She appeared genuinely distressed.

'That's kinda tough,' she agreed. 'I hate to do a thing like this to you, Pop, because you're a good old scout. Listen. Here's the best way out. We'll cut you in for twenty-five per.'

Anne looked up. Her face was twisted.

'I believe he's dead,' she whispered.

'Oh, I shouldn't think so,' said Dolly.

Lord Uffenham betrayed a certain petulance.

'Don't interrupt now, my dear. We're talking business. Yer'll do what?'

'Slip you twenty-five per cent of the gross receipts. I wouldn't do it for everyone, mind you. It's a lot of money. And that's not a firm offer,' Dolly warned him. 'It all depends on whether we can freeze Chimp out of the deal. How about it, Pop? Think on your feet. I'm in a hurry.'

Lord Uffenham was breathing stertorously. He seemed unimpressed by the magnanimity of the concession.

'Twenty-five per cent? Are you aware that my niece's little bit of stuff is in that jar, too?'

'You don't say? How did that happen?'

'I had charge of it. It was my sacred trust, dash it. I'll have to make it good to her. D'yer realize what this means? It means that I've got to marry Mrs Cork!'

Dolly's grave, concerned face broke into a relieved smile.

'Well, why didn't you tell me before that you and the Corko were that way? Why, this makes us all happy. If you're all set to marry Mrs Cork, there's nothing to worry about. She's got more dough than you could shake a stick at. You won't miss this little bit of chicken-feed I and Soapy are taking. Listen, Pop. She's in the cellar. Here's the key. Go let her out, and don't do it till she says "Yes" through the keyhole. Good-bye, I must rush,' said Dolly, and vanished.

For some moments after she had gone, Lord Uffenham stood motionless, his eyes fixed on the key in his hand. He heard dimly, as in a dream, his niece saying something about somebody not being dead, but he was unable to give her his attention. He was thinking of Mrs Cork as a life-partner and using all his powerful will to force himself to the dread task before him.

Then suddenly he turned and started for the door, moving slowly but with steady eye and squared jaw, like an aristocrat of the French Revolution walking to the tumbril.

It was at this moment that there came from without the sound of a car gathering speed down the drive.

It had not taken Dolly long to reach the car. Like Myrtle

Shoesmith and Anne Benedick, she could move quickly when she chose.

Her mood, as she hastened to where the tail-light shone redly in the darkness, was one of quiet happiness. And her first suspicion that all might not be for the best in the best of all possible worlds came when, arriving where the car waited, its engine purring softly, she saw standing beside it not only her husband but the cheese-mite Twist.

'Oh, hello,' she said, not a little taken aback.

Chimp was in excellent humour. The pistol-shot had come to him as a refreshing surprise. He had been so certain that Dolly would have forgotten that item in the programme.

'At-a-girl,' he said, quite amiably. 'Let's go.'

Dolly was still trying to adjust herself to his unwelcome presence.

'What have you done with the prunes?'

'Locked 'em in. How about the Cork dame?'

Relief flooded over Dolly. She had seen the way.

'She's in the cellar,' she said, then started dramatically, with a quick intake of the breath. Her eyes had widened, and she was staring past Chimp. 'Cheese!' she exclaimed. 'She isn't, neither. Here she comes!'

Chimp started.

'Where?' he cried, wheeling.

'There,' said Dolly, bringing the butt-end of the pistol into smart contact with his averted head.

Between a smallish pistol and a stout tobacco jar ornamented with the arms of Trinity Hall, Cambridge, there is really no comparison, considering each in the light of a mechanism for socking people on the occipital bone. Where Jeff had collapsed like a wet sock, Chimp Twist merely tottered.

But it takes a man several seconds to totter, and a woman accustomed to acting promptly finds a few seconds an ample margin for pushing her husband into a two-seater car, leaping in herself and driving off.

Mr Molloy, who had been an entranced spectator, was overcome with admiration.

'You're certainly hitting 'em right to-night, pettie.'

'It's all in the follow-through,' said Dolly.

She relapsed into silence, her eyes on the road.

CHAPTER 28

In the study, Jeff had risen and was propping himself against the desk from which Mrs Cork had dictated so much good stuff about elephants. He found its solidity comforting. There was something about it that seemed to support the theory that he was awake, and this was a point on which he particularly desired assurance. A man cannot be bumped on the back of the head with a stout tobacco jar without undergoing a certain amount of mental disorder, and it seemed to Jeff that there were aspects of his recent experience which might quite easily have been the phantasmagoria of delirium.

Anne had perched herself on the arm of a chair, and was looking at him with the tender eyes of a mother whose first-born has come safely through a testing attack of mumps. She, too, was conscious that the late happenings had not been without their bizarre side. But of one thing she was sure, quite sure, and that was that this was the man she loved.

'How are you feeling now?' she asked gently.

Jeff passed a hand across his forehead.

'I'm feeling stunned.'

'Well, nobody has a better right to.'

'I was never more surprised in my life.'

'Than when Mrs Molloy hit you with that jar?'

'Than when I came out of my swoon and found you kissing me.'

'Oh, that?'

'You *were* kissing me? It was not just a lovely dream?'

'No. I was kissing you. You see, I thought you were dead.'

Jeff paused. They were approaching the nub. From this point, he would have to follow her answers very carefully.

'Do I have to be dead for you to kiss me?'

'Not at all. I would prefer it otherwise.'

Jeff's brain was still a little clouded.

'I don't quite follow this.'

'What's puzzling you?'

'Well, only a short while back, your manner suggested that you were not particularly fond of me.'

'It was meant to.'

'But now —?'

'It looks as if I had changed my mind, doesn't it?'

'You *are* fond of me?'

'Very.'

Once more, Jeff paused. Much depended on her answer to his next question.

'You don't by any chance – love me?'

'I do.'

'This is amazing.'

'I must say it surprised me, too. It seemed to come over me like a wave, when I saw Mrs Molloy hit you with the tobacco jar.'

Jeff's head was still singing, but now his heart was singing, too.

'Then Heaven bless Mrs Molloy!' he cried. 'Three rousing cheers for the sweet little woman.'

Convinced at last, he delayed no longer. He drew Anne into his arms, and for a while there was silence.

'Mind you,' he said, at length, 'I don't believe this is happening. It isn't fooling me for a second. I know perfectly well that I shall wake up and find we're back in the Ice Age, with you saying "Oh?" I wonder if you have the remotest conception what it's like for a fellow when you catch him without his warm winter underclothing and say "Oh?" to him.'

Anne uttered a remorseful cry.

'My poor angel! Was I very haughty?'

'Cleopatra could have taken your correspondence course.'

'I'm sorry. The fact is, I don't know my own strength. Still, you deserved it.'

'If you're going to freeze me to the marrow every time I deserve it, my future looks pretty bleak.'

'Oh, no, it won't happen again. Whatever you do, I shall just say to myself "Oh, it's only that old idiot Jeff. He can't help it, and he has many good points and I love him." That will be better?'

'That will be fine. I see a singularly placid and happy married life before us. But, you know, you came very near to losing me.'

'You mean, you might have gone off and fallen in love with some other girl?'

'Good Lord, no. How on earth could I fall in love with another girl after I'd seen you? What I meant was that a little more of that iciness of yours, and I'd have been like the chap in Excelsior. That's a bit above your head, of course. You've never heard of Excelsior.'

'I have!'

'Extraordinary, that private education of yours. It's like your uncle's memory – you never know when it's going to work.'

'It worked all right this time,' said Anne ruefully. 'I suppose you know the Molloys went off with the diamonds?'

'No, did they? By the way, what's become of your uncle?'

'I don't know. He went out.'

'Probably to fetch a grasshopper, so that he could tell what the temperature was. Like the chap in Excelsior, I was saying. They sent out the St Bernard dogs, and found him lying in the snow, lifeless and beautiful. That's how I should have been.'

'Not beautiful.'

'You think not?'

'Definitely not, thank goodness. I never want to see another beautiful man as long as I live. I should call yours a good, honest face, no more.'

'Perhaps you're right. Though you aren't seeing me at my best. Being swatted like a fly with tobacco jars does something to a man. It removes the bloom. Still, I know what you mean. It's pretty tough for girls, isn't it? They start out dreaming that some day they will marry a Prince Charming, and they wind up with fellows like me.'

'I have no regrets.'

'None?'

'None.'

'Anne, you angel,' said Jeff, with deep emotion, 'if you knew what an angel you were, you would be staggered.'

The embrace in which he folded her was one which Lord Uffenham, sternest of critics, would have passed as well up to standard. Anne emerged from it, looking thoughtful.

'You know,' she said, with a little sigh, 'life's very hard.'

Jeff could not agree to this.

'Not a bit. I won't hear a word against life. It's terrific. What do you mean?'

'I told you the Molloys went off with the family diamonds.'

'What of it?'

'Well, it's a pity, don't you think?'

Jeff seemed bewildered.

'I can't follow you. You tell me you love me ... You did say that?'

'Yes, I remember saying that.'

'And you're going to marry me?'

'Yes.'

'And yet you seem to be expecting me to make a song and dance because the Molloys have gone off with a few diamonds.'

'I only said it was a pity. Wouldn't you have liked your wife to have brought you a *dot*?'

'You don't know what *dot* means?'

'Yes, I do.'

'It's amazing. French and everything.'

'But wouldn't you?'

'Have liked some *dot*? Of course not. What's money? Be she never so broke, a pure, sweet English girl is a fitting mate for the highest in the land.'

'An English girl can be just as pure and sweet with a bit of stuff in the bank. I must say, dearly as I love him, I could get a good deal of simple pleasure out of hitting my Lord Uffenham with a tobacco jar.'

'Well, now's your chance. Here he comes. I dare say he has another jar somewhere that he could lend you.'

George, Viscount Uffenham, was a man who always walked heavily, and he was seldom seen without a glassy look in his eyes, but it seemed to Jeff, as he watched him enter the study now, that his tread was even more measured than usual and that the glassiness of his eyes had become a super-glassiness.

Except for the fact that his face was covered with coal dust, which at such a ceremony it would not have been, he might have been attending the funeral of a dear friend.

Anne, womanlike, noticed this physical blemish rather than the evidences of a bruised soul.

'Darling! What have you been doing to your face?'

Lord Uffenham's eye lost its glassiness, and became a smouldering eye. It was plain that some memory, some vision of things past, was disturbing him.

'It's not what I have been doing to my dashed face, it's what that little squirt Trumper's been doing to it. He threw coal at me.'

'Coal!'

'Excellent stuff for throwing purposes,' Jeff assured her. 'A good marksman can get a lot of value out of coal. Why was this?' he asked. 'Or didn't he say?'

'He didn't like me kissing Mrs Cork.'

The sensation of having strayed into a rather eccentric dream, which had never quite left Anne this evening, became intensified.

'You kissed Mrs Cork? Why?'

'I wanted her to marry me.'

'So naturally,' said Jeff, 'he kissed her. The first move when you want someone to marry you is to kiss them. Look at you and me. If it hadn't been for you kissing me, I might never have yielded. I was in two minds.'

Anne eyed him coldly.

'I don't know if you know it, young J. G. Miller, but you're in grave danger of having "Oh?" said to you again.'

'Who cares? I'm a very different man from the craven who curled up beneath your eye earlier in the evening. You've no notion how it bucks a fellow up, knowing he's going to marry you. I defy you.' He turned to Lord Uffenham. 'Pay no attention to this. Just a lovers' tiff. We're engaged.'

'Lord-love-a-duck! Are you?'

'We are. You, I take it from something in your manner, are not. Couldn't you draw the Cork? What went wrong?'

'The whole dashed thing went wrong. I opened the cellar door, and she came leaping out, and I kissed her—'

'Did you tell her that you were really the missing Lord Uffenham?'

'Hey? No. Why?'

'It only occurred to me that she might have thought it odd, the butler kissing her.'

'Lord-love-a-duck! I never thought of that.' Lord Uffenham nodded sagely, like a man to whom all things have been made clear. 'That must have been why she said I was tight and told me to go and sleep it off.'

'I expect so.'

'Not that it mattered, because she had already fixed it up in the cellar that she was going to marry Trumper. That was why he threw coal at me. The upshot of the whole thing was that she sacked me, and I'm leaving first thing to-morrow. Month's wages in lieu of notice, thank goodness. Come in handy, that will.'

'Halves, partner. But I thought she couldn't sack you.'

'That reminds me of the story of the feller who was in prison, and his friend comes and asks why, and the feller tells him, and the friend says "Lord-love-a-duck, they can't put you in prison for that." "I know they can't," says the feller, "but they have." She says she doesn't care if a million clauses in a million leases say she can't sack me. "If Lord Uffenham sues me," she said, "I shall fight him to the House of Lords." I doubt if I will, though. Lot of trouble and expense.'

Anne, who had been experiencing her usual difficulty in insinuating herself into an Uffenham–Miller duologue, seized the opportunity afforded by a slight pause at this point to speak.

'Poor Anne!' she said. 'Poor unfortunate girl! What a future for that sweet creature, with a crazy husband and a gibbering uncle. Jeff!'

'My lamb?'

'Will you kindly tell me what all this is about?'

'I will, indeed. There before you stands the whitest man I know.' He paused. 'No, that was in the circumstances rather unfortunately put. I mean, he's a hero. He's a sort of cross between a knight of old and a Boy Scout. He was going to marry Mrs Cork, so as to be in a position to dip into her doubloons and repay you your lost capital.'

'Uncle Gee-orge!' cried Anne, overcome.

'Quite all right, my dear,' said Lord Uffenham. 'Only possible course. *Noblesse oblige*, you know, *noblesse oblige*.'

His smugness was so intense that Jeff regretted having given him such a build-up. How often it happens, he felt, that a kindly word of praise proves too heady for its recipient.

'It's all very well, you standing there trying to look like Sidney Carton,' he said, coldly administering the corrective. 'The necessity for all this self-sacrificing stuff would never have arisen, if you had had one ounce more sense than a coot.'

'These are strong words, Jeff,' said Lord Uffenham, stung.

Anne agreed with him.

'It looks to me,' she said, 'as if this Miller had got thoroughly above himself. A haughty, arrogant, domineering blighter, of a type I very much dislike.'

'I cannot recede from my position,' said Jeff. 'I said a coot, and I meant a coot. Why didn't the silly ass put those diamonds in the bank?'

'Are you calling my uncle a silly ass?'

'I am.'

'Well, it's about time somebody did,' said Anne. 'Of course, he doesn't believe in banks.'

'So he told me.'

'And I suppose, if you don't believe in banks, you hate the idea of them having your diamonds.'

'I can't see that it's any worse, a bank having them, than the Molloys.'

'There's that, of course.'

Lord Uffenham had not been giving his attention to these exchanges. After registering that protest, he had withdrawn into himself, and the twitching of his eyebrows showed that his brain was working. He now came shooting back to his young companions.

'Wait a minute!' he cried. 'I believe something's coming. Jeff!'

'My lord?'

'Keep saying "Bank" for a bit, will yer, my dear feller.'

'Bank?'

'He means "Bank",' said Anne.

'Oh, does he? Very well. Bank ... Bank ... Bank ... How long has this got to go on?' asked Jeff. 'It's making me feel like a bus-conductor.'

'I'll tell yer something,' said Lord Uffenham. 'I'm beginning to have grave doubts as to whether I put those diamonds in that tobacco jar, after all. And yet that word "pond" still seems significant. So does the word "bank". You remember I found it in that diary of mine, entered against the date April the Fourth.'

Anne uttered a cry.

'That was the day before you had your accident!'

'Exactly. That's what makes it so dashed significant. Don't speak to me for a moment. I want to think.'

He fell into a profound reverie, and Jeff and Anne conversed in low whispers.

'I love you,' said Jeff.

'That's the way to talk,' said Anne.

'I shall never love anyone but you.'

'Better and better.'

'Did you know that ants run faster in warm weather?'

'No, really? Faster than what?'

'Faster than other ants in cold weather.'

'You wouldn't fool me?'

'Certainly not. I had it from your uncle in person. It appears that they sprint like billy-o in the dog days. I knew you would be glad to hear that. And, I was nearly forgetting to mention it, I love you.'

Lord Uffenham heaved himself from his chair. Satisfaction radiated from every feature of his vast face – from the eyebrow, from the nose, from the eyes, from the chin and from the upper lip. Even his ears seemed to be vibrating in silent ecstasy.

'Knew I'd get it,' he said. 'I never forget anything, not permanently. You just have to give me time and let me concentrate. I did put those diamonds in the bank.'

'You did?' cried Jeff.

'What bank?' cried Anne.

'The bank at the far end of the pond,' said Lord Uffenham, 'just by that lead statue of the naked boy with the large stomach. I remember it distinctly. I was strolling round there, and I had a trowel with me because I'd been doing a bit of weeding in the sunken garden, and it suddenly came over me that here was a good spot. I'll go and get 'em.'

He stumped ponderously through the french window, and Jeff and Anne looked at each other with a wild surmise.

Anne was the first to speak.

'Do you think they're really there?'

Jeff shook his head.

'Not a hope.'

'You're not very cheerful.'

'I'm a realist. You aren't going to make me believe at this late hour that your uncle would ever have chosen a sane, conservative place like the bank of a pond as a repository for diamonds. No, let's face it, this is just another of his false starts. What we have to do is plan out our future quietly and calmly and forget all about those diamonds.'

'My *dot*!'

'Come, come.'

'I know, but I did want to bring you a *dot*.'

'I tell you I don't want your dashed *dot*. It will be a cold day when a Halsey Court Miller cannot support his wife without the help of her money. In modest comfort, of course, not luxury. At first, no doubt, we shall have to live fairly smally. You will cook our simple meals, I shall wash the dishes. No, by Jove, I jolly well shan't. Your uncle shall wash the dishes. He will, of course, come to live with us, and there's no sense in having a well-trained butler in the home if you don't set him to work. Here, as I see it, is the set-up. You cook the meals. He washes the dishes, waits at table, answers the door, runs errands, cleans the silver—'

'What silver?'

'I have a small cup which I won at school for proficiency in the quarter-mile.'

'And what will you do?'

'I see myself lying on a settee with a pipe and a little something in a glass, generally supervising things.'

'You do, do you?'

'Adding, as it were, the Miller Touch.'

There came from without the tramp of heavy feet. Lord Uffenham home from the hunt.

He loomed up against the evening sky, and having stood framed in the french window for an instant, as if bestowing a silent benediction, came clumping into the room.

'Here you are,' he said. 'I told yer so.'

And with a careless gesture he started spraying diamonds all over the desk.

Twenty miles away, in a lane off the London road, Dolly Molloy had stopped the two-seater, and was telling her Soapy to fetch out the l'il old jar so that she might take a gander at its contents before proceeding to the metropolis.

She said she felt like a child about to open its Christmas stocking.

THE END

TITLES IN THE COLLECTOR'S WODEHOUSE

This edition of P. G. Wodehouse has been prepared from the first British printing of each title.

The Collector's Wodehouse is printed on acid-free paper and set in Caslon, a typeface designed and engraved by William Caslon of William Caslon & Son, Letter-Founders in London around 1740.